Latin American Populism
In Comparative
Perspective

Latin American Populism In Comparative Perspective

Edited by
Michael L. Conniff

University of New Mexico Press
Albuquerque

Library of Congress Cataloging in Publication Data
Main entry under title:

Latin American populism in comparative perspective.

Includes bibliographical references and index.
1. Latin America—Politics and government—Addresses, essays, lectures. 2. Populism—
Latin America—Addresses, essays, lectures. 3. Soviet Union—Politics and government—
1894–1917—Addresses, essays, lectures. 4. United States—Politics and government—
Addresses, essays, lectures.
I. Conniff, Michael L.
JL966.L36   320.98   80-54572
ISBN 0-8263-0580-6   AACR2
ISBN 0-8263-0581-4 (pbk.)

Library of Congress Catalog Card Number 80-54572
International Standard Book Number 0-8263-0580-6 (Cloth) 0-8263-0581-4 (Paper)
International Standard Book Number 0-8263-0578-4
First edition.

To John J. Johnson

Contents

Tables

FOREWORD

John D. Wirth
Stanford University

Populism is dead. . . . Long live populism! This variety of Latin American politics—urban-based, multiclass coalitional, hierarchical, cooptive, ad hoc and nonrevolutionary—has supposedly run its course. Leaders such as Argentina's Perón, Brazil's Vargas and Mexico's Cárdenas belong to another era; their successors, including most recently President Echeverría of Mexico, have failed to revive the style and substance of populism. In this period of postpopulist politics, the field belongs to other actors with more modern styles. Whereas the populists sought integration of the masses without fundamental change, revolutionaries, heartened by the cycle of Central American upheavals beginning in 1979 after two decades of dismal failures in South America, seek ways to sustain mobilization of the masses in order to root out the old society. Yet the vested interests, represented by the post-1960 technocrats, military planners, and many economists, preside over Latin America's bureaucratic authoritarian regimes, which stress productivity and capital formation while warning against premature redistribution. Democrats are also alive and well, as evidenced by the spread of pluralist politics, open information flows, intersectoral competition, and the stress on human rights—none of these emphasized in classic populism. What, then, of populism?

Historically, populism flourished from roughly 1930 to about 1960, although as Michael Conniff points out the preconditions existed well before the Great Depression, when the main structures sustaining populist politics definitively came together. These were urban growth, industrialization, and the rise of national welfare states.

The phenomenal growth of cities by World War I marked Latin America as a newly urbanizing continent undergoing vast population shifts from countryside to city and town. The new masses who moved to industrial suburbs and the shantytowns were, as it turned out, upwardly mobile in their self-image and aspirations for their children. Thus they were "available" to populist leaders under very favorable conditions. The populist idea of an expanding economic pie held great appeal, and the leaders mostly and until the end stopped short of redistributionist politics. This reassured established elites except in the countryside, where landed wealth was neglected, taxed more severely, but rarely (except in Mexico) expropriated. Swelling cities were part and parcel of populist optimism. Gone, it seemed, was the ancient and fatalistic zero-sum game (my gain is your loss) of Iberian political economy.

These new and available masses, employed in industry or the mushrooming service sector, participated in the expanding economies of Latin America's more industrially advanced nations. This was the age of import-substitution industrialization (ISI), when Argentina, Brazil, and Mexico moved from the production of basic consumer goods to complex industrial economies. Other nations such as Chile, Colombia, Cuba, and Peru industrialized as they could, the point being that the masses with their purchasing power and their labor were fundamental to ISI.[1] By 1950 national growth through industry had become the populist stock in trade. This was a policy on which national industrialists, the middle classes, and organized labor could all agree.

The third main structure necessary to the rise of populism was the rapid spread of social security legislation after 1930. Upon workers in their cities, but not in the countryside, Latin American governments bestowed the benefits of minimum wages, accident insurance, and better regulated work conditions of the sort then becoming standard in most of the Western world. That these expanded government services also opened many jobs for the middle classes was a happy bonus to populist leaders who played loose with, when they did not repudiate outright, the norms of democratic politics. Millions were made beholden to those who dispensed the benefits from the top down, while unions and class associations were weakened and coopted by the more powerful state.

Populism also was part of the Latin American self-discovery in the arts, social thought, and political economy after decades of subservience to metropolitan nations that had been fostered in the period of export-led growth after 1850. Decolonized at last, Latin America seemed to find its own path. The cities concentrated people for jobs and services, but also for indoctrination in national norms and symbols, not to mention participation through the vote. ISI was the proof of populist policies based on economic nationalism looking to the growth of national economies, greater national power, and hence more national independence. Activist nation states did more for citizens and, as the case studies in this volume reveal, there were many forms of populism. It was a hopeful, experimental period, in which past and future were congruent enough to sustain the promise of progress without upheaval.

In the clarity of hindsight, populist politics probably failed because of, not despite, its considerable success. Certainly, by the late 1950s, it was losing the capacity to deliver more goods and services to more people: benefits to the cities and for industry, but little or nothing for the countryside and agriculture. It had been a logical but temporary solution to rising social pressures. Industry itself became more, not less, dependent on foreign suppliers and capital. The large industrial parks, based increasingly on multi-nationals, sold and serviced a smaller, if richer, share of the electorate. Expanding the social benefits could only be sustained by rapid economic growth, which slowed. Furthermore, the growth process became more difficult, complex, and demanding of sacrifices and deferred expenditures than in the ISI phase.[2] Concurrently, swelling electorates rendered the Latin American state less able to insulate itself from populist pressures for redistribution. Control of the masses, always fundamental to the success of populist politics, was now in doubt.

After the Cuban revolution, it appeared that conflict rather than conciliation between classes was the order of the day. Military

regimes rose to repress uprisings that were now universally anticipated on a massive scale. In the political climate of the 1960s, Latin
American populism was thoroughly discredited. Its solutions to the
political economy were held to be anachronistic and lacking in
rigor. Its optimistic stance on the potential for national growth and
development was now labeled an illusion, especially by the creators
of dependency theory whose pessimistic analysis swept the field.
The period of postpopulist politics began.

Yet an afterglow at least persists. No political style or movement
entirely disappears in Latin America, where political discontinuities
and uncompleted social changes sustain what Charles Anderson has
called a "living museum" of politics. Populistic styles of integrative
politics are by now well established in Latin American political
culture. Leaders from Pinochet to the Sandinistas use guitars, folk
music, and national costumes to demonstrate at multi-sector rallies
their encompassing appeal, concern, and care for fellow citizens.
The more important question is whether populism is still a vehicle
for the popular sector to play a significant role in national politics.

It is conceivable that as Latin America's integration into the
international economy accelerates in the 1980s, some form of
populism will arise as a corrective, nationally acceptable force.
Production sharing, whereby favored regions of the hemisphere
supply cheap labor and heavy industrial production in return for
know-how and access to foreign markets,[3] will increase wealth at
the probable cost of accelerating the process of uneven growth and
benefits. One wonders what politics could sustain such a burden of
inequality and seemingly open-ended social and economic change
as promised in the era of production sharing?

Productivity and participation are the twin, linked problems of
our day. The revolutionary left in Latin America would probably
settle for less integration into world markets at the cost of productivity. Authoritarian military regimes are vulnerable to repudiation
by even their own controlled electorates and may well be more
harmful than supportive of the long-term development process.
Capitalist solutions that do not kill the goose of productivity while
diverting some of the golden eggs to mass consumption may yet
evolve. Consider the recent growth of peasant unions, ignored by
the classic populists except Cárdenas.[4] They will need urban sector
allies. The ecclectic, ad hoc nature of populism could be a tactical
asset in the search for new coalitions to support a balancing of

exports with national consumption. Strong central governments might find this politics attractive to swing support for land reform and the production of more domestic goods and services, including food and social services, for example. Yet populism from the bottom up was not successful in the classic period, and the weak states that might accompany such movements open pathways to the left. On the other hand, mass organizations with internal leadership and some autonomy from the state might sustain democratic solutions, as happened in Venezuela and in Colombia and Costa Rica under different circumstances. Whether in today's world a revamped populism can offer viable political solutions to the twin problems of productivity and participation is problematic, but it cannot be ruled out.

Notes

1. In a brief, judicious review of populism David Collier maintains there was no clear link between the onset of industrialization and populism after 1930. Rather, each example must be taken case by case. David Collier, chapter 9, pp. 371—77 in his edited volume *The New Authoritarianism in Latin America* (Princeton, 1979).

2. The causal links between political and economic change after 1960 are probed extensively and from many vantage points in the Collier volume. See especially the chapters by Albert Hirschman and José Serra.

3. Production sharing is introduced provocatively by Peter Drucker (pp. 95ff.) in his *Managing in Turbulent Times* (New York, 1980).

4. The rise of a Latin American rural populism might offer interesting comparisons with the United States and Russian cases discussed in this volume. Interestingly, both the U.S. and Russian movements failed in part because they failed to link up with urban groups.

Part I

Latin American Case Studies

1

Introduction: Toward a Comparative Definition of Populism

Michael L. Conniff
University of New Mexico

Urban populism is a new and relatively unstudied political phenomenon that has appeared throughout much of the Western World in the twentieth century. In general, one may say that populist, or *people's,* movements were multiclass, expansive electoral coalitions, urban in Latin America but rural in North America, that were led by charismatic figures who promised to redress popular grievances and to build social solidarity. Presented in this volume are eight original essays on populism in Latin America, Russia, and the United States. In addition, the viewpoints advanced in the essays are discussed in the opening and closing chapters to find an overall, workable definition. Any collection of essays on such a broad subject is bound to contain some disagreements among individual authors. Nevertheless, as this manuscript moved through the planning, discussion, writing, and editing stages, we tried to single out and emphasize the most important common aspects of populism. We have tried to achieve the elusive goal of comparative history.

Most of the essays in this book stress formative characteristics of the movements they examine—socioeconomic antecedents, composition of the movements, attainment of cohesion and legitimacy,

3

and ties between leaders and followers. Relatively less attention is devoted to such traditional lines of analysis as ideology, policy output, nationalism, and international influences. This is not to say that the latter concerns are not consequential or even crucial to understanding populism in individual countries and regions. Nevertheless we believe that good reasons recommend the approach adopted. First, it penetrates beyond appearances, styles, and pronouncements to the inner makeup of populism. It permits definition without stressing the immediate political environment. Second, transnational comparisons are easier to make using the formational approach because properties common to most political movements are examined. Third, such analysis highlights the early dynamism of populism rather than the later stages when routinization obscured critical relationships. Finally, it emphasizes variables that are in large part dependent on urbanization, reflecting our conviction that twentieth-century populism could not have occurred without the massive growth of cities in the nineteenth century.

By the early twentieth century, urbanization had transformed life in the Western World. It is little exaggeration to speak of a "metropolitan revolution," which consisted of vast cityward migration plus rapid advances in medicine, manufacturing, education, construction, communications, and transportation.[1] By bringing people closer together and promoting interaction, the metropolitan revolution seemed to promise more citizen participation in public decision-making and a reduction of inequalities in their standards of living. The enlightenment ideals of government with the consent of the governed, social mobility, and economic equity seemed within the grasp of millions who now lived in the cities of Europe and the Americas.

Yet paradoxically urbanization in Europe and the Americas also brought increasingly *un*democratic government, as well as politics which exacerbated socioeconomic disparities. Bismarck and Napoleon III established a trend toward centralized imperial rule in Europe, followed in other countries by a resurgence of monarchism. Latin America underwent similar changes, with the Maximilian episode in Mexico, the consolidation of Pedro II's rule in Brazil, the Spanish restoration in Santo Domingo, and the general rise of autocratic regimes (for example, those of Porfirio Díaz, Guzmán Blanco, and Julio Roca). Even the United States experienced an erosion of democracy following the Civil War, through widespread corruption and the rising power of plutocratic "Robber Barons." Traditional forms of citizen participation and distribution of wealth were often suppressed during these years. A major justification for this was the perceived need for elite management of large cities, especially to ensure continued control over what seemed to be markedly more dangerous social and economic circumstances. Therefore, the second half of the nineteenth and the early years of this century saw increasingly autocratic governments in the Western World.

Many forces operated simultaneously to thwart realization of the earlier ideals. One of the most powerful was capitalism, which had undergone a stupendous expansion in organizational and productive capacity around the world. International capitalism, or informal imperialism, was enormously efficient, but it depended among other things on concentrating capital and decision-making in the metropolitan centers. Thus corporate bureaucratic administration became a universal norm. Whenever farmers, miners, craftsmen, and other small scale producers objected to working conditions or prices, they were silenced, often brutally. Related to this expansion of capitalism was the marked concentration of income in those countries that joined the international market. In both industrial and primary producing countries, the wealthy profited while conditions for the working classes often deteriorated. These two developments—relative decline in political and economic power of the masses plus the promise of improved conditions due to the metropolitan revolution—formed the immediate antecedents of twentieth century populism. Stated simply, populism was a repudiation of those forces hindering popular representation, social mobility, and rising standards of living for the masses.

Almost all the early populist movements contained a mixture of reactionary and progressive sentiments: reactionary in their wish to restore rights formerly enjoyed by citizens; progressive in their desire for expanded benefits for the disfranchised masses. The measures of these two elements, of course, depended upon the time and place. In the United States, where democratic freedoms were a citizen's birthright, populism seemed to hark back to earlier traditions. In Russia, where few rights had ever existed, populism seemed more forward-looking and reformist. It was frankly socialist in program and envisioned radical action to obtain an egalitarian society. In fact, populist programs frequently overlapped with those of socialism. As one author stated, ". . . there is no socialism without populism, and the highest form of populism can only be socialist." While this may be overstated, the progressive side of populism could be quite reformist.[2]

The fates of the U.S. and Russian populist movements also depended upon specific circumstances in each country. The People's Party movement (1892–1900) died quickly, yet most of its goals and many of its campaign techniques became permanent fixtures of American politics.[3] In Russia, the Socialist Revolutionary Party of the early twentieth century was nearly killed off by internal division and Imperial persecution. But it endured, and in 1917 the well-organized Bolsheviks captured control to create a communist state. Despite the brief existence of the U.S. and Russian populist movements, they drew upon the same popular aspirations for democracy and economic leveling that inspired the later movements in Latin America.

Populism in Latin America proved to be stronger, more widespread, and longer lasting than in other regions. This is because it appeared at an exceptionally propitious moment in the region's history. During the second half of the nineteenth century, Latin America became engaged in the international division of labor effected by the British. The region derived substantial benefits from the world market: investment, technology, manpower, trade, and culture flowed from Europe to Latin America, provoking a veritable roller-coaster ride of progress.[4] The metropolitan revolution, postponed by political and economic turmoil after Independence, occurred in Latin America during the last quarter of the nineteenth century, and in some respects it still continues today. Populism emerged as the predominant form of politics during much of that period.

In Latin America, populism may be dated from about 1920 to 1965. Some parties prior to 1920 contained elements of populism (for example Batlle y Ordóñez's Colorado Party and Yrigoyen's Radicals), but the general prosperity of the 1920s fostered the new urban politics that became populism. By the 1920s a new generation of adults was available in the cities—children of foreigners, migrants from smaller towns, clerks and merchants—who now took an interest in public affairs and self-determination. The decline of populism may be dated approximately in the mid-1960s, with the rise of authoritarian military governments. We will discuss the interaction of populism and authoritarianism in a later section.

Two major phases of Latin American populism may be discerned. In the years between the two world wars, the issues sparking populist movements concerned legitimacy and representation, and the movements expanded easily to address such problems. This first era can be called *reformist* or *consensual,* due to the broad spectrum of social groups they drew upon. The early populist movements made only modest changes, such as political and social reform of a preservative nature, but they did take irreversible steps toward mass politics.

After World War II, more complex movements arose to confront more challenging problems. They now faced issues of economic growth and redistribution of income, as the region shifted from export to industrial production. A common strategy was to transfer investments from agriculture to industry and to expand labor's share of income, so this phase may be termed the *national developmentalist era.* Populist leaders in this period grappled with problems of political economy and required more power to impose solutions. They used aggressive voter recruitment aided by mass media. The working class vote became crucial in elections, and labor's share of income became an important payoff. Inflation brought debate over redistributive policies. The later movements, while still multiclass, tended to retrench in several sectors of society, typically the urban labor force and the industrial bourgeoisie. Development became the goal and mass political support the means, so consensual politics faded from the scene. Having established this brief introduction and chronology, we must now turn to the historical antecedents of populism.

THE ORIGINS OF LATIN AMERICAN POPULISM

Because of the high level of development it achieved, Latin American populism warrants concentrated attention here. The cultural similarities of the region also argue for such an approach. The colonial heritage of Latin America was rich and still deeply felt in the early twentieth century, and this provided a tradition that could be easily invoked by populists. This heritage, moreover, was eminently urban and was fundamental to the emergence of populism.

Colonial Latin American cities were not mere administrative centers. Instead, they were authentic social entities with most of the attributes of European cities. From Spain and Portugal they inherited municipal laws whose origins could be traced to three legal traditions: communal, patrimonial, and Natural Law.[5] The communal heritage gave Christians the right to band together in defense of themselves and their belongings and to found towns and places of worship. The patrimonial tradition was a similar right, granted by a king or his agent, in exchange for pledges of fealty and taxes from the townspeople. Natural Law regulated the whole of Christendom according to divine will, protecting the subjects from despots and assuring their right to pursue just and moral lives. A basic tension in these laws pitted the king's authority against that of the people in city administration; later theorists have termed such a bifurcation as between the oriental and occidental city traditions, the latter being largely self-governing.[6] As a result of these origins, Iberian legal traditions contained ambiguities that defied the codifying efforts of several generations of legal scholars.

Inconsistencies in urban law allowed considerable independence of local government in the Americas, a situation that became more pronounced with the decline of Iberian authority in the seventeenth century. The general formula for disobeying royal commands was the famous phrase, *obedezco pero no cumplo* (I obey but do not comply), and in many places local elites brazenly put their own interests ahead of the king's. The rise of smuggling, illegal manufacturing, and tax evasion in the seventeenth century were symptoms of growing autonomy in the American colonies. As Richard M. Morse noted, "the colonial Latin American town is therefore sometimes more appropriately conceived as a semiautonomous agrourban polis than as an outpost of empire."[7] The degree of autonomy achieved depended upon many factors, of course, paramount among which were the forcefulness of local leadership and the coercive powers of the king.

It is worth noting that the Bourbon and Pombaline reforms of the eighteenth century severely curbed local autonomy and thereby contributed to the struggles that culminated in the independence movements of the early nineteenth century. What needs stressing is that urban society in colonial America was not always rigidly governed by a far-away metropolis, even though that was often the intent of the Iberian monarchs. Rather, a pronounced tradition of municipal self-government had been inherited from Spain and Portugal, and it could be upheld without much disloyalty. The legacy was strongest in the seventeenth and early eighteenth centuries, and it inspired the independence movements as well. It was a heritage that would be invoked, albeit unconsciously, by the populists.

Both the communal and the patrimonial legal traditions in colonial Latin America tended to reinforce the supremacy of public power over private, so that in cities "municipal communalism" prevailed. Capitalist enterprise was typically rural or extramural, in the mines and plantations and in overseas commerce. Within the city walls, retail and artisan trades were strictly monitored to serve the needs of local citizens. Virtually all urban trade and employment had to be licensed for the well-being of the collectivity. Nowadays such a government would be termed *interventionist,* for it gave broad powers to public officials to regulate private business. This too would conflict with the metropolitan revolution.

Another important attribute of colonial Latin American cities was social solidarity. This meant that everyone, no matter how poor or wretched, had a definite place. To be sure, places were hierarchically arranged. Though inequality was accepted, charity and concern for the downtrodden were important, and this responsibility became vested in both Church leaders and the wealthy. From monasteries and convents to brotherhoods and guilds, many institutions administered charity and maintained an interconnectedness between all persons, rich and poor. In this way colonial urban society was holistic and organic.[8]

European urbanism of the second half of the nineteenth century also had a major impact on the metropolitan revolution, and together with capitalism it helped undermine the autonomy, public power, and organic solidarity of Latin American cities. The great French urbanist Baron Georges Haussmann had combined social control and physical grandeur in his famous administration of Paris during the Second Empire. Haussmann's accomplishments included grandiose public buildings to embody Imperial might, neoclassical architecture, grand boulevards and suburban railways, modern water and sewage systems, and crowd control through deployment of well-trained police squads. Haussmann's influence on Latin American officials was enormous: his reforms were imitated in Rio, Mexico City, Caracas, Buenos Aires, and other cities as well.[9]

9

The social control contained in Haussmann's work was embodied in Latin America by the urban dictatorships of the late nineteenth century. This was the age of the Porfiriato in Mexico, the Generation of 1880 in Argentina, Guzmán Blanco and Juan Vicente Gómez in Venezuela, the undemocratic "Republic" in Brazil, and the elitist Parliament in Chile. Cities that previously had enjoyed considerable self-government through legal systems, councils, elections, and business regulation came under the sway of autocrats who ruled town and country alike through national institutions legitimized by fraudulent elections. The effect for cities was disfranchisement of centuries-old rights. By the first decades of this century intellectuals, the middle classes, and even some elite groups began to protest against autocratic regimes. This protest sometimes erupted in violence, as during the Mexican Revolution, but more often it manifested itself as the electoral reform movements that were the early stages of populism.

The loss of social solidarity provided another urban objection to the metropolitan revolution. During the *fin de siècle* years, the organic ideal of society was abandoned for the elitist doctrines of positivism, Spencerianism, and social Darwinism. By exalting individual qualities and ambitions, these and other so-called popular philosophies induced the elite, and even some middle classes, to abandon the poor, sick, illiterate, and disabled to their own devices. To the extent that the masses were the object of public policy at all, it was only to prevent their slipping into delinquency and crime, not to uplift them. And whereas guilds had traditionally enjoyed official existence in colonial Latin America, the newer labor unions were not welcomed by the generation of the metropolitan revolution.[10]

Abandonment of charity and discouragement of unionization provoked the growth of voluntary beneficent associations among lower-middle and working-class people in Latin America. Government officials during this era congratulated themselves that citizens were satisfying their own needs for social protection (and were following European practices too). But a few criticized the laissez-faire social policy on the grounds that self-help efforts could only benefit those who were employed, literate, and socially aware, not the genuinely needy. Soon critics spoke of the "social question" in Brazil, the United States, Argentina, Chile, and elsewhere—the plight of the poor in burgeoning cities. Drawing from the works of

Emile Durkheim, the encyclicals of Pope Leo XIII, and others, these writers claimed that the government should adopt measures to integrate the "marginal" population into society as a whole. Otherwise, they predicted, the masses might explode in a social revolution. The social question and its solution—integration—were to become major components of Latin American populism.[11]

Social integration of the masses may be regarded as the ideology of populism, although for our purposes its significance is less as a philosophy than as an indicator of how movements were formed. Populists tended to draw upon eclectic philosophical sources, and they sometimes espoused naïve and contradictory programs. It is our contention, however, that the call for social integration was crucial to twentieth century populism because it simultaneously satisfied the desire for organic society, addressed the social question, promised citizen participation in government, and provided a winning strategy for reform-minded groups to come to power peaceably. Integration was, in short, the ideal program for virtually anyone except an elitist ruling group or a revolutionary opposition. It offered nonviolent solutions to some of the most perplexing dilemmas of modern urban society. It rejected both oligarchic government and socialist revolution (with the exception of the Russian case), preferring a reformist middle ground. The populists promised to reconcile colonial and modern traditions through purposive, interventionist government.

As for organic society and the social question, populist integration held obvious appeal. People concerned with the social question believed that something needed to be done to curb the disorganizing effect of urban industrial life on the working class. As men and women from stable rural environments now worked ten or more hours a day in factories, family life became fragmented and education of children difficult. The result was individual and group alienation, known to sociologists as *anomie.* Many social theorists argued that the way to combat anomie was to reinforce social solidarity in urban industrial society, and they turned to theories of organicism.

The organicism that most informed Latin American populism was that described by Émile Durkheim, sometimes called "mechanical solidarity." Durkheim believed that the cause of widespread anomie in nineteenth century Europe was the excessive individualism of modern industrial capitalism. This eroded the individual's sense of

11

belonging in society. Durkheim called for renewed commitment to religious and family life, as well as more stress on the interrelatedness of all occupations, the so-called division of labor. Recognition of the importance of all occupations, managerial as well as menial, would produce a sense of social cohesion such as had existed in medieval times, when Church, family, and guild had fixed man's place in the cosmos. Durkheim suggested the creation of large private corporations (we might call them super-guilds) based on occupational sectors, which would mediate between the individual and the state. This concept, from which most modern corporatist theories derived, could be conservative or progressive, depending upon the size, degree of self-governance, and social responsibility of the corporations. The metropolitan revolution brought on a search for restoring social solidarity, and both populists and authoritarians in Latin America would find value in the Durkheimian concept of organicism. To their mind it resembled the holistic society of colonial times.[12]

Social integration as we have used the term above suggests the insertion of an individual into a complex society in which he will be free to move vertically or horizontally according to his talents. It also implies a pluralistic political system in which his fortunes may be improved by the pursuit of interests shared with other individuals. Yet not all populist movements allowed free social mobility and interest group politics, and for those that did not organicism had a distinctly conservative character. It served to designate a fixed place for the individual in the hierarchical order. The term *incorporation* might best be reserved for this sort of populist mobilization of the masses.

Before moving on to the principal characteristics of populism, it is worth reviewing the origins of the Latin American movements in comparison with those of Russia and the United States. In all these places, populism was a response to the metropolitan revolution and the host of changes it brought. In some cases a strong desire arose to return to a colonial tradition of social wholeness, self-government, and public authority that could check the excesses of private enterprise. Lawrence Goodwyn writes of the late nineteenth century "disappearance of a visible [American] public ethic and sense of commonweal," and the need to restore such ideals.[13] Even where such rights had never existed, they became mass aspirations. Because populism pursued integration of marginal groups, it was everywhere reformist and often quite progressive in its goals; hence populism was both backward- and forward-looking, a bridge between tradition and progress. And above all, it wished to ameliorate some of the harshest aspects of the metropolitan revolution—elitist government, abandonment of the poverty-stricken, maldistribution of wealth, and rapacious capitalism. In all of these ways, early populist movements in Russia, the United States, and Latin America were remarkably similar.

CHARACTERISTICS OF POPULISM

Many of the elements of early populism already mentioned require more definition and specification, especially as they apply to the Latin American variants. The most important characteristics were *urban, multiclass, electoral, expansive, "popular,"* and *led by charismatic figures.* This section will discuss each of these attributes separately and then conclude by making a distinction between populism and authoritarianism.

Populism was urban in Latin America because it was a reaction against the authoritarian nature of the late nineteenth century metropolitan revolution. Many of the traditional rights and characteristics of colonial cities discussed throughout this chapter were suppressed by wealthy elites. Thus populist movements and programs nearly always appeared in major cities. Several exceptions merit mention, however, if only to prove the rule. The earliest Russian movement to be labelled populist was that of the *narodniks,* in the 1870s and 1880s, who formed several groups dedicated to agrarian socialism, especially their People's Party. But Russian populism was largely created by intellectuals in the cities, and their periodic attempts to establish peasant communes were usually unsuccessful. There is no question that the *narodniks* were urbanites.[14]

A similar movement arose in Peru in the 1920s, the Alianza Popular Revolucionaria Americana (APRA), led by Víctor Raúl Haya de la Torre. It too was urban-based and student-organized, though it did recruit a following among sugar cane workers around Trujillo. Like Russian populism, APRA aspired to leadership of a politicized peasantry, especially with its pro-Indian doctrine of *indigenismo.* But most of its effective support came from rural wage earners, students, and urban labor.[15] Thus, both the Russian and Peruvian populist movements were largely urban, despite their attempts to recruit rural followings.

The populist movement in the United States during the 1890s is an exception to the generalization that populism was urban, for the People's Party (1892–1900) was unquestionably based in the farming communities of the South and Midwest and in mining towns of the Mountain West. Indeed North American populism is best described as an *antiurban* political movement, a reaction to the big cities, industrialism, and the kind of government they sustained. Yet half of our definition applies here, too, for U.S. populism was also a response to the metropolitan revolution, as seen in the growth and power of Philadelphia, New York, and Chicago. What made this case exceptional was that it actually mobilized the people who were adversely affected, whereas in Russia and Latin America it fell to urbanites to speak up for the peasants, or, more often, simply to wait until they migrated to the cities.

The foregoing discussion and the studies in this volume largely confirm the urban dimension of populism. At no time in the history of the world did so many cities grow so fast or so large as during the period between 1880 and 1930.[16] But the metropolitan revolution was far more than a demographic phenomenon, and the populist reaction was not against the mere numbers—indeed some saw hope in mass urban society. Instead it reacted against the forms of governance, social relations, economic organization, and culture which came to prevail in big cities. To ignore this relationship is to misunderstand the nature of populism.

The term *multiclass* is often used to describe Latin American populism, and by this we mean that the movements recruited from all levels of society.[17] The term highlights two important aspects of populism. First, it was usually a movement of the masses, in which the latter were defined so broadly as to eliminate specific class identity or action. Typically the "masses" included the urban workers, the petit bourgeoisie, the economically inactive, rural migrants, and even such "nonaligned" groups as students, intellectuals, and foot soldiers. The formation of such an amorphous population is sometimes referred to as "massification" or "urbanization without industrialization."[18] The unspoken outcome of this sort of analysis (and sometimes an explicit promise of the populists) was the achievement of a "classless society without revolution," or a holistic society in the terms utilized above.

Regardless of what populists promised or implied, their movements did have consequences that warrant class analysis because power, status, and economic benefits were not distributed equally to all followers. Moreover, some sectors were denied access. In general, the largest and most favored groups were urban labor and the middle classes. The former received union recognition, electoral power, welfare benefits, and a recognized place in society. The latter received more public jobs, better educational facilities, decision-making authority in the bureaucracy, and a higher social standing at the vanguard of reformism. These sectors became so secure that in most countries they retain special status. They have only been dislodged at the expense of curtailed civil liberties and constitutional government.

Some groups were ignored or excluded by populists. Peasants rarely took part in mass electoral movements because they were too difficult to recruit; however, at times such rural laborers as plantation workers, who were employed near towns, could be mobilized and included. But in general peasant mobilization did not occur, and this probably derived from the absence of concern for rural folk in pretwentieth century Western political philosophy. For each exceptional instance of urbanites reaching out to peasants, many contrary examples of rural-urban antagonism could be cited. The extension of mass politics to the country was usually too difficult, unpleasant, and unrewarding. Those movements that did mobilize rural poor, such as the Zapatistas and Villistas in the Mexican Revolution, were soon excluded from the political alliances formed to stabilize and rule the country. In some cases, for example, during Getúlio Vargas's long rule in Brazil, tacit agreements may have existed with the landowning class not to politicize the peasantry. Peasants, therefore, were only present as a part of the rhetoric in most populist movements.

Moreover, traditional elites such as major landowners, ranking military officers, financiers, and prominent merchants were rarely included in populist movements, for the obvious reason that their interests conflicted with those of the disfranchised masses. Finally, revolutionaries did not join or support populist movements (except in Russia) because the latters' approach was antithetical to the strategy of class struggle.

A second implication of the term *multiclass* is that singleclass hegemony had become impossible. Several Latin American political analysts have argued that since about 1930, traditional ruling groups have been unable to maintain their control and have been forced to ally themselves with other sectors, notably the masses (whom they manipulated in various ways) or the military. Such a situation, called a "hegemonic crisis" by José Nun and a "compromise state" by Francisco Weffort, gave rise to Bonapartist regimes: ones in which opportunistic and resourceful leaders managed very large but hardly coherent coalitions.[19] Some populist movements, notably those in Brazil, Argentina, and Mexico, may be interpreted in this framework.

Finally, the concept *multiclass* is the political side of social organicism and integration. The logical outcome of social integration and political incorporation of the masses was a classless electorate. Such a concept is obviously more applicable to the complex Latin American movements than to those of Russia and the United States.

Twentieth century populism was usually electoral and encouraged citizen participation in politics, which differentiated it from other forms of mass movement in which followers did not vote. The earliest populist parties arose to demand restitution of electoral rights or their extension to disfranchised groups, such as immigrants, the propertyless, and peasants. The U.S. People's Party encouraged rural voters to pursue their interests through the ballot box; Batlle y Ordóñez in Uruguay campaigned for expanded voting and competitive elections; the Mexican hero of 1910, Francisco Madero, raised the banner of "effective suffrage and no reelection"; and Yrigoyen's Radical Party in Argentina pressured the government to enfranchise adult male citizens, which occurred with the famous Sáenz Peña Law of 1912. For the next fifty years, the populists continued to pursue electoral government, some more assiduously than others. By the 1960s most of the countries in which populism had existed possessed electorates of between 40 and 50 percent of the population, which is to say that most of the adult urban population was enfranchised.[20] The rapidity of electoral incorporation is impressive, given the lack of such participation at the turn of this century (see Table 1).

Populist movements required dynamism, a sense of achievement and growth, to renew constantly their mandate from the people.

Therefore they expanded to embrace new groups and new causes. By *expansive* we mean that the movements established new contacts, curried support, registered voters, organized local committees, stimulated rallies, encouraged direct action, and got new voters to the polls. Populists politicized new sectors for several reasons. First, their charismatic authority demanded periodic confirmation. Second, the movements rarely began with the allegiance of "all of the people" for whom they spoke, and hence they continually strove for universal representation. Of course all political movements attempt to grow, but they must also be prepared to accept stable or even declining portions of the electorate. Populists found it constitutionally difficult (though not impossible) to lead stagnating movements. A final reason for the populist compulsion to expand derived from the fact that the movements arose in opposition to entrenched, elitist government and were therefore obliged to struggle for power. Once they were accustomed to fight for victory, many populists seemed unable to desist—Argentina's Yrigoyen was a classic example. The continual search for new support led to serious problems and instability, however. Sometimes promises to prospective supporters alienated stalwarts. More complex coalitions required delegation of authority, which was troublesome for a charismatic leader.

Neither U.S. nor Russian populism ever reached the point of electoral saturation, but some of the Latin American movements saw their voter expansion taper off due to the lack of new groups to recruit. For example, during Perón's first presidency the electorate rose from 18 to 50 percent of the total Argentine population. Subsequent stagnation sometimes constituted a crisis, which caused leaders to take radical action. Some abandoned the populist approach (for example, Perón in 1955), while others turned to the rural masses for new recruits (such as Goulart in 1964). This need to expand helps explain the generally unstable character of Latin American populism. It may be the single most important factor in the decline of populism after mid-century, when new groups became harder to recruit and when expansion was effectively blocked by entrenched opposition. Landed classes in particular objected to politicization of peasants.

In some instances, populist movements passed from expansive to institutional stages without severe problems. This could occur if the movement lost its leader unexpectedly and was taken over by

17

Table 1. Voting in Selected Presidential Elections

Decade beginning	Argentina	Bolivia	Brazil	Chile	Colombia	Ecuador	Mexico	Peru	Uruguay	Venezuela
1900	—	—	—	—	—	'01 74	—	—	—	—
	—	—	'02 600	—	—	—	—	—	—	—
	—	—	—ª	—	—	'05 79	—	—	—	—
	—	—	'06 300	—	—	—	—	—	—	—
	—	—	—	—	—	—	—	—	'07 44ª	—
1910	—	—	'10 600	—	—	—	'10 19	—	—	—
	—	—	—	—	—	'11 110	'11 20	—	—	—
	—	—	—	—	—	'12 63	—	—	—	—
	—	—	'14 600	—	—	—	—	—	'14 110ª	—
	—	—	—	'15 139	—	—	—	—	—	—
	'16 747	—	—	—	—	'16 136	—	—	—	—
	—	—	—	—	—	—	'17 813	—	—	—
	—	—	'18 400	—	—	—	—	—	—	—
1920	—	—	—	'20 166	—	'20 128	'20 1,182	—	—	—
	'22 878	—	'22 800	—	—	—	—	—	—	—
	—	—	—	—	—	'24 187	'24 1,593	—	—	—
	—	—	—	'25 261	—	—	—	—	—	—
	—	—	'26 700	—	—	—	—	—	'26 282	—
	—	—	—	'27 233	—	—	—	—	—	—
	'28 1,462	—	—	—	—	—	—	—	—	—
	—	—	—	—	—	—	'29 2,082	—	—	—
1930	—	—	'30 1,900	—	'30 825	—	—	—	'30 316	—
	'31 1,562	—	—	'31 286	—	—	—	'31 323	—	—
	—	—	—	'32 344	—	'32 80	—	—	—	—
	—	—	—	—	'34 942	'34 64	'34 2,266	—	—	—
	—	—	—	—	—	—	—	'36 192	—	—
	'37 2,036	—	—	—	—	—	—	—	—	—
	—	—	—	'38 444	'38 516	—	—	—	—	—
	—	—	—	—	—	—	—	'39 339	—	—

Rounded to nearest 1,000, except Brazil 1902–45.

ªLegislative only—presidential elections were indirect.

ᵇFrom Kenneth Ruddle and Philip Gillette, eds., *Latin American Political Statistics* (Los Angeles: Latin American Center, UCLA, 1972), pp. 105–14.

Table 1, other sources: Chile, 1920: Paul W. Drake, *Socialism and Populism in Chile, 1932-1952* (Urbana: University of Illinois Press, 1978), p. 99; Chile, 1925-70: Brian Loveman, *Chile, the Legacy of Hispanic Capitalism* (New York: Oxford University Press, 1979), p. 260; Argentina, 1916-37: Darío Cantón, *Elecciones y partidos políticos en la Argentina* (Buenos Aires; Siglo Veintiuno, 1973), pp. 267-77; Brazil, 1902-30: Joseph L. Love, "Political Participation in Brazil, 1881-1969," *Luso-Brazilian Review,* 7, no. 2 (December 1970): 9; Colombia,

Decade beginning	Argentina	Bolivia	Brazil	Chile	Colombia	Ecuador	Mexico	Peru	Uruguay	Venezuela
1940	—	—	—	—	—	'40 82	'40 2,638	—	—	—
	—	—	—	'42 467	'42 1,148	—	—	—	—	—
	—	—	'45 6,200[b]	—	—	—	—	'45 456	—	—
	'46 2,868[b]	—	—	'46 479	'46 1,366	—	'46 2,299[b]	—	—	'46 1,385
	—	—	—	—	—	—	—	—	—	'47 1,170
	—	—	—	—	—	'48 282[b]	—	—	—	—
	—	—	—	—	'49 1,141	—	—	—	—	—
1950	—	—	'50 8,255[b]	—	—	—	—	—	'50 907[b]	—
	'51 7,582[b]	'51 126[b]	—	—	—	—	—	—	—	—
	—	—	—	'52 955	—	'52 358	'52 3,651[b]	—	—	—
	—	—	—	—	—	—	—	—	'54 879[b]	—
	—	—	'55 9,097[b]	—	—	—	—	—	—	—
	—	'56 958[b]	—	—	—	'56 614	—	'56 1,321[b]	—	—
	—	—	—	—	'57 4,397	—	—	—	—	—
	'58 9,065[b]	—	—	'58 1,250	'58 3,109[b]	—	'58 7,485[b]	—	'58 1,005[b]	'58 2,722[b]
1960	—	'60 988[b]	'60 12,586[b]	—	—	'60 767	—	—	—	—
	—	—	—	—	'62 2,635[b]	—	—	—	'62 1,171[b]	—
	'63 9,326[b]	—	—	—	—	—	—	'63 1,954[b]	—	'63 3,126[b]
	—	'64 1,324[b]	—	'64 2,531	—	—	'64 9,422[b]	—	—	—
	—	—	—	—	'66 2,535[b]	—	—	—	—	—
	—	—	—	—	—	'68 853	—	—	—	'68 3,742[b]
1970	—	—	—	'70 2,955	'70 4,028[b]	—	'70 14,066[b]	—	—	—
	—	—	—	—	—	—	—	—	'71 1,655[b]	—
	—	—	—	—	—	—	—	—	—	'73 4,351[b]
	—	—	—	—	—	'78 1,376	—	—	—	—

1930–57: Colombia, Registradoría Nacional del Estado Civil, *Organización y estadísticas electorales* (Bogota, 1964), pp. 134–36; Mexico, 1910–40: Pablo González Casanova, *La democracia en México*, 2nd ed. (Mexico: Ediciones ERA, 1965), pp. 180–81; Ecuador, 1901–40: newspaper clipping file, April 1979; Peru, 1931, 1945: Jorge Basadre, *La vida y la historia* (Lima: Banco Industrial del Perú, 1975), p. 576; Peru, 1936–39: Baltazar Caravedo Molinari, *Burguesía e industria en el Peru, 1933–1945* (Lima: Instituto de Estudios Peruanos, 1976), pp. 100, 140; Uruguay, 1907–14: Milton I. Vanger, *The Model Country: José Batlle y Ordoñez of Uruguay, 1907–1915* (Hanover, N.H.: University Press of New England, 1981), pp. 23, 333; 1926–30: Benjamin Nahum, *La historia uruguaya,* vol. 6: *La época batllista, 1905–1930* (Montevideo: Ediciones de la Banda Oriental, 1975), pp. 116–21; Venezuela, 1946–47: Edwin Lieuwen, *Venezuela,* 2nd ed. (London: Oxford University Press, 1965), pp. 73, 76; Venezuela, 1973: José Rodríguez Iturbe et al., *Polarización y bipartidarismo el las elecciones de 1973* (Caracas: Colección Análisis Político, 1974).

19

uncharismatic lieutenants, or if the opportunities for compromise were great and sanctions against confrontation stiff. Although this book does not stress established populist movements, their existence merits a brief discussion. Abandonment of active politicization induced populists to stabilize their followings and to improve bargaining strength through parliamentary alliances, something unusual for dynamic movements. Institutionalization encouraged development of an ideological appeal with which to supplant the charismatic authority necessary in the formative stages. The middle class had a greater voice in the established populist movements. Examples of such movements are Peronismo from 1955–73; the Chilean Socialist Party; APRA; and the Mexican Partido Revolucionario Institucional (PRI).

Populism everywhere forged a new cultural awareness among the masses, which has been one of its enduring legacies. It encouraged study of folkways and popular art forms, rescuing them from the disdain of elite European tastes. The search for a popular culture answered an existential need to define the "people" whose role in national life was expanding, and in whose name the populists campaigned. The metropolitan revolution projected outward the ideals of an ordered civilization, such as existed in Paris, London, Vienna, and Amsterdam. That ideal had no room for the illiterate, unwashed, nonwhite, malnourished people who made up the majority of the world's population. Nor did it value the accouterments with which those people made their lives a little less miserable: their music, painting, carving, weaving, storytelling, dancing, and sundry crafts. Today it is hard to imagine a time when Eurocentrism was so strong as to deny all value to native cultures, but elites in many underdeveloped countries tried to be more European than Europe itself by rejecting what was indigenous to their lands. Populism, therefore, helped revive interest in native cultures.

We can cite several examples of indigenous revivals spurred by populism. The *narodniks* idealized the Russian peasantry. The U.S. crusade glorified the American farmer. In Mexico and the Andean countries, populism fostered a strong interest in Indian culture, called *indigenismo*. The Mexican philosopher Vasconcelos even spoke of a "cosmic" mestizo race. In Brazil the revival traced the intertwining of three distinct lineages, the Amerindian, the African, and the European, to explain the country's uniqiue "civilization in the tropics." In each case the cultural revival stimulated an inward search by intellectuals and artists for the so-called true people, and usually it produced folk art forms that were highly prized by the populists. One thinks of primitive painting, sociological and anthropological studies of the masses, popular music given an audience by the radio, and the literature of social protest. Of course populism was not solely responsible for the rising interest in folk culture, but it certainly provided a propitious climate. The populist quest for the "people" sanctified indigenous culture; in turn, populism was legitimated by it.

Sometimes the search for an authentic folk past revived traditional forms of participation, which had been suppressed by the metropolitan revolution. The Mexican *ejido* was a fine example, as were the community *mingas* in the Andean countries and African cult organizations in Brazilian cities. So were patron-client arrangements based on traditional deference patterns. As Morse noted, populism "means not merely the participation of urban 'masses' in politics but also the cultural form of participation."[21] Such revivals of traditional political forms reinforce our argument that in Latin America populism drew upon colonial legacies.

One of the most important but elusive attributes of populism was charismatic authority. Charisma is generally defined as leadership authority conferred on a person who is perceived to have special personal qualities. In early Christian usage, the term (meaning "the gift of grace") was applied to religious or messianic leaders. In modern times charisma is employed in a secular sense. According to Max Weber, pure charisma is attributed to an individual who is "set apart from ordinary men and treated as endowed with supernatural, superhuman, or at least specifically exceptional qualities."[22] Weber used as examples popular kings, prophets, and military heroes. The authority conferred on such persons is in contrast to two other forms of legitimacy, the rational-legal and the traditional. Charismatic legitimacy is most likely to arise during times of crisis, when the other two forms are in eclipse. In chapter 3, Weber's theory of charisma is used to explain Argentina's Evita Perón.

Two aspects of charisma provide special insights on the nature of populism. First, pure charismatic leadership is unstable, but it often can be institutionalized. As Weber said, charismatic authority "may be said to exist only in the process of originating. It cannot remain stable, but becomes either traditionalized or rationalized, or a combination of both."[23] This accounts for the dynamic quality of

21

populism, the constant drive to renew and expand the people's will. Even when routinized, charismatic authority may be unstable, for then it is subject to the ordinary pressures and dangers of political bargaining.

Second, charismatic leadership can be democratic and antiauthoritarian. This derives from the fact that charisma does not exist without its perception by followers. Hence in many cases followers "democratically" elect and depose leaders by recognizing and denying their leaders' charisma. Weber stated that this was always the case ". . . where the chief feels himself to be acting on behalf of the masses and where his recognition is based on . . . ." the use of plebiscites.[24] It is true that once he possesses charisma, the leader may use his power to guarantee that he retains it, so withdrawal of authority may not be as voluntary as was its conferral. Moreover, recall for loss of charisma may not be for rational or even purely representational reasons. Nevertheless, the relationship between leader and follower under these circumstances is semidemocratic.

Because populist leadership was charismatic and because the movements sought electoral expansion, populism could be antiauthoritarian. It needs stressing that this is an assertion about populism *as a political phenomenon and not about individual leaders or particular episodes.* The chapters which follow reveal such a great variety of personality types among populist leaders that no useful generalization could be made. Yet antiauthoritarian tendencies in populism warrant emphasis because some writers, extrapolating from leaders or events, have concluded that populism is necessarily authoritarian, especially in the Latin American setting. Such a view fits the stereotype of undemocratic politics in the region and seems to flow from corporatist or patrimonial traditions in medieval and Renaissance Iberia.[25] We believe, however, that populism in fact descends from the *communal* tradition, as the terms *popular* and *people's* clearly indicate. Therefore populists could champion the interests of the citizenry over those of the king. The chapter on Brazil develops this argument further, by positing the emergence of a populist-authoritarian dialectic during the 1930s.

The view that populists were always authoritarians derives some strength from the notion that they were the direct descendants of the nineteenth century caudillos, dressed in modern attire. However, the similarities between them—for example, charismatic authority and mass appeal—are offset by larger differences. For one thing, the caudillos were authoritarians to a man and indeed were usually military officers, whereas populists were often not. For another, populists were a good deal more representative, due to the necessity of expanding their movements through electoral politics. Caudillos were rural-based and distrusted the European enlightenment, while populists not only accepted its ideals but tried to extend their application to the lower classes. Along these lines, Morse refutes the idea that populism in São Paulo was "urban coronelismo." Perhaps a better case could be made that some of the recent so-called new military governments (those of Juan Velasco Alvarado in Peru and Omar Torrijos in Panama, for example) were protopopulist. These regimes did encourage participation, social integration, and lower class cultures, although they did not seek legitimacy at the ballot box.[26]

To conclude this section, we will restate some of the important characteristics of populism. First, it was overwhelmingly urban, in the dual senses of being a reaction to the metropolitan revolution and also nearly always occurring in large cities. Second, populism was polyclass and attempted to reintegrate society into a coherent whole. It drew supporters from all walks of urban life, though its main appeal was to the working and middle classes. Third, populism was electoral and representative. Fourth, it was expansive, pursuing universal consensus and continually renewing its mandate from the people. Fifth, populism sought its roots in popular culture, folkways, and the people's sense of justice. In fact, it stimulated interest in an indigenous cultural revival. Finally, populist leaders were imbued with charisma. When their charisma required frequent validation by their followers, the populists tended to be antiauthoritarian. These are for the most part formative characteristics having to do with the social composition of the movements, their leadership, and their relationship to society as a whole. This approach seems to offer the best framework for a comparative definition.

THE HISTORIOGRAPHY OF LATIN AMERICAN POPULISM

Leaving aside, for a moment, populism in the United States and Russia, we must assess the literature on populism in Latin America, for here is where the movements reached their greatest development. Writings on populism did not appear in this area until the 1950s, and they did not achieve conceptual rigor until the 1960s.

Leaders now regarded as populists did not use that designation, because of the generally negative connotation given to the Russian and U.S. populist movements. Nor did social scientists perceive the similarities discussed above. Therefore, most writers viewed the growth of the electorates as normal, albeit tardy, forms of the political development that had occurred in Europe and the United States after the eighteenth century. To the extent that analysts in the 1950s like Gino Germani, Robert Alexander, and Victor Alba differentiated mass democratic movements from others, they called them "national-popular."[27]

In the early 1960s, however, several scholars began to develop theories of populism with which to explain the mass electoral movements that had arisen since World War II. Argentine sociologist Torcuato S. di Tella proposed different categories of Latin American political parties, of which populism was one.[28] In a 1965 London conference on Latin America, di Tella formulated the first cogent discussion of populism, in a paper that has been reprinted many times. He defined populism as

> ... a political movement which enjoys the support of the mass of the urban working class and/or the peasantry but which does not result from the autonomous organizational power of either of these two sectors. It is also supported by non-working-class sectors upholding an anti-*status quo* ideology.

He also touched on such factors as dissatisfied elites, aroused masses, and an emotional state that facilitated communication between the leader and the followers. In attempting to explain the great diversity of movements by the early 1960s without looking for historical unities, he utilized a model of populist "progression," in which movements went from simple (multiclass integrative) to complex (revolutionary), depending on the political development and sophistication of each country in different historical moments. This was an ingenious approach, especially useful for post-World War II South American politics.[29]

The Brazilian political scientist Francisco Weffort, also writing in the mid-1960s, developed a fruitful analysis based on his country's experience since World War II. Although his definition was more vague than di Tella's, he explored the leader-and-masses relationship with great subtlety. He was one of the first from the left to criticize populists for failing to accomplish radical reforms and for allowing the military to eradicate democracy. His pessimistic assessment was that, regardless of their personal intentions, the populists were bound to serve the interests of capitalism and thus betray the masses. Weffort's concept of the "compromise state" was mentioned above. Perhaps his most important contribution was the idea of an exchange relationship between the leader and masses whereby the former used the latter but also awakened in them a desire for representation.[30]

Octavio Ianni, a Brazilian sociologist, began working on populism in the late 1960s, especially with his book, *O colapso do populismo no Brasil.* Ianni's vision was longer, for he traced the origins of populism to the processes of modernization occurring after World War I and especially after Brazil's 1930 revolution. His interpretation was largely favorable, for as he summed up, "Brazilian populist democracy was a political form adopted by mass society . . . ." Like Weffort, he recognized the antipopulist nature of the post-1964 military regimes. He believed that the subsequent economic penetration by transnational companies, which in his terms involved "associated dependent development," was basically incompatible with mass democratic movements.[31]

In mid-1967 a number of European scholars met in London to discuss comparative aspects of populism, and the papers were published two years later. The lack of agreement, even after the conference, was conveyed by the opening line of the editor's introduction: "A spectre is haunting the world—populism."[32] The participants did, however, endorse a short definition drafted by G. Hall:

> Populist movements are movements aimed at power for the benefit of the people as a whole which result from the reaction of those, usually intellectuals, alienated from the existing power structure, to the stresses of rapid economic, social, cultural, or political change. These movements are characterized by a belief in a return to, or adaptation of, more simple and traditional forms and values emanating from the people, particularly the more archaic sections of the people who are taken to be the repository of virtue.[33]

This definition, while more general than that employed in this book, is nonetheless compatible with ours.

The reader compiled from the London conference contained a number of exploratory essays, which examined populism from geographical and topical perspectives. Alistair Hennessy's chapter on Latin America contained a masterful synthesis of what the Latin Americans had theorized up to that point, plus many fine insights by Hennessy himself. Although he did not develop a workable definition, he introduced a genuinely pan-Latin American perspective.[34]

In the 1970s demand for studies of populism produced a number of books based on the Latin American experience: four anthologies, four single-country studies, and two attempted syntheses. Some of the original 1960s articles have been reprinted many times, and several writers have recast their arguments to accommodate newer sociopolitical theories in vogue. The most influential theory in the past decade was "dependency," a neo-Marxist interpretation of Third World underdevelopment as primarily the result of imperialistic capitalism. Fernando Henrique Cardoso, an early pioneer of this approach, reinterpreted populism as a continuing phase of dependency in Latin America.[35]

Cardoso's argument began with the observation (at odds with our view) that colonial towns did *not* enjoy any self-government or autonomy and that they left a legacy of domination and exploitation to modern cities. In the twentieth century, capitalist penetration of Latin America was aided by the urban oligarchies, which profited from the continued exploitation of their people and resources. He characterized populism as

> a regime of domination . . . an alliance between a sector of the ruling classes . . . and certain sectors of the popular masses . . . the determining factor in Latin American populism seems to have been its ability to define itself structurally by a "downward alliance" . . . .

Cardoso held that populism undermined the significance of elections and that the relationship between the leader and followers was one of "opportunistic paternalism allied with the impetuous masses." This interpretive framework has been utilized by a number of social scientists, including Octavio Ianni, but relatively few researchers have tested it with empirical or case studies.[36] The most important studies on populism are listed in the Annotated Bibliography in this volume.

It is our conviction that populism will continue to be a valuable concept for understanding twentieth century urban politics, regardless of the final historical verdict on its character and accomplishments. The decade of the 1980s must witness substantial new research on the topic before achieving theoretical maturity; for that reason Drake's concluding suggestions are particularly valuable. This volume, we hope, stands not only as a review of past studies but as a suggested strategy for the research tasks ahead. Hypotheses informed by the theories discussed herein must be examined empirically and then reassembled with historical imagination to form a coherent new interpretation. That is the challenge of comparative history which we have attempted to confront.

Notes

1. For the general outlines, see Lewis Mumford, *The City in History: Its Origins, Its Transformations, and Its Prospects* (New York: Harcourt, Brace, & World, 1961), chapters 15-17.

2. On the interaction of socialism and populism in Chile, see Paul W. Drake, *Socialism and Populism in Chile, 1932–52* (Urbana: University of Illinois Press, 1978). Quote from Ernesto Laclau, *Politics and Ideology in Marxist Theory: Capitalism, Fascism, Populism* (London: NLF, 1977), p. 196.

3. Among the best brief treatments is Lawrence Goodwyn, *The Populist Movement: Short History of the Agrarian Revolt in America* (New York: Oxford University Press, 1978).

4. Sanford Mosk, "Latin America and the World Economy, 1850–1914," *Inter-American Economic Affairs* 2 (1948): 53–82; Roberto Cortés Conde, *The First Stages of Modernization in Spanish America* (New York: Harper and Row, 1974).

5. A seminal article on these issues is Richard M. Morse's "The Heritage of Latin America," in *The Founding of New Societies,* by Louis Hartz et al. (New York: Harcourt, Brace, & World, 1964), pp. 123–77. See also Paul E. Sigmund, *Natural Law in Political Thought* (Cambridge, Mass.: Winthrop Publishers, 1971).

6. Vatro Murvar, "Some Tentative Modifications of Weber's Typology: Occidental Versus Oriental City," *Social Forces* 44 (1966): 381–89.

7. Richard M. Morse, "A Prolegomenon to Latin American Urban History," *Hispanic American Historical Review* 52 (1972): 369. The same author stresses the autonomy of Brazilian cities in "Brazil's Urban Development: Colony and Empire," *Journal of Urban History* 1 (1974): 43–46. Cf. Charles R. Boxer, *The Dutch in Brazil, 1624–1654* (Oxford: The Clarendon Press, 1957), p. 19.

8. See Joaquín Capelo, *Lima in 1900,* intro. Richard M. Morse (Lima: Instituto de Estudios Peruanos, 1973), and Richard M. Morse, "The Lima of Joaquín Capelo: A Latin American Archetype," *Journal of Contemporary History* 4 (1969):95–110.

9. David H. Pinkney, *Napoleon III and the Rebuilding of Paris* (Princeton: Princeton University Press, 1968); John H. Galey, "A City Comes of Age: Caracas in the Era of Antonio Guzmán Blanco (1870–1888)," *Boletín del Centro de Investigaciones Históricas y Estéticas* (Caracas), 15 (1973): 77–113; James R. Scobie, *Buenos Aires: Plaza to Suburb, 1870–1910* (New York: Oxford, 1974); María Dolores Morales, "La expansión de la ciudad de México en el Siglo XIX: El caso de los fraccionamientos," *Seminario de historia urbana* (Mexico: Cadernos de Trabajo, INAH, 1974), pp. 71–103.

10. For a brief sketch, see Germán Arciniegas, *Latin America: A Culture History*, trans. Joan MacLean (New York: Alfred A. Knopf, 1967), chapter 16.

11. Michael L. Conniff, "Voluntary Associations in Rio de Janeiro, 1870-1945: A New Approach to Urban Social Dynamics," *Journal of Inter-American Studies* 17 (1975):64-81; James O. Morris, *Elites, Intellectuals, and Consensus: A Study of the Social Question and the Industrial Relations System of Chile* (Ithaca, N. Y.: Cornell University Press, 1966). See also the general discussion by Gino Germani, "The Concept of Social Integration," in *The Urban Explosion in Latin America*, ed. Glenn H. Beyer (Ithaca, N. Y.: Cornell University Press, 1967), pp. 175–89.

12. Émile Durkheim, *Suicide, a Study in Sociology*, trans. John A. Spaulding and George Simpson (New York: The Free Press, 1951), pp. 378–90, and *De la division du travail social*, 4th ed. (Paris: Librairie Felix Alcan, 1922), pp. i–xxxvi.

13. Goodwyn, *Populist Movement*, p. xiv.

14. Avrahm Yarmolinsky, *Road to Revolution: A Century of Russian Revolution* (New York: Collier, 1962), chapters 9–16.

15. Steve Stein, *Populism in Peru* (Madison: University of Wisconsin Press, 1980); Peter F. Klaren, *Modernization, Dislocation, and Aprismo: Origins of the Peruvian Aprista Party, 1870-1932* (Austin: Institute of Latin American Studies, 1973), chapters 6–7.

16. See, for example, Adna Ferrin Weber, *The Growth of Cities in the Nineteenth Century: A Study in Statistics,* 2nd ed. (New York: Cornell University Press, 1963), and Richard M. Morse, with Michael L. Conniff and John Wibel, eds., *The Urban Development of Latin America, 1750–1920* (Stanford: Center for Latin American Studies, 1971).

17. Torcuato di Tella, cited below in n. 29.

18. An early statement is, "Que é o Adhemarismo," *Cadernos do nosso tempo* (Rio), Jan.-June 1954, pp. 139–49.

19. José Nun, *Latin America: The Hegemonic Crisis and the Military Coup* (Berkeley: Institute of International Studies, 1969); Francisco Weffort, *O Populismo na política brasileira* (Rio: Paz e Terra, 1978), p. 50.

20. Kenneth Ruddle and Philip Gillette, eds. *Latin American Political Statistics* (Los Angeles: Latin American Center, 1972), pp. 105–14.

21. Richard M. Morse, "Recent Research on Latin American Urbanization: A Selective Survey with Commentary," *Latin American Research Review* 1 (1965):61.

22. Max Weber, *On Charisma and Institution Building: Selected Papers*, ed. and intro. S. N. Eisenstadt (Chicago: University of Chicago Press, 1968), p. 48.

23. Ibid., p. 54.

24. Ibid., pp. 61–62.

25. See, for example, Ronald C. Newton, "Natural Corporatism and the Passing of Populism in Spanish America," in *The New Corporatism: Social-Political Structures in the Iberian World,* ed. Frederick B. Pike and Thomas Stritch (Notre Dame: University of Notre Dame Press, 1974), pp. 34–51; and James M. Malloy, "Authoritarianism and Corporatism in Latin America: The Modal Pattern," in *Authoritarianism and Corporatism in Latin America,* ed. James M. Malloy (Pittsburgh: University of Pittsburgh Press, 1977), pp. 3–19.

26. Morse, "São Paulo: Case Study of a Latin American Metropolis," *Latin American Urban Research* I (1971): 164–65; and Julio Cotler, "Crise política e populismo militar no Peru," in *Ideologias-populismo,* ed. Fanny Tabak (Rio: Eldorado, 1973), pp. 123–72.

27. Gino Germani, "Classes populares y democracía representativa en América Latina," *Desarrollo económico* 2 (1962): 23–43; Victor Alba, "Populism and National Awareness in Latin America," (Lawrence: University of Kansas Center of Latin American Studies, 1966). The South American writers were probably influenced by Alain Touraine's work on labor sociology.

28. "Los procesos políticos y sociales de la industrialización," *Desarrollo económico* 2 (1962): 19–48; "Ideologias monolíticas en sistemas políticos pluripartidistas: el caso

latinoamericano," in *Argentina, sociedad de masas,* ed. Gino Germani (Buenos Aires: EUDEBA, 1965), pp. 272−84.

29. "Populismo y reforma en America Latina," *Desarrollo económico* 4 (1965): 391−425. The quotation is from an abridged translation in *Obstacles to Change in Latin America,* ed. Cláudio Véliz (New York: Oxford University Press, 1965), p. 47.

30. Weffort, *Populismo na política brasileira,* is a collection of mid-1960s essays plus unpublished material from his 1968 dissertation.

31. Octavio Ianni, *O Colapso do populismo no Brazil* (Rio: Civilização Brasileira, 1968); English trans. Phyllis B. Eveleth, *Crisis in Brazil* (New York: Columbia University Press, 1970), quote from p. 198.

32. Ghiţa Ionescu and Ernest Gellner, eds., *Populism: Its Meaning and National Characteristics* (New York: The Macmillan Co., 1969), p. 1.

33. Isaiah Berlin, et al., "Populism," *Government and Opposition* 3 (1968):179.

34. Alistair Hennessy, "Latin America," in Ionescu and Gellner, *Populism,* pp. 28−61. See also his "Fascism and Populism in Latin America," in *Fascism, a Reader's Guide, Analyses, Interpretations, Bibliography,* ed. Walter Laquer (London: Wildwood House, 1976), pp. 255−94.

35. See especially "The City and Politics," in *Urbanization in Latin America: Approaches and Issues,* ed. Jorge E. Hardoy (Garden City, N. Y.: Anchor Books, 1975), pp. 157−90.

36. Ibid., pp. 179, 182. This analysis is put into larger dependency theory in Fernando Henrique Cardoso and Enzo Faletto, *Dependency and Development in Latin America,* trans. Marjory Mattingly Urquidi (Berkeley: University of California Press, 1979), esp. ch. 5, and in Octávio Ianni, *A formação do estado populista na América Latina* (Rio: Civilização Brasileira, 1975). An interesting case study in this framework is Kenneth Paul Erickson. "Populism and Political Control of the Working Class in Brazil," in *Ideology and Social Change in Latin America,* ed. Juan E. Corradi, June Nash, and Hobart A. Spalding, Jr. (New York: Gordon and Breach, 1977), pp. 200−36.

Annotated Bibliography

In addition to the references cited in the individual chapters, the interested reader will want to consult the following studies to gain an understanding of populism:

Alba, Victor. "Populism and National Awareness in Latin America." Center of Latin American Studies, Occasional Publications No. 6. Lawrence: University of Kansas, 1966.
Short paper which argues that populism was an early stage in the formation of national identity. Haya de la Torre was the foremost populist, for he devised a nationalist, reformist, antiimperialist movement which drew electoral support from different classes.

Cardoso, Fernando Henrique, and Faletto, Enzo. *Dependency in Latin America.* Translated by Marjory Mattingly Urquidi. Berkeley: University of California Press, 1979.
One of the most read and cited works of the "dependency school," this book devotes a chapter to nationalism and populism, treating them as a phase of consolidation of the domestic market. Discussed in the text.

Di Tella, Torcuato S. "Populismo y reforma en América Latina." *Desarrollo económico* 4 (1965):391−425.
This is one of the first coherent interpretations of populism, and as such it has been widely utilized and reprinted. This version is preferred over others, for it has useful diagrams. Discussed in the text.

Gallaga, Roberto. "El Populismo latinoamericano." *Pensamiento político* 15 (1970):67−74.

A short article which looks at rural and urban populism and argues that Mexico has not experienced either.

Germani, Gino; Di Tella, Torcuato S.; and Ianni, Octávio. *Populismo y contradicciones de clase en Latinoamérica.* México: Ediciones Era, 1973.
Reprint of an early 1960s article by Germani; reprint of Di Tella's cited above; and an early 1970s attempt by Ianni to interpret populism throughout Latin America. All are discussed in the text.

Hennessy, Alistair. "Latin America." In *Populism: Its Meaning and National Characteristics,* edited by Ghiţa Ionescu and Ernest Gellner. New York: The Macmillan Company, 1969.
An imaginative assessment of both populism and studies about populism, prepared for a 1967 London conference. Discussed in the text.

—. "Fascism and Populism in Latin America." In *Fascism, a Reader's Guide, Analyses, Interpretations, Bibliography,* edited by Walter Laquer. London: Wildwood House, 1976.
A timely update, with individual treatment for major countries and considerable bibliography. Argues that fascism did not take firm root in Latin America, but that populism was an alternative.

Ianni, Octávio. *A formação do estado populista na América Latina.* Rio: Civilização Brasileira, 1975.
Based on dependency theory, the book argues that populism ". . . seems to correspond to a specific period in the evolution of contradictions between national society and dependent economy." This book is discussed in the text.

Ionescu, Ghiţa, and Gellner, Ernest, eds. *Populism: Its Meaning and National Characteristics.* New York: The Macmillan Company, 1969.
A selection of papers from the 1967 London conference on populism, this reader contains both geographical and topical approaches. Discussed in the text.

Laclau, Ernesto. *Politics and Ideology in Marxist Theory: Capitalism, Fascism, Populism.* London: NLB, 1977.
Probably the most rigorous attempt to analyze populism in Marxist theory. Definition: "Our thesis is that populism consists in the presentation of popular-democratic interpellations as a synthetic-antagonistic complex with respect to the dominant ideology" (pp. 172–73).

Niekerk, A. E. van. *Populism and Political Development in Latin America.* Rotterdam: University of Rotterdam Press, 1974.
A very superficial treatment of the leading countries, based entirely on secondary sources. No definition nor theoretical framework is offered.

Quijano, Aníbal, and Weffort, Francisco C. *Populismo, marginalización, y dependencia.* San Jose, Costa Rica: EDUCA, 1973.
Several of Weffort's articles are translated into Spanish here; Quijano's section deals with marginality rather than populism.

Skidmore, Thomas E. "A Case Study in Comparative Public Policy: The Economic Dimensions of Populism in Argentina and Brazil." *The New Scholar* 7 (1979):129–66.
A valuable comparison of the political and economic strategies pursued by Perón and Vargas during the late 1940s and 1950s. Stress is on the balancing of political demands with economic necessities.

2

Yrigoyen and Perón: The Limits of Argentine Populism

David Tamarin
University of Oregon

Twentieth-century Argentina has been dominated by populism as perhaps no other country in Latin America. Two great populist movements, first Radicalism and later Peronism, shaped the contours of Argentine political life for most of this century and the legacies of both—particularly Peronism—continue to manifest themselves in the raw conflicts of contemporary Argentina. Consequently, the Argentine case affords a particularly valuable opportunity to examine the development of populism over a period of three or four generations while comparing two distinct populist movements within a single evolving national context. These two movements, in turn, correspond to the two major phases of Latin American populism: Radicalism is a classic representative of "reformist era" populism, as Peronism is of the "national developmentalist era." Both of these movements, for all their practical differences, held forth similar promises to their partisans that they would create an Argentina freed from the political control of the traditional agrarian oligarchy, sovereign in economic decision making, socially just and unencumbered by class conflict, and culturally emancipated from the dominance of imported values and styles. In brief, both movements claimed to represent the struggle for the revindication of *argentinidad*—the Argentine essence—in almost all realms of national life.

In this chapter the major features of Radicalism and Peronism are reviewed in their formative stages and "in power" (although both subsequently played important roles as opposition movements). In particular, the focus is on the nature of the crises in Argentine society that engendered these populist movements, their social bases, ideological tenets and programs, their relation to the labor movement, and the role of personalist leadership in each. It is demonstrated that despite their deep impact on many aspects of national life, Argentine populist movements fell far short of achieving the promises held out to their followers.

Radicalism grew out of intraelite conflicts of the late nineteenth century. The Radical Civic Union (U.C.R.), founded in the early 1890s, was composed originally of "estranged patrician groups" that, for one reason or another, were virtually excluded from direct participation in government. Promising to end fraudulent elections and closed political rule, and to do away with the traditional spoils system, personalism, jobbery, cronyism and backroom political deals, the U.C.R. committed itself to revolutionary action against the so-called *régimen* of the ruling conservative elite.[1] The failure of several revolutionary attempts to seize power in the period 1890–1905, together with the defection of an important stratum of its leadership, prompted the upper-class U.C.R. to widen its base of political support by appealing for the sympathies of urban middle-class groups, especially in Buenos Aires. By and large, however, the U.C.R. only began to resemble a mass movement after 1905, when Argentina's crisis of political legitimacy extended beyond the confines of intraelite rivalry.

By the turn of the century, the maturation of Argentina's traditional primary export economy had created a highly urbanized (53 percent in 1914) and stratified society. Middle-class groups, predominantly linked to the commercial and service sectors and composed largely of sons-of-immigrants, basically shared the agrarian elite's commitment to Argentina's traditional economic structures. At the same time, however, the middle classes found their aspirations for social mobility and political representation substantially blocked by the elite's virtual monopolization of political power, as well as by its control of higher education, entrance into the professions, and jobs in the expanding state bureaucracy. Middle-class resentment was further agitated by the fact that suffrage was limited and that commonplace governmental fraud, bribery, and institutionalized political bargaining seemed to mock and subvert the democratic intent of the 1853 Constitution.[2]

Under the leadership of Hipólito Yrigoyen (who was the nephew of the U.C.R.'s founder), the U.C.R. tapped this middle-class frustration and restiveness by championing the introduction of "representative democracy." However, beyond a commitment to universal male suffrage, to revitalizing the Constitution, and to allowing contradictory tendencies within the movement, Radical ideology was vague.[3] In effect, Radicalism became a moral crusade, a quasi-religious movement that called for the spiritual rejuvenation of Argentine society in order to free it from the imported and decadent "positivist materialism" of the ruling oligarchy. U.C.R. partisans addressed one another as *coreligionarios,* referred to their movement as *la causa* (the cause) and viewed Yrigoyen as their spiritual leader as well as their political *jefe* (chief).

Yrigoyen's personality and political acumen became the linch pin of the movement, and any thorough analysis of Radicalism and Yrigoyen as a populist leader would delve deeply into the personality and career of the man, as well as into Argentine social psychology. Several aspects of his career remain an enigma, for he was introverted and his oratory was weak. Yrigoyen actively cultivated an aura of mystery and paternal aloofness. This mode of behavior, in fact, served Yrigoyen as an effective political style, provoking popular wonderment and fascination, and imbuing him with an air of detached, even majestic, superiority. He refused to make public political speeches or issue conventional political statements except on rare occasions. In contrast with the U.C.R.'s rhetorical rejection of personalism as an evil associated with the *régimen,* Yrigoyen became (and earned a well deserved reputation as) a master of machine politics. This "man of mystery," as Manuel Gálvez aptly described him, was to remain the domineering political *caudillo* among middle-class partisans within the U.C.R.[4]

In point of fact, though, personalism pervaded every level of the Radical movement. The U.C.R.'s success among the middle classes after 1905 depended in large part upon its system of local party bosses and their machine organization. As allocators of patronage and charity, the local machine symbolized the style of government implicitly promised by the radicals and aspired to by the disfranchised middle classes: a government that would wrest spoils from the oligarchy and redistribute favors and opportunities in their direction. In essence, Radical populism was a movement that functioned superlatively at two extremes but remained devoid of a center. At one end it offered an abstract set of moral principles and at the other, an effective organizational machine. What it virtually lacked was a coherent political and economic doctrine or program. Linkage, instead, depended upon Yrigoyen's mystique and personal command. This proved to be the strength of Radicalism in its formative stage as an opposition movement seeking power, enabling it by 1912 to become a truly cross-regional, popular party. Still, it retained much of its initial character as a mass movement led by upper status groups rather than a grass-roots movement responding to pressures and direction from the base.[5]

By 1910, segments of the ruling elite became convinced that the Radicals and their middle-class followers had to be accommodated. First, the reform minded among the elite considered the Radicals a greater threat as an insurrectionary movement than they would be as an institutionalized "loyal opposition." Second, the implications of the Radical and middle-class challenge to traditional Argentine society seemed slight compared to expanding activity of the militant anarchist labor movement. In 1912, elite reformers under the leadership of President Roque Sáenz Peña held sway, enacting universal adult male suffrage and cleansing Argentine electoral procedure of its worst abuses. Thus the principal Radical demand had been met, prompting the U.C.R. to abandon its strategy of intransigence (refusal to vote or hold office as a protest) and thereby paving the way for Yrigoyen's election to the presidency in 1916.

In power, Yrigoyenist populism retained many of the features it had exhibited in its formative opposition stage, thereby revealing the tenuous foundations of its multiclass composition and appeal. The patrician character of the leadership was manifested in Yrigoyen's appointment of several upper class landholders to cabinet positions as well as the continued representation of "aristocrats" in U.C.R. congressional delegations. Furthermore, the Radical government's economic policies basically followed traditional liberal tenets to the advantage of the agrarian export economy.[6] Concomitantly, the Radicals cemented their linkage to urban middle-class elements, primarily in the littoral. Among its major policies intended to achieve these goals, the government: (1) extended its patronage system of party control; (2) inflated public spending, thereby speeding the growth of the bureaucracy to the advantage of middle-class job seekers; (3) increased the tributary relationship between the provinces and Buenos Aires to the advantage of the urban consumer; and (4) extended middle-class access to higher education with a series of university reforms enacted in 1918.[7]

In the area of Yrigoyen's labor policies, however, are to be found extremely illuminating insights into the social character of Argentine populism during this early "reformist era" as well as into its limited ability to integrate Argentine society. For the most part, prior to 1916 the U.C.R. had not articulated a position regarding social and labor problems. Other than affirming a commitment to the interests of "all the people," its rejection of "socialist materialism" with its concept of intrinsic class antagonism, and its implacable opposition to the Socialist Party (which it regarded as great an adversary as the oligarchic *régimen*), the U.C.R. had given little hint of how it would approach the so-called social question. By contrast, the response of the pre-1916 conservative elite governments to social and labor unrest had been unequivocal: labor strife and social unrest were first and foremost matters for the police. The prevailing elite attitude had dismissed any thought of social legislation as utopian nonsense. Instead, the dominant sectors of the traditionalist conservative elite had championed restrictive immigration policies, "antisubversive" laws, and stern police action to protect Argentine society from foreign-born "misanthropes" and revolutionaries.[8]

Yrigoyen's ascent to the presidency temporarily signalled a departure from many of these policies. First, it coincided with a critical juncture in the development of the Argentine labor movement. In 1910 the anarchist movement, which had led Argentine labor in its first heroic stage, reached its apogee. Great numbers of workers (many first generation Argentines) began to turn to other labor factions, particularly to the syndicalists, who rejected the ideological accouterments of anarchism and socialism, propounding instead an apolitical "bread and butter" unionism.[9]

For Yrigoyen and the U.C.R., the urgent social question, together with developments in the labor movement itself, presented a unique opportunity. Abandoning the approach of his conservative predecessors, Yrigoyen attempted to formulate an "even-handed" labor policy sympathetic to workers' "just demands." The formulation of this so-called *obrerismo*—or labor policy—included plans for protective and regulatory social legislation; however, little of it passed due to congressional opposition. It was reinforced by paternalistic acts of charity and patronage, occasionally issuing directly from Yrigoyen's hands. In part, this policy obeyed real convictions that the laboring classes had to be integrated peacefully into Argentine society and that they should share more equitably in the nation's wealth. Beyond this, however, little doubt exists that *obrerismo* was principally a calculated form of electoral strategy designed to woo the native and naturalized worker into the U.C.R.'s orbit. In Buenos Aires in particular, *obrerismo* was consciously promoted as a means of challenging the Socialist Party for the votes of workers.[10]

In addition to these facets of *obrerismo*, between 1916 and 1919 Yrigoyen lent support to several strikes, especially in the railway and maritime transport sectors dominated by foreign capital. More often than not, this support came in the simple form of government nonintervention, that is, police power was not utilized to break strike activity as had been the previous practice. Occasionally, however, Yrigoyen would use the power of the presidency directly to persuade recalcitrant employers to arbitrate their conflict with striking workers.[11] Undoubtedly, these policies lent credence to Yrigoyen's claim that Radicalism stood for the redemption of Argentine nationalism exploited by foreign business interests, as well as for the redemption of the workers and the poor.

Obrerismo, in its various manifestations, contributed to a dramatic upsurge in labor activity and unionization between 1916 and 1920. Led overwhelmingly by syndicalists, whose doctrine complemented the Radicals' own antisocialism, the level of unionization in 1920 grew to over 700,000 members, a high point not to be duplicated for twenty-five years, until the advent of Peronism.[12] The relationship between labor and the Radical government, however, retained a personalistic character. Neither the union movement itself nor the protective role of the state became institutionalized features of Argentine society. And ultimately, Yrigoyen found it impossible to maintain harmony between his middle-class supporters and his benevolent *obrerismo*.

By 1919 the middle and upper classes reacted violently to what they considered government capitulation to unbridled labor militancy and threatened to assume strike-breaking functions themselves by forming antilabor militias. Following the infamous "Tragic Week" of January 1919, during which Buenos Aires was convulsed by violent vigilante repression of a city-wide general strike, Yrigoyen obeyed middle- and upper-class Radical opinion by retreating from *obrerismo*. Thereafter, Yrigoyen's bid for labor support was limited primarily to the extension of party patronage and charity to working-class elements. Once again police and military force were regularly employed to check labor militancy.[13] Radical populism thus proved unable to forge solid links to the working class: from their inception, Yrigoyen's labor policies had been *ad hoc* responses to social conflict, devoid, like Radicalism in general, of any basic commitment to structural reform or any solid grounding in social theory. Nevertheless, *obrerismo* did instill an important segment of the working class with Yrigoyenist sympathies and with an abiding faith in the potentialities of state benevolence on behalf of working class aspirations, which would later be tapped by Juan D. Perón.

Other factors, as well, undermined the Radicals' construction of a broad, national, multiclass coalition. Yrigoyen's personal domination over the party, which had served as a cohesive force at the level of mass political organizing, nonetheless engendered antipersonalist opposition to him within sectors of the party itself—especially among the U.C.R.'s patrician leadership. By the late 1910s, antipersonalism within the party was strong enough to jeopardize Radical performance at the polls during congressional and municipal elections. Furthermore, the struggle over personalism was accompanied by dissent over the Radicals' failure to articulate a conventional political program.[14] Finally, the presidential succession in 1922 brought the issue of personalism to a head. The election of Marcelo T. Alvear (one of the U.C.R.'s "prominent blue-bloods") was soon followed by internal party controversy over Yrigoyen's attempts to control the government of his hand-picked successor, leading in 1924 to a formal schism in the U.C.R. between Yrigoyenist and antipersonalist Radicals. Likewise, Yrigoyen's heavy-handed policies of provincial interventions and his subordination of interior interests to those of the littoral during his administration had alienated provincial sympathies. In Mendoza and San Juan, for instance, local populist leaders who had originally identified with the U.C.R. broke away from the national Radical movement. Championing local "popular" interests, these provincial populists became implacable foes of Yrigoyenist centralism. [15]

The general retreat from *obrerismo* together with the defection of patrician and provincial elements rendered *yrigoyenismo* a popular, urban, middle-class movement. When Yrigoyen returned to the presidency in 1928, his government was more thoroughly middle-class in character than ever before. Yrigoyen attempted to cement his middle-class constituency by increasing government spending and patronage (as opposed to the fiscal conservatism of his antipersonalist predecessor) and by directing appeals of economic nationalism (particularly with regard to the fledgling national oil industry) to the urban middle classes.[16] Without a wide social and regional base of support, however, Yrigoyen's second government became embroiled in fierce political and economic disputes. The exaggerated personalism of his second presidency hindered governmental functions and antagonized the military. Finally, the impact of the world depression in 1929 forced Yrigoyen to curb government spending, to the disillusionment of much of his middle-class following. It is significant that the *golpe* of September 1930 encountered virtually no popular resistance: Yrigoyenist populism had dissipated itself even before the restoration of the oligarchic *régimen*.[17]

The 1930s were a critical watershed in Argentine history. Through the direct military intervention of September 1930, the oligarchy was restored to power; the fiction of representative democracy was retained but fraud—"patriotic fraud," as it was cynically called—ruled in the political arena.[18] Ironically, by their mere willingness to participate in the corrupt and fraudulent system, the opposition Personalist Radical and Socialist parties were tainted along with the ruling *concordancia*—or "concordance"— of conservatives. However, the crisis of the 1930s, which led ultimately to the emergence of a new populism, was much deeper than the *concordancia's* mere lack of legitimacy.

The thirteen years following the *golpe* of September 1930 produced profound changes in Argentina's economic and social structure. Ironically the conservative governments of this so-called infamous decade (which in many respects represented a throwback to pre-1916 political norms) largely initiated and oversaw the transformation of Argentina's traditional primary-export economy to a "nonintegrated industrial economy." Supporting limited and what it hoped would be temporary import substitution industrialization, the agrarian oligarchy struck a coalition of convenience with Argentine industrialists. The oligarchy hoped that expansion of domestic industry would ameliorate the drastic effects the world depression had upon the agrarian sector.[19]

Several points should be stressed about these developments in relation to the emergence of a new populism. The agrarian oligarchy did not accept industrialization as a permanent or in the long-run desirable situation. Its acceptance of emergency industrialization did not entail any commitment to a new, modern social order. Rather, they intended that it would alleviate the crisis without endangering Argentina's traditional political values and institutions or its fundamental class structure.[20] In fact, by the early 1940s the functional coalition between agrarian and industrial interests began to erode. The ruling agrarian elite retreated from proindustrial policies in anticipation of a postwar return to normalcy, that is, to the autonomous recovery of the primary export economy. Industrial interests were severely threatened by this retreat, to be sure. However, it must be remembered that industrial as well as agrarian interests did not intend that industrialization—temporary or permanent—should change Argentina's rigid class structure or upset the fraudulent political system which upheld it. Although the industrial sector sought a more powerful political role for itself and wished to guarantee the postwar survival of industrial development, it nevertheless relied heavily during this period on the state's police powers in its own struggle with a growing and increasingly restive industrial proletariat.[21] Furthermore, Argentine industrialists had expressed longstanding admiration for the oligarchy's social status, wishing to be assimilated rather than to challenge or supplant it. [22]

Thus by the early 1940s Argentina was faced with a generalized political and structural crisis. Industrialization had led to the rapid growth of the urban working class, large numbers of which were recently urbanized *criollos* from the interior provinces. Despite harsh police repression, the pronounced antilabor orientation of the government (reminiscent of the pre-1916 period), and debilitating interunion conflict, militancy among workers was on the upswing. Communist labor organizers, in particular, led the difficult drive to unionize the new industrial proletariat against the overt hostility of industrial interests and the covert opposition of many older, established unions. At the same time, industrialists themselves faced the grim prospect of a postwar attack on domestic industry by both the agrarian elite and foreign capital. Furthermore, the industrialists' concern for the survival of domestic industry was echoed by various segments of Argentine society: the labor movement had adopted a protectionist position during the course of the 1930s; middle-class intellectuals had become fervent economic nationalists; and the Argentine military had developed strong nationalist currents and championed Argentine industrial development.[23]

Juan Domingo Perón emerged as the arbiter among these various groups and tendencies. In sharp contrast to Yrigoyen, Perón's claim to a mass popular following and his ascent to power were not the product of a long and arduous struggle nor of political organizing. As one leader of the 1943 military *golpe,* Perón's accession to power preceded his formation of a mass political base. The significance of this simple truth can be easily overlooked: Perón built his populist movement not with the promise of an opposition politician nor with vague metaphysical pronouncements about political morality, but instead with immediate and concrete acts decreed and enforced by an authoritarian military government. "To act is better than to speak. To deliver is better than to promise." This, in Perón's own words, was the guiding principle in his construction of a mass, populist movement.[24]

From its inception, the mass social base of Peronism lay in the working class. For Yrigoyenist populism, the working class and the social question had always been peripheral elements, social and labor reform secondary and expedient concerns. For Peronism they were the core of the movement, representing Perón's principal electoral base as well as a massive counterweight against his inconsistent military, industrial, and middle-class supporters. Unlike Yrigoyen, Perón never denied that there was an intrinsic antagonism between labor and capital. He did not promise to eliminate class differences and class conflict but rather to make the state act as an arbiter to guarantee social justice, civil peace, and economic development.

In two years—from October 1943 to October 1945—Perón managed to win the overwhelming support of labor to his side.[25] The major components of his labor policy were to enforce existing labor legislation, to extend it to groups of workers previously excluded, to intervene in labor conflicts on the workers' behalf, and to broaden social security, medical, and other fringe benefits. Perón made extensive personal contact with workers, both in Buenos Aires and the interior, to generate support for his national labor program. He readily admitted, even boasted, that his approach was eclectic. He claimed that his reforms continued the historical struggles of labor yet broke fundamentally with the past. He promised to respect the autonomous and free development of the labor movement but offered to make the state labor's guardian and tutor. He spoke of Marxist class struggle but also of "social collaboration," an ideology of authoritarian corporativism. Finally, while directing his appeal to and basing his popular support on the working class, Perón consistently linked labor to socioeconomic integration, which he hoped would hold broad appeal for other sectors of society.[26]

Acutely aware of the economic transformations that had occurred since 1930 and of the difficulties the nation would face in the postwar era, Perón and other members of the military saw continued industrial progress as the basis of Argentina's power. "The future of the nation will be industrial or we will continue to be a semicolonial country," Perón declared.[27] Equitable and just solutions to labor and other social problems, he argued, were prerequisites for guaranteeing future industrial development. Therefore, for instance, Perón defended his concession of higher industrial wage rates not only in terms of social justice but also as a necessary element of rational economic planning. Wage hikes would stimulate internal demand and help domestic industry; alleviating the plight of the rural masses was partly justified as an attempt to stabilize the interior's social structure and curtail the rural exodus to urban industrial centers. Throughout, Perón attempted to sell his program to reluctant Argentine industrialists as being in their own best interests. He characterized his labor policies as insuring "social peace" and retarding militant communist unionism.[28]

Between 1943 and 1948, Perón forged a multiclass alliance amidst a steady growth of the G.N.P., which resulted from the wartime and immediate postwar export boom. This gave him great latitude to assign larger shares of the national income to the working class, to industrial investment, and (through government patronage) to many members of the nonentrepreneurial middle class *without* reducing the real incomes of other sectors.[29] The opposition to Perón from segments of the entrepreneurial and middle class did not stem from direct economic hardship but rather was motivated by a variety of other concerns: limitations the regime placed on wartime agrarian and other profits; concern about the regime's authoritarian political tendencies (despite the formal maintenance of elections, congress, and opposition parties); and, for many, simply the sociocultural transformation Peronism promoted.

In this last regard, Peronist populism signalled something of a cultural revolution. As a vindication of native *criollo* culture and as a movement that propounded the dignity of the common worker and the deprofessionalization of politics, Peronist populism was a profoundly democratizing social force—perhaps, one should add, in spite of itself.[30] The authoritarian, centralizing, and bureaucratic nature of Peronism as well as its heavy reliance (especially after 1950) on personalism and the cults of Perón and his charismatic wife, Evita Duarte, should not obscure the fact of Peronism's long-range integrative impact on Argentine society. Among other things, the extension of primary and technical education (especially in the interior provinces), the enfranchisement of women, and the institution of limited workers' control in the work place, all elevated the degree of popular participation and sovereignty. Peronism was the vehicle by which the Argentine masses began to pass from ascriptive norms of behavior in everyday affairs to elective norms—in other words, began to demand and to take control over their own lives.[31]

With the collapse of the postwar export boom in 1948 and generalized economic recession thereafter, Peronist populism began to erode. The Peronist state no longer merely allocated relative economic advantages but became genuinely redistributive: what was given to one sector came from some other because there was not an absolute rise in national income.[32] The economic emphasis of the regime shifted to revitalizing the agrarian sector and to promoting further industrialization by attracting foreign investment, thereby seeming to abandon Peronism's earlier fervent economic nationalism. This shift was accompanied by industrial unemployment, inflation, and a decline in the working classes' share of the national income, reflected by a steady reduction of real wages. The regime attempted to counterbalance these developments with greater fringe benefits and social welfare. Increasingly, however, Peronism relied on bureaucratic centralization, personalism, demagoguery, and repression to maintain its mass following.[33] Without disavowing the Peronist regime, militant sectors of the labor movement engaged in unsanctioned strike activity. They demanded a return to Peronism's earlier emphasis on fulfilling working class aspirations and protecting the patrimony against foreign capital. By 1955, Perón's popular following had waned sufficiently so as to preclude any mass resistance to the military movement that toppled his regime. The maintenance of multiclass Peronist populism during the "national development era" could not survive the debilitating impact of economic stagnation.[34]

As political and socially integrative populist movements, Radicalism and Peronism made great strides in the direction of democratizing Argentine society. Neither, however, was inclined, prepared, or able to transform Argentina's fundamental economic and class structures, nor to free Argentina from its dependency on foreign penetration of the national economy. The essential analagous qualities of these populist experiences—appeals to *argentinidad,* nationalism, social justice for all "the people," faith in the leader— ultimately failed to transcend basic class antagonisms, which economic adversity placed in particularly sharp relief. The symbols and rhetoric of Peronism remained capable of rallying mass resistance to exploitative society after 1955, and the continued appeal of Perón culminated in his brief return to the presidency after an exile of eighteen years.[35] However, the overwhelming failure of the Peronist restoration of 1973 to maintain a contemporary Argentine populism, together with Perón's death, strongly suggest the demise of populist politics in Argentina.

Notes

1. For the origins of the Unión Cívica Radical, see: Roberto Etcheapareborda, *La revolución argentina del 90* (Buenos Aires, 1966); Luis Alberto Romero, "El sugimiento y la llegada al poder," *El radicalismo* (Buenos Aires, 1968), pp. 7–21; David Rock, *Politics in Argentina 1890–1930: The Rise and Fall of Radicalism* (London, 1975), pp. 1–47, passim.

2. For a review of the epoch, see: Roberto Cortés Conde, "Auge de la economía y vicisitudes del régimen conservador (1890–1916)," *Historia argentina,* vol. 5: *La república conservadora* (Buenos Aires, 1972), pp. 97–233.

3. Romero, "El surgimiento," pp. 30–31; Rock, *Politics,* p. 55.

4. A definitive study of Yrigoyen has yet to be written. The classic work is: Manuel Gálvez, *Vida de Hipólito Yrigoyen—el hombre de misterio* (Buenos Aires, 1939). Also see: Félix Luna *Yrigoyen* (Buenos Aires. 1964). The great Argentine essayist and social critic Ezequiel Martínez Estrada wrote of Yrigoyen that he "embodied [a] transcendental and

magic reality in his person, in his mentality and in his acts as apostle and martyr. . ." in Ezequiel Martínez Estrada, *X-Ray of the Pampa,* trans. Alan Swietlicki (Austin, 1971), p. 281.

5. Peter H. Smith, *Argentina and the Failure of Democracy. Conflict among Political Elites 1904 –1955* (Madison, 1974), pp. 30 – 31; Rock, *Politics, p. 58.*

6. Smith, *Argentina,* pp. 30 – 31, treats the issue of the social composition of Radical Party office holders. Yrigoyen's economic policies are discussed in: Peter H. Smith, "Los radicales argentinos y la defensa de los intereses ganaderos, 1916–1930," *Desarrollo económico* 7 (April-June 1967): 795 – 829; and Carl Solberg, "The Tariff and Politics in Argentina, 1916 – 1930," *Hispanic American Historical Review* 53 (May 1973): 260 – 84.

7. The university reforms of 1918 and the Argentine university student movement associated with it have served as models for similar activities and reforms in many other Latin America countries since that year. See: Tulio Halperín Donghi, *Historia de la universidad de Buenos Aires* (Buenos Aires, 1962), pp. 110 – 20, passim.

8. Ricardo M. Ortiz, "El aspecto económico-social de la crisis de 1930," *Revista de historia* 3 (1958): 41 – 72; Hobart Spalding (ed.), *La clase trabajadora argentina: Documentos para su historia 1890–1912* (Buenos Aires, 1970), pp. 46 – 49; Carl Solberg, *Immigration and Nationalism: Argentina and Chile, 1890–1914* (Austin, 1970), pp. 93 – 117, passim.

9. José Panettieri, *Los trabajadores* (Buenos Aires, 1967), pp. 125 – 34.

10. For the content of Yrigoyen's *obrerismo,* see: Juan Carlos Grosso, "Los problemas económicos y sociales y la repuesta radical en el gobierno (1916 – 1930)," *El radicalismo* (Buenos Aires, 1968) pp. 163 – 69; Alfredo N. Morrone, *El derecho obrero y el Presidente Yrigoyen* (Buenos Aires, 1928). Rock, *Politics,* pp. 119 – 20, treats the political aspect of *obrerismo.*

11. Rock, *Politics,* chapter 6, passim.

12. The growth of syndicalist union membership is discussed in Alfredo L. Palacios, *El nuevo derecho,* 5th ed. (Buenos Aires, 1960), p. 226.

13. The most complete account of the Semana Trágica is to be found in: Julio Godío, *La Semana Trágica de enero de 1919* (Buenos Aires, 1966).

14. Richard J. Walter, "Elections in the City of Buenos Aires during the First Yrigoyen Administration: Social Class and Political Preferences," *Hispanic American Historical Review* 58 (November 1978): 595 – 624.

15. The most important of these provincial populist movements were those of Federico Cantoni in San Juan and Carlos Wáshington Lencinas in Mendoza.

16. See Carl Solberg, *Oil and Nationalism in Argentina: A History* (Stanford, 1979), chapter 5, passim; Rock, *Politics,* pp. 241 – 46.

17. An excellent analysis and review of the events surrounding the revolution of September 1930 can be found in *Revista de historia* 3 (1958). The entire volume is dedicated to "La crisis de 1930."

18. Alberto Ciria, *Partidos y poder en la Argentina moderna (1930 –46),* 2nd ed. (Buenos Aires, 1968), pp. 53–55, passim.

19. Miguel Murmis and Juan Carlos Portantiero, *Estudios sobre los orígenes del peronismo,* 2nd ed. (Buenos Aires, 1972), pp. 3 – 25. Government policy goals are elaborated in Argentine Republic, Ministerio de Hacienda, *El plan de acción económica nacional* (Buenos Aires, 1934).

20. Mónica Peralta Ramos, *Etapas de acumulación y alianzas de clases en la Argentina (1930 –1970)* (Buenos Aires, 1972), pp. 75 – 91.

21. See: David Tamarin, "The Argentine Labor Movement in an Age of Transition, 1930 – 1945" (Ph.D. diss. University of Washington, 1977), pp. 137 – 49, passim.

22. Peter H. Smith, *Politics and Beef in Argentina* (New York and London, 1969), pp. 134 – 35.

23. Tamarin, "The Argentine Labor Movement," pp. 268–70; Ciria, *Partidos,* pp. 172–76, 246–53.

24. Juan Perón, *El pueblo quiere saber de qué se trata* (Buenos Aires, 1944), p. 32.

25. Juan Carlos Torre, "La C. G. T. y el 17 de octubre de 1945," *Todo es Historia* 197 (March 1976): 70-90; Tamarin, "The Argentine Labor Movement," chapter 7, passim.

26. See, Luis F. Boulin Zapata, "La intervención del estado en la vida económica," *Boletín de la Secretaría de Industria y Comercio* (November 1944): 139–50.

27. Perón's speech to Argentine industrialists, 18 January 1945, reprinted in *Boletín de la Secretaría de Industria y Comercio* (January 1945): 313.

28. *La Prensa,* 12 November 1943; *La Nación,* 28 July and 29 September 1944.

29. Argentine Republic, Secretaría de Asuntos Económicos, *Producto e ingreso de la República Argentina en el período 1935-54* (Buenos Aires, 1955), pp. 116–121.

30. See: Pedro Getlam, "Mitos, símbolos y héroes en el peronismo," *El peronismo,* ed. Beatriz Sarlo Sabajanes (Buenos Aires, 1969) pp. 109–37.

31. Gino Germani, *Política y sociedad en una época de transición* (Buenos Aires, 1962).

32. David Rock, "The Survival and Restoration of Peronism," *Argentina in the Twentieth Century,* ed. David Rock (London, 1975), p. 191.

33. Walter Little, "Party and State in Peronist Argentina, 1945–55," *Hispanic American Historical Review* 53 (November 1973): 644–62. The evolution from emphasis on integrative ideology to emphasis on an exaggerated cultism of Perón and Evita can be traced through the pages of *Mundo Peronista* between 1951 and 1955.

34. The working-class and labor movement were sufficiently dissatisfied with Peronism by 1955 to accept the "Liberating Revolution" of September 1955 with its false promise that the earlier advances achieved by labor through the aegis of the Peronist state would be protected. See: Juan Carlos Torre and Santiago Senén Gonzales, *Ejército y sindicatos (los 60 dias de Lonardi)* (Buenos Aires, 1969), pp. 11–45.

35. Rock, "The Survival," pp. 194–220; Daniel James, "The Peronist Left, 1955–1975," *Journal of Latin American Studies* 8 (November 1976): 273–96. For a review of post-1955 development in Argentina, see: Félix Luna, *Argentina, de Perón a Lanusse 1943–1973* (Buenos Aires, 1973).

3

Evita's Charismatic Leadership

Marysa Navarro
Dartmouth College

The most striking and unusual characteristic of Peronism, when compared with other forms of populism, is its dual leadership. Indeed, from 1946, when General Juan Domingo Perón was elected president, until July 26, 1952, when Evita died, Argentina was headed by two charismatic leaders who complemented each other totally, although the origins and the nature of their leadership differed greatly.

Perón and Evita's charismatic relationship with their followers has been a significant factor in Argentine politics since the mid-1940s. It survived her death, his ousting by a military coup in 1955, and his eighteen-year exile. Yet the subject of charismatic leadership in Peronism has received little attention.[1] What follows is an attempt to examine one aspect of this question: Evita's leadership during Perón's first term in office from 1946 to 1952.

Max Weber first discussed the concept of charismatic leadership in *The Theory of Social and Economic Organization,* where he described three possible forms of legitimate authority: traditional, rational or legal, and personal or charismatic. The latter, he explained, was defined by the possession of charisma,

a certain quality of an individual personality by virtue of which

> he is set apart from ordinary men and treated as endowed with supernatural, superhuman, or at last specifically exceptional powers or qualities. These are such as are not accessible to the ordinary person, but are regarded as of divine origin or as exemplary, and on the basis of them the individual concerned is treated as a leader.[2]

According to Weber, a charismatic leader is distinguished by his sense of mission and his capacity to inspire devotion, loyalty, and "absolute trust" on the part of his followers. His charisma, revealed through some " 'sign' or proof, originally always a miracle" is not by itself the basis of his legitimacy; it "lies rather in the conception that it is the *duty* of those who have been called to a charismatic mission to recognize its quality and to act accordingly."[3] "Recognition," he pointed out, may arise "out of enthusiasm, or of despair, or hope."[4]

Weber identified charisma as "a phenomenon typical of prophetic religious movements or of expansive political movements in their early stages. But as soon as the position of authority is well established, and above all as soon as control over large masses of people exists, it gives way to the forces of everyday routine."[5] He further emphasized that "in its pure form charismatic authority may be said to exist only in the process of originating. It cannot remain stable, but becomes either traditionalized or routinized, or a combination of both."[6]

For Weber, the concept of charismatic leadership was value-neutral. How charisma "would be ultimately judged from any ethical, aesthetic, or other such point of view is naturally entirely indifferent for purposes of definition."[7] He mentioned several types of charismatic leaders—war heroes, "berserkers," "shamans," and such people as Joseph Smith, the Bavarian Communist intellectual Kurt Eisner, and prophets—but he did not offer an extensive analysis of political charismatic leadership. However, it is precisely in the realm of politics that his ideas have proved to be most fruitful. In recent years, for example, social scientists have used the concept of charismatic leadership to analyze the transition of certain colonial societies into independent nations.[8] On the other hand, despite these and other attempts to elaborate a theory of charismatic leadership, the very concept remains elusive. Substantial disagreement exists among scholars about its usefulness, its applicability, the conditions in which charismatic leaders may emerge, their characteristics, or what happens when they die.[9]

At first sight, Weber's ideas on charismatic leadership appear to be neither useful nor applicable in the case of Evita. First and foremost, charismatic leadership is usually identified with men. Indeed, the concept is generally infused with specifically male characteristics.[10] Yet during her short public life, Evita inspired as much devotion, obedience, and "absolute trust" as Perón. Second although charismatic leadership is found in moments of crisis, when a movement is striving to change specific conditions, Evita's leadership emerged when "the process of originating" was completed, as a result of Perón's decision to allow her to act as his liaison with labor after he was elected president. Third she *shared* her leadership with Perón, yet the concept of "shared charisma" seems incongruent, self-negating.

Moreover Evita cannot be studied isolated from Perón because her leadership originated in him. It was explicitly exercised as a complement of his, yet he, in turn, presents additional difficulties. Perón's leadership was proclaimed and "recognized" during a massive demonstration that took place some four months before his election to the presidency, that is to say, after "the process of originating" was over. Indeed, throughout his first two terms in office (1946−55), Perón was president as well leader of the *descamisados* (shirtless ones), as his followers were known. Charisma, in Perón's case, did not "give way to the forces of everyday routine," but continued to coexist with his "control of large masses of people" and remained "stable."

Despite these difficulties and even the contradictions with Weber's model enumerated above, a closer look will reveal that his ideas are useful and applicable to the study of Evita as a charismatic leader.

Although Evita is undoubtedly Latin America's most famous female politician, for most of her life she was far more interested in her acting career than in politics. Born in 1919, of a lower-class background, illegitimate and barely educated, she was a successful radio actress when she met Colonel Perón in early 1944. He was then the most controversial political figure among the group of military officers who had ruled Argentina since June 4, 1943. Her interest in politics began to develop as a result of her relationship with him and of her participation in a propaganda program sponsored by the secretariat of labor. Nevertheless, her career as a soap opera and film actress continued to be her main concern until

October 23, 1945, when she abandoned it to marry Perón. His election to the presidency in February 1946 altered her life to such an extent that by 1949 she had become the second most powerful and influential person in the Peronist administration. By the time she died on July 26, 1952, she was Eva Perón, Argentina's First Lady; "Evita," *la abanderada de los descamisados* (the standard bearer of the shirtless ones); Perón's liaison with labor; president of the Partido Peronista Femenino (the women's branch of the Peronist party); and head of the Eva Perón Foundation.

Perón's involvement in politics also began in the early forties. When the June 4 coup took place, he was a forty-eight-year-old colonel who had taught military history at the National War College and was highly respected by his fellow officers. Although he had taken part in Gen. José Félix Uriburu's military coup of September 6, 1930, his interest in social and political matters was recent and had been aroused by a training tour to Italy and other fascist countries in 1939–41. These experiences would guide him for several years. On October 27, 1943, Perón took over the department of labor, which until then had been a second echelon agency whose role was primarily to suppress labor independence. Perón had it raised to secretariat by the end of the next month and soon transformed it into the symbol of a new era in Argentine labor relations by implementing old laws, enacting new ones, supporting demands for unionization, and in general developing a social policy that raised the standards of living and working conditions of rural, urban, and white collar workers.[11]

The origins of Perón's leadership are to be found in his actions as secretary of labor and in the relationship he established with labor from 1943 to 1945. He was helped by several factors, among others Argentina's favorable economic conditions because of World War II, the existence of a fast-growing working class with large numbers of nonunionized workers, a highly bureaucratized labor movement, and an entirely new political style. He met daily with labor leaders and the rank and file in the secretariat of labor, visited their headquarters and factories, and attended their rallies. When he addressed them, he spoke of social justice, emphasized workers' rights, and proclaimed the beginning of a new era in which the state would end inhumane exploitation of workers.[12] He used a radical language, previously unheard in government officials but appreciated by the workers because it was their own.

Perón's policies found strong resistance among all political parties, which already opposed the military government because of its neutralist stand in World War II (in fact pro-Axis) and its suspension of constitutional guarantees. The Communists and Socialists, who controlled much of organized labor until 1943, were particularly antagonistic toward Perón and denounced him as a demagogue and a Nazi. Yet his personal support among labor continued to grow, even among the Socialists, and his relationship with workers remained close. In October 1945, during a crisis that gripped Argentina for nine days, it was put to a test, only to emerge strengthened.

The crisis erupted on October 9 when Perón, then also minister of war and vice-president, was forced to resign from his three posts by his military opponents in the Campo de Mayo garrison. His dismissal precipitated a cabinet crisis for the president, Gen. Edelmiro J. Farrell. Cabinet members presented their resignations and Farrell set out to form a new government. Before abandoning the secretariat, however, Perón had addressed a workers' rally where he announced several measures favorable to labor. His speech so angered his enemies that on October 13 he was detained and jailed on Martín García Island. The news of Perón's arrest triggered the reaction of labor leaders and the rank and file; helped by his collaborators in the secretariat of labor, they began to mobilize to obtain his release. On October 15, sugar workers in Tucumán province went on strike and that same day the General Confederation of Workers (CGT) met to consider a motion to declare a general strike. It was voted for the 18th but on the morning of the 17th, workers abandoned their factories en masse and invaded Buenos Aires. Demanding Perón's release, they converged on the Plaza de Mayo. Neither the police nor the Campo de Mayo garrison stopped them, and they were joined by throngs of men and women throughout the day. They did not leave until late that night, after Perón finally appeared on a balcony of the Casa Rosada and spoke to them.[13]

Perón's presence in the government house and his speech, frequently interrupted by expressions of delirious enthusiasm, marked the transformation of his relationship with the Argentine working class into a bond that would unite them for the following thirty years.[14] It was then that he emerged explicitly as "the leader" and his followers "the *descamisados*"—indeed the terms were used shortly after to describe Perón and the crowds that flocked to the

Plaza de Mayo.[15] The latter recognized him as their "hero," their "leader," because in a decisive and unprecedented action, he had taken up their defense and in a short time had changed their lives in tangible ways. Socialist and Communist accusations notwithstanding, they knew that the secretariat of labor had become a different institution since he began directing it. His broad smile inspired confidence when he received labor leaders in his office, and they soon found themselves at ease, chatting amicably with him. Furthermore, he knew how to address a workers' rally as if he were a seasoned labor leader. Because of his actions in support of labor, his enemies had demanded his resignation, jailed him, and even threatened his life. In the workers' eyes, Perón's enemies were therefore their enemies. In attacking him, they had threatened the gains they had achieved since 1943. Their fears were augmented by the inaugural speech of the newly appointed secretary of labor, the reaction of employers when workers went to get their October 12 salary, and the rumors about the composition of Farrell's cabinet, which indicated that the conservative oligarchy would soon be back in power.[16] Identifying their gains with Perón, they went on strike, forcing the CGT leadership to declare it. They made themselves his followers and as a result of their action, their hero was freed and returned to them. Their mobilization signified their express recognition of Perón's leadership, a collective recognition according to Weber, "decisive for the validity of charisma."[7]

The events of October 17 had the significance of a founding act: the symbolic proclamation of Perón's leadership and the surrender of the collective will because he embodied it. In the years to come, the ceremony would be reenacted every October 17 with a massive rally held in the same plaza; Perón, standing on the same balcony, would speak to the *descamisados* as he did that night. The ritual would take place on a national holiday officially called Loyalty Day, in remembrance of the loyalty he had shown to the *descamisados,* comparable only to the loyalty they had demonstrated toward him.

By their actions, both Perón and his followers had broken the accepted rules and roles of political and social behavior and repudiated past practices. Their meeting on October 17 can thus be characterized in Weber's words as revolutionary.[18] But the charismatic relationship that revealed itself on that day did not in fact invalidate existing institutions, did not altogether destroy the accepted rules. It might better be said to have superimposed itself on top of them. Instead of acting in accordance with the new authority vested in him, Perón, the newly anointed leader, became that very day a candidate in the forthcoming presidential elections. Indeed, the following month Perón announced his candidacy, and the mandate he received on October 17 was formalized and confirmed in February 1946, when he was elected president.

According to Weber's model, Perón's leadership had undergone its "process of originating." From then on "routinization" should take over and inevitably erode his relationship with the *descamisados*. Instead, it remained intact until 1952 and became even stronger. The key to this unexpected transformation was the incorporation of Evita into Perón's leadership.

Perón won the 1946 election in a campaign that pitted him against all the political parties that existed prior to the 1943 coup. From Communists to conservatives, they were united in an anti-Perón front, but he received 1,527,231 votes out of a total of 2,734,386. He also won all but two of the provincial governorships, all of the Senate seats, and a large majority in the Chamber of Deputies. Nevertheless, his position was far from secure. He lacked a solid political party, having entered the presidential race backed by two organizations created after October 17. The Unión Cívica Radical (Junta Renovadora), a small offshoot of the Unión Cívica Radical, and the Partido Laborista, organized by labor leaders, were united only by the person of Perón himself, and their disagreements flared up as soon as the campaign got underway. The Labor Party itself presented a serious danger to Perón because it was headed by seasoned labor leaders who had the respect of the rank and file and who, though committed to him, also wanted to maintain some independence. Furthermore, its leadership overlapped with that of the CGT, and as late as October 15, 1945, the labor leaders had clearly refused to put their organizations entirely in Perón's hands.

On October 15, the CGT met to consider a motion to declare a general strike. The minutes of that meeting indicate that the delegates understood the full impact of Perón's policies on Argentine labor. Like the rank and file, the labor leaders supported him because these policies had put an end to long-standing grievances. They did not disagree with the course adopted by the workers who had abandoned their jobs in protest against Perón's arrest. In fact, they saw no other alternative but to declare a general strike. However, they resisted calling a general strike for the purpose of releasing Perón because such an action would signify the surrender of their leadership to him. The motion finally adopted setting the strike for October 18 did not include Perón's name.[19]

The CGT attempt to maintain its legitimacy as a labor organization was thwarted by the workers' mobilization of the 17th, which left the labor leaders in a difficult position. They tried to regain some ground by founding the Labor Party, but it was too late, and in May 1946 Perón dissolved it. His action was openly resisted by some labor leaders, while others accepted it but persisted in trying to maintain a labor movement independent from him.[20]

Perón's position was further endangered by the rapid expansion of organized labor, the massive incorporation of industrial workers, which changed the composition of the CGT membership, and the high level of worker mobilization, which led them to strike for higher wages and better working conditions. All this occurred at a time when the secretariat of labor—newly transformed into a ministry—was unprepared to meet their demands.

If Perón was to maintain the social basis of his power, he needed to continue to satisfy these demands and tighten his control of the labor movement. He also needed to be assured that the minister of labor would not undermine his contact with the *descamisados* and find some means to continue the political style he had established as secretary of labor. His election in fact threatened his relationship with the *descamisados,* but he was able to circumvent the problems posed by his presidential duties by adopting the following steps. On the one hand, he named to the ministry of labor a barely known labor leader, José María Freire, who owed his preeminence to Perón and thus could not easily become his rival. On the other hand, he allowed Evita to be his substitute and thus delegated to her his personal contact with the rank and file.

Shortly after Perón was inaugurated, Evita began to undertake certain activities very unusual for an Argentine first lady. Not only did she accompany the president wherever he went, but she also met with workers' delegations in an office made available to her in the Post Office building, visited factories and union headquarters, attended rallies, and everywhere made speeches in the name of Perón. In September 1946 her office was transferred to the ministry of labor, which was located where Perón's *old* secretariat had been. By this move he informed his followers that from then on Evita was his liaison with them, that he relied on her to keep in contact with them, and that, though he was the president of Argentina, he had not ceased to be secretary of labor—a point repeatedly implied by Evita in her speeches when she called Perón "the colonel" (although he had been promoted to general) and mentioned "the secretariat" (although it had become a ministry). Furthermore, by December 1946 her role as Perón's liaison with labor was made official by a presidential press release.[21]

Discussion of Perón's and Evita's personal reasons for undertaking such an extraordinary course lies beyond the scope of the paper.[22] What matters here is that by delegating his personal contact with labor to her, he gave her the legitimacy she needed to be accepted by the *descamisados,* transferred to her part of his leadership, and in so doing prevented its "routinization." Evita's charismatic leadership, however, did not emerge overnight, as a result of Perón's decision. It developed gradually, as she established her usefulness to the *descamisados* and Perón, during his first two years in office. While maintaining her close identification with him, she nevertheless began to individualize her role; she acquired a political language of her own, and her personality became more distinct.

Her transformation took place during the period in which Perón asserted his control over organized labor and isolated the remnants of Laborista opposition among his followers. The process was completed in 1948: by then José Espejo was secretary general of the CGT, and that year congressional elections reinforced Perón's hold on the Chamber of Deputies. It was crowned by a constitutional reform which permitted his reelection in 1951. By the time Perón consolidated his power, Evita had become an integral part of it, and her own relationship with the *descamisados* was already clearly established. In a symbolic recognition of her new status, on October 17, 1948 she addressed for the first time the crowds in the Plaza de Mayo with Perón.

Her presence on the balcony of the Casa Rosada confirmed the legitimacy of her leadership. It was the "proof" or "sign" of her charisma, but it also had an additional symbolic meaning. As co-leader of the *descamisados,* she had to be a participant in the alliance that emerged on October 17, 1945. Since she had not been part of the original "covenant," she had to be integrated into the process that began that day. Her 1948 speech therefore established her link with the earlier events and made her a participant after the fact in the founding of Peronism.

The 1948 confirmation of Evita's role in Peronism is doubly important, for many writers have erroneously ascribed to her a greater part in the workers mobilization of October 1945. Such portrayals of her forceful actions are unsubstantiated accounts, void of concrete details but rich in adjectives depicting her supposed attitude.[23] They are creations a posteriori which reflect the fiery personality she exhibited in the late forties but not the person she was in 1945. What Evita did during the October crisis was to try to obtain a writ of habeas corpus for Perón's release. While the days he spent on Martín García Island may have been intensely painful for her, she had neither the experience nor the contacts with labor leaders and the rank and file to be an organizer of the workers' demonstration.

Although Perón was the ultimate source of Evita's authority, the basis of her leadership came from the actual work she performed with the rank and file. Every day she met with countless delegations of workers in her ministry office. They went to see her for a variety of reasons: in some cases, they wanted help because they were organizing a union or were involved in contract negotiations. In others, they needed her support to win an internal election, to force an employer to implement a specific labor law, or to improve the working conditions in a particular factory. What she did essentially was to listen to all requests, relay them to the appropriate office, and, (acting in Perón's name) exert enough pressure to speed up paper work and obtain prompt results. She soon acquired the reputation of being efficient, and workers were quick to realize that in order to get what they wanted, it was to their advantage to channel their requests through her.

Evita undoubtedly helped the ministry of labor to maintain its frantic pace of recruitment by her constant and forceful intervention—membership in the CGT rose from 441,412 in 1941 to 528,523 in 1945 to 1,532,925 in 1948.[24] Furthermore, at a time when the CGT secretariat was headed by old labor leaders like Luis F. Gay or Aurelio Hernández, who resisted the "peronization" of organized labor, she weakened the effectiveness of the secretariat by establishing an alternative line of communication with the ministry of labor. Indeed, the labor leaders with whom she met in this early period were intermediate cadres, and her relations with the leaders of the largest unions were cool—a situation which changed radically in December 1947, when a new secretariat was elected and its members, from the Secretary General José Espejo down to the last man, were all enthusiastic Peronists. By establishing contact with men who could replace old labor leaders, head new unions, be candidates in the 1948 elections, and lead the Peronist Party, she also contributed to the consolidation of Perón's power.

Evita's meetings with labor delegations remained the center of her political activities. Even after she began spending long hours—sometimes until 3 or 4 in the morning—taking care of matters related to the Fundación Eva Perón and started organizing the women's branch of the Peronist Party she still managed to meet with the CGT secretariat and labor delegations every day.

There is no doubt that favorable economic conditions in Argentina following World War II enabled Perón to pursue the same type of policy he had devised as secretary of labor. But as workers continued to sign generous labor contracts, form new unions, receive more fringe benefits or improve their working conditions, Evita became identified with these gains, and she was perceived as responsible for the continuation of Perón's social policy.

Although the workers' allegiance to Evita was emphasized by the new CGT secretariat, which constantly stated its debt to her, as her power and influence augmented, she was able not only to satisfy more requests but also to obtain funds for projects that directly benefited the *descamisados.* In this respect, the Fundación Eva Perón, whose funds she controlled exclusively, was particularly useful to her. From 1949 on she subsidized vacations of *descamisados,* gave them funds for their union headquarters, and built luxurious hospitals, modern clinics, low cost housing projects, and elegant hotels for them.

Evita's leadership did not separate the *descamisados* from Perón. On the contrary, it strengthened the bond that united them to him because she was his wife, therefore part of him and at all times acted on his behalf—a point she never failed to make in her speeches.

One of her main functions from 1946–52 was to give speeches. Her effectiveness as a public speaker was a valuable asset to Perón, and in fact, together with the work she performed on a daily basis with the rank and file, it may have been what thrust her into political prominence. Her first public speech, part of the government campaign to lower the cost of living, was followed by many others in which she explained the goals of the Five-Year Plan, urged the adoption of women's suffrage, asked unions to remain faithful to

Perón as they had done in October 1945, backed Peronist deputies in the 1948 congressional elections, advocated the need of a constitutional reform, eulogized Perón's doctrine—Justicialismo and The Third Position—warned against the threats posed by Communists and oligarchs, and, even when she was very sick, begged Peronists to reelect Perón in 1951.

Although she occasionally spoke on the radio, most of these speeches were given when she was visited by labor delegations or at meetings organized by the CGT, individual unions, and the Peronist Party. Whatever the specific occasion, however, the same themes reappeared, constantly repeated with very few changes: the terrible conditions in which workers lived before 1943; the benefits they had obtained when Perón took over the secretariat of labor; the accomplishments of the June 1943 Revolution—multiplied tenfold by Perón who had transformed Argentina into a country "economically independent, socially just, and politically sovereign" where workers could now live in happiness and joy; the absolute necessity for Perón to remain in power so as to further social justice in Argentina; Perón's love for the *descamisados;* his greatness and the extraordinary significance of his doctrine; the *descamisados'* duty to fight for their rights and for Perón and to defend them from their enemies—the Communists, the oligarchy, capitalism, and imperialism.

When Evita spoke from the balcony of the Casa Rosada during the May 1 or October 17 celebrations, she did not alter her themes or her objectives, but she worded and delivered her speeches very differently. They became explosions of passion and fury, veritable harangues calculated to arouse an emotional response from the audience. They contrasted with Perón's speeches, which explained and argued in a simple and clear language and were delivered in a calm, reassuring, fatherly tone. When Evita spoke, her long hands clutched the microphone or slashed the air. Her voice would rise tense and urging, and at a rapid pace she sent blast after blast against Perón's enemies, slowing down only to pronounce caressingly his name or the word *descamisados.*

Using a language that was extracted from soap operas, she transformed politics into dramas dominated by relentless invocations of love: Perón's work in the secretariat of labor was prompted by his love for workers; they had saved him on October 17 because they loved him; she was sacrificing her life for all because of her love for them; and the love that united Perón, Evita, and the *descamisados* was the cause of the oligarchy's hatred towards them. Her scenarios never changed and her characters were stereotyped by the same adjectives: Perón was always "glorious," the people "marvelous," the oligarchy *egoista y vendepatria* (selfish and corrupt), and she was a "humble" or "weak" woman, "burning her life for them" so that social justice could be achieved, *cueste lo que cueste y caiga quien caiga* (at whatever cost and regardless of consequences). On May 1, 1951, she ended her speech with the following words:

> "And if I could choose among all the things of this world, I would choose the infinite grace to die for the cause of Perón, which is to die for you. Because I, too, like the comrade workers, am capable of dying and ending the last moment of my life with our war cry, our salvation cry: our lives for Perón.[25]

Evita did not display the full range of her rhetoric, with its unique style and extraordinary vocabulary and sentence structure, until the last two years of her life. But it was already noticeable in 1946 when she began to act as Perón's substitute and visited factories or met with labor delegations in the ministry. With an aggressive language, which was the same Perón had used while secretary of labor but which he had abandoned since taking office, she reminded her audiences that "the colonel" had brought social justice to Argentina and was committed to pursue the same policy as president. As the years went by, her speaking style became increasingly violent, especially after the aborted military coup of September 1951. It is therefore not surprising that twenty years after her death, it was Evita's radical statements that would be adopted as revolutionary slogans by a new generation of Peronists and used as demonstrations of the revolutionary potential of Peronism, a potential thwarted by the enemies she had singled out.

But the radicalism of Evita's discourse cannot be viewed isolated from Perón's own discourse. Whether in 1946, 1949, or 1951, her speeches had the unmistakable purpose of establishing the continuity between the past and the present, reinforcing the *descamisados'* allegiance to Perón—and therefore their control—and exalting his personality as the symbol of their will, their rights, and their welfare.

a's leadership was defined from the very start on the basis of
s superiority. He was the undisputed leader, *el líder* or *el conductor,* the ideologue who elaborated the doctrine, the strategist who defined the goals and articulated the plans to achieve them.[26] As for Evita, she concerned herself only with repeating Perón's ideas time and again to his followers, innovating only insofar as his cause would be furthered and carrying out the tactics which he outlined. As she stated in her autobiography: "He is the leader. I am only the shadow of his superior presence."[27] She never used the word *leader* to describe herself and neither did the *descamisados,* although a few weeks before her death, Congress granted her the title of Spiritual Leader of the Nation. As the "shadow" of Perón, however, she had numerous titles: *la abanderada de los humildes* or *la abanderada de los trabajadores* (the standard bearer of the poor or the workers); *el escudo de Perón* (Perón's shield); *la esperanza y la eterna vigía de la revolución* (the hope and the eternal guardian of the revolution); *la plenipotenciaria de los descamisados* (the plenipotentiary of the shirtless ones); and the one she seems to have preferred, because she used it most often to describe herself, *el puente de amor entre Perón y al pueblo* (the bridge of love between Perón and the people). These titles were not mere rhetorical devices created by the peronist propaganda machinery or herself in order to satisfy her vanity, which was great, but rather they were accurate descriptions of the role she performed between 1946 and 1952, as well as reflections of her own relationship with the *descamisados.*

Perhaps the best way to understand their significance is to examine the structure of her speeches, especially those she pronounced from the balcony of the Casa Rosada during the October 17 or May 1 celebrations. On such occasions, Evita's speeches were composed of three basic elements: Perón, the *descamisados,* and herself as the nexus between them. If she began addressing the latter, she usually spoke to them as if she were Perón but keeping a certain distance from him. She would then change the direction of speech and address herself to Perón, calling him *mi general,* as if she were part of the public but speaking in its name. Finally, she would separate herself from Perón and the *descamisados* to reaffirm that she was only a humble woman who loved both Perón and the *descamisados* and who was dedicated to work until death for their happiness.

In a speech she gave during the final session of a CGT congress, for example, she began by establishing her identification with Perón: "I, who had the great honor of sharing with the general his concerns, his dreams, and his patriotic achievements, feel proud to have followed the good path, that is to say, the path pointed out to us by General Perón." Later on, she switched sides and in her inimitable syntax she spoke to him identifying herself with the *descamisados* but separated from them. "My general: here is the CGT with its *descamisado* vanguard, with your glorious and beloved *descamisado* vanguards, present to honor you and to support you, not in a circumstantial fashion, because that support comes from men who when they shout 'our lives for Perón' did it on October 17, 1945 . . . ." Still speaking to Perón, she proceeded as if she were part of the public:

> "Because my general, we fight for economic independence; we fight for social justice; we fight for sovereignty and for the honor of our flag; we fight for the happiness of our children and for the humanization of a capitalism that has only brought us sterile struggles among brothers; we fight for the consolidation in our Fatherland of the extraordinary doctrine of our celebrated workers' leader."

Finally, she separated herself from all:

> "I thank you comrade workers for the honor bestowed upon this humble woman who works trying to interpret the patriotic dreams of General Perón. . . . This stimulates me and spurs me to continue; it is the most honorable decoration in the breast of a woman who comes from the people, who is proud to belong to the people, and whose work is to listen to the palpitations of the working people."[28]

Evita could speak *to* the *descamisados* because she was Perón's delegate, his interpreter, his "shield," his intermediary with them. She could speak *to* Perón, because she was their intermediary with him, their standard bearer, their plenipotenciary. And in relation to *both,* she was "the hope and the eternal guard of the revolution," "the bridge of love between Perón and the people."

Evita never failed to emphasize Perón's superiority and praised him lavishly and tirelessly. Although the government propaganda machine, party officials, and Peronist congressmen echoed her words, they could not compete with her passionate declarations of nending love for Perón and the *descamisados*. She proclaimed her fanatic allegiance to them, her willingness to sacrifice her life for them, and demanded in turn from his followers comparable assertions of love, fidelity, gratitude, obedience, and commitment to die for Perón. She never spared superlatives when referring to him. He was "glorious," "superior," "incomparable," heaven could not exist without him.[29] In a speech she delivered at the Escuela Superior Peronista she explained that the study of world history proved conclusively that he was a genius superior in all respects to such men as Lycurgus, Alexander the Great, Napoleon, or Karl Marx. "I have analyzed him deeply. Perón is perfect."[30]

Her pleas and demands for unity, discipline, faith in Perón, trust in Perón, and obedience to Perón, all of which were repeated endlessly, created an atmosphere where self-criticism and challenge were successfully eliminated. By 1949, subjection to the leader's will had become a cardinal principle of Peronism. In so doing, Evita gave it another one of its striking, but this time not exclusive, characteristics: a cult of the leader so powerful that it survived Perón's eighteen-year exile. When he returned to Argentina, it was even given a new name: *verticalismo* (verticalism).

Blond, pale, and beautiful, Evita was the incarnation of the Mediator, a Virgin-like figure who despite her origins, shared the perfection of the Father because of her closeness to him. Her mission was to love infinitely, give herself to others and "burn her life" for others, a point made painfully literal when she fell sick with cancer and refused to interrupt her activities. She was the Blessed Mother, chosen by God to be near "the leader of the new world: Perón."[31] She was the childless mother who became the Mother of all the *descamisados,* the Mater Dolorosa who "sacrificed" her life so that the poor, the old, and the downtrodden could find some happiness.

This image of Evita was a mask that hid another woman: the shrewd and jealous politician who bullied ministers, worked at a frantic pace, and ran the Eva Perón Foundation and the Partido Peronista Femenino with an iron hand. The mediator image was nurtured by her and repeated ad nauseam by government officials, party members, and labor leaders, and it became real for many peronists. A few days after her death in July 1952, a labor union sent a telegram to the Pope requesting her canonization, and twenty years later Peronists still bought Madonna pictures of her.

Perón and Evita offer an interesting example of what may be called institutionalized charisma or, in Weber's words, routinized charisma. Of the two, Evita clearly represented pure charismatic authority since she did not hold an elected post or an official government position. She moved outside of the institutional structure, tied to it only informally, and therefore free to exert her influence without institutional constraints. She was checked only by Perón, as when her inflamatory speeches would be tempered by him. As president and leader of the *descamisados,* however, Perón embodied both charismatic and routinized or legal authority. He was able to overcome "the forces of everyday routine" because he transferred part of his charisma to Evita. She, in turn, by accepting at all times his supremacy and defining herself as his complement, not only insured that Perón's own relationship with the *descamisados* would remain intact but also infused new life into his charisma.

Because of Evita, Perón did not have to share his leadership with another man, someone who might have used the ministry of labor against him, as he had done against Farrell. He avoided reliance on a potential rival like Col. Domingo A. Mercante, a son of a railroad worker who was also very popular among organized labor in the early forties. She freed Perón from certain activities essential to his style of politics so as to give him time to perform his presidential duties. She shielded him from the kind of daily contact that is wearing for a leader whose movement is no longer fighting for power but is in power. She protected him from troublesome confrontations or negotiations when conflicts erupted and thus allowed him to play the role of the final arbiter, the wise man who could solve problems when everything else had failed, the statesman, the judge, the teacher, the ideologue, the father, in a word, *el conductor.*

Evita could define herself as Perón's complement because she was a woman and his wife. As a woman, she was an outsider to the world of politics—Argentine women could not vote in national elections until 1951—and therefore no one initially could conceive her as a threat. Perón, for example, could not think of her as a rival and the *descamisados* could not see her as an obstacle to their relationship with him. By the time she demonstrated her political ability, she could no longer be stopped because she had become too useful to Perón and the *descamisados.* As Perón's wife, Evita was his extension, therefore part of him. Because of her illegitimate

63

h, her career as an actress, and their eighteen-month extramari-
iaison, without Perón she could never have achieved political
power and legitimacy. "Everything I am, everything I have, everything I think and everything I feel belongs to Perón," she wrote in
her autobiography. At no time could she forget

> that I was a sparrow and that I am still one. If I fly high it is
> because of him. If I walk among the mountaintops, it is because
> of him. If I sometimes touch the sky with my wings, it is
> because of him. If I see clearly what my people are and I love
> my people and I feel the love of my people caressing my name,
> it is because of him.[32]

Following Evita's death in 1952 (at the age of thirty-three) Perón's
ties with labor, the military, the church and industrialists began to
weaken considerably. His new economic policies, his growing
authoritarianism, and the political vacuum created by Evita's death
eroded his support; he was finally ousted by a military coup in
September 1955. Perón's own charismatic relationship with the
descamisados underwent a period of estrangement, but during his
eighteen-year exile his leadership was never seriously threatened.
By the early sixties he was once again the undisputed leader of the
descamisados. In 1973, he returned to Argentina to win a third
term in office with his third wife, Isabel, vice-president; however,
Peronism's dual leadership died with Evita.

Notes

1. See Alberto Ciria, *Perón y el justicialismo* (Buenos Aires, 1971) and José Luis de Imaz, *Los que mandan,* trans. Carlos A. Astiz with Mary E. McCarthy (Albany, N.Y., 1979).

2. Max Weber, *The Theory of Social and Economic Organization,* trans. A. M. Henderson and Talcott Parsons (New York, 1947), pp. 358–59.

3. Ibid. p. 359.

4. Ibid.

5. Ibid. p. 37.

6. Ibid., p. 364.

7. Ibid., p. 539.

8. See David E. Apter, "Knrumah, Charisma and the Coup," *Daedalus* 97, no. 2 (Summer 1969), 757–792, and Ann Ruth Willner and Dorothy Willner, "The Rise and Role of Charismatic Leaders," *The Annals of the American Academy of Political and Social Science* 358 (March 1965), 77–88.

9. See Robert C. Tucker, "The Theory of Charismatic Leadership," *Daedalus,* 97 no. 2 (Summer 1969): 731–56 and K. J. Ratnam, "Charisma and Political Leadership," *Political Studies* 12, no. 3 (October 1964), 341–54.

10. In his discussion of "The Routinization of Charisma and its consequences," Weber writes that the "individual who has not successfully gone through the initiation, remains a 'woman'; that is, is excluded from the charismatic group." Weber, *The Theory of Social and Economic Organization* p. 367.

11. See Miguel Murmis and Juan Carlos Portantiero, *Estudios sobre los orígenes del peronismo* (Buenos Aires, 1971); Samuel L. Bailey, *Labor, Nationalism and Politics in Argentina* (New Brunswick, N.J., 1967); Alberto Ciria et al., *La década infame* (Buenos Aires, 1969); Carlos Fayt, *La naturaleza del peronismo* (Buenos Aires, 1967); Hobart A. Spalding, Jr., *Organized Labor in Latin America* (New York, 1977); Ruben Rotondaro, *Realidad y cambio en el sindicalismo* (Buenos Aires, 1971); Peter H. Smith, "The Social Base of Peronismo," *Hispanic American Historical Review* 52, no. 1 (February 1972), 55–72; and David Tamarin, "Argentine Industrial Unionism During the 'Infamous Decade' and the Emergence of Perón" (Paper delivered at the 1979 meeting of LASA, Pittsburgh, 1979).

12. Perón's language in these speeches was not the same as he used on other occasions during this period. See, for example, his speech to the Bolsa de Comercio of August 25, 1948, reprinted in: Colonel Juan Perón, *El pueblo quiere saber de qué se trata* (Buenos Aires, 1945).

13. For the best detailed account of events between 1943 and 1946, see Félix Luna, *El 45: Crónica de un año decisivo* (Buenos Aires, 1969).

14. This statement does not imply that Perón's support came exclusively from the working class. But whereas other classes or sectors of classes supported Perón in different periods, they were not as consistently Peronist as the working class. On the other hand, Perón continued to find resistance and even active opposition among the working class throughout his first two terms in office. For an analysis of his relationship with labor see Walter Little, "The Popular Origins of Peronism," in David Rock, ed., *Argentina in the Twentieth Century* (Pittsburgh, 1975), and Louise M. Doyon, "Conflictos obreros durante el régimen peronista (1946–55)," *Desarrollo Económico* 17, no. 67 (October-December 1977), 437–73.

15. The word *descamisado* really means coatless rather than shirtless. Social conventions being what they were in Argentina in 1945, it was inconceivable for a gentlemen or any man aspiring to be one to be seen on the streets without coat and tie; only workers and other riffraff went about in such casual attire. Throughout this chapter, the word *descamisados* is used as a generic term that describes the men and women, workers and white collar workers, rural and urban, who supported Perón. For the latest round in the debate over the social composition of Peronism, see Peter H. Smith, "The Social Base of Peronism"; Gino Germani, "El surgimiento del peronismo: el rol de los obreros y de los migrantes internos," *Desarrollo Económico* 13, no. 51 (October-December 1973), 435–88; Peter H. Smith, "Las elecciones argentinas de 1946 y las inferencias ecológicas," *Desarrollo Económico* 14, no. 54 (July-September, 1974), pp. 385–98; Eldon Kenworthy, "Interpretaciones ortodoxas y revisionistas del apoyo inicial del peronismo," *Desarrollo Económico* 14, no. 56 (January-March 1975), pp. 749–63; and Walter Little, "The Popular Origins of Peronism."

16. When the new cabinet was finally announced on 17 October, the workers' fears were confirmed.

17. Weber, *The Theory of Social and Economic Organization*, p. 359.

18. Ibid., pp. 262–63.

19. See *Pasado y Presente* (Buenos Aires, July and December 1973).

20. For an analysis of the CGT during this period, see Juan Carlos Torre, "La caída de Luis Gay," *Todo es Historia* (Buenos Aires, October 1974).

21. *La Nación,* 19 December 1946.

22. See Marysa Navarro, "The Case of Eva Perón," in *Signs, Women and National Development: The Complexities of Change,* ed. Wellesley Editorial Committee (Chicago, 1977).

23. George I. Blanksten for example, explains that

> when the officers came to arrest Perón, they "discovered that it was much easier to overthrow Perón than to dislodge his mistress. Perón, as is perhaps proper on such occasions, frantically begged his captors not to kill him. Evita was another matter. She flew into a tantrum, screamed and spat at the conspirators, and shouted defiant obscenities at them . . . . She then proceeded to play a major role in frustrating the coup against Perón. She alerted his political lieutenants, and the machinery for restoring the colonel to power was rushed into operation."

George I. Blanksten, *Perón's Argentina* (Chicago, 1953), p. 91. Mary Main writes that while Perón remained in his room in Martín García

> and grumbled about the weather, and the Opposition quibbled over points of leadership, Eva showed neither weakness nor hesitation. She had wept and stormed with fury when they had taken her lover off but no sooner was he gone that she began to fly around among her erstwhile friends, shrieking at them, bullying them, cajoling them and threatening them, demanding his release."

Mary Main (María Flores), *The Woman with the Whip: Eva Perón* (New York, 1952), p. 79.

24. See, Louise M. Doyon, "El crecimiento sindical bajo el peronismo," *Desarrollo Económico* 15, no. 57 (April-June 1975), 151–61.

25. Argentina, Presidencia de la Nación, Subsecretaría de Informaciones, *Perón y Eva Perón hablan en el día de los trabajadores* (Buenos Aires, 1951).

26. See Juan Perón, *Conducción política* (Buenos Aires, 1952).

27. Eva Perón, *La razón de mi vida* (Buenos Aires, 1951), p. 14.

28. Argentina, Subsecretaría de Informaciones de la Presidencia de la Nación, *Perón y Evita hablan en el acto de clausura del Congreso Extraordinario de la Confederación General del Trabajo* (Buenos Aires, 1950).

29. *Eva Perón habla a las trabajadoras del país* (Buenos Aires, 1949).

30. Eva Perón, *Historia del peronismo* (Buenos Aires, 1971), p. 136.

31. Eva Perón, *La razón de mi vida,* p. 211.

32. Ibid., p. 10.

4

Populism in Brazil, 1925–1945

Michael L. Conniff
University of New Mexico

A distinctive urban politics arose in Rio de Janeiro during the 1920s, which led to Brazil's first genuine populist movement in the 1930s. Populism emerged as a response to the metropolitan revolution of the early twentieth century, and in particular against the political generation of the First Republic (1889–1930). The changes in social and economic relations were pronounced: abandonment of the poor to their own devices; transfer of power to several major states through the "politics of the governors" and *coronelismo;* emergence of an ethic that gave profitable public services and land development opportunities to individual entrepreneurs; growing disparities in wealth and standard of living; and fostering of a public works strategy that stressed grandiose projects of little value to the populace. Campaigns against this "new urbanism," as its critics labeled it, were led by reformers in the 1920s and afterward by Brazil's first populist, Pedro Ernesto Baptista, a tenente leader and mayor of Rio from 1931 to 1936.[1] Populism quickly became a powerful means of extending the vote to lower- and working-class citizens and for generating debate on public issues. Pedro Ernesto (as he was known popularly) made good use of mass media, which had just become available. His movement, in short, became a model for urban politics in other big cities.

The rise of populism followed closely the 1930 revolution of Getúlio Vargas, and many of the important changes of the decade may be traced to growing state intervention common to both. Intervention had so-called soft and hard sides, for populism stressed social programs for uplifting the lower classes, whereas Vargas' federal team emphasized social control and depoliticization of the masses. These differences led to a confrontation between the two men and their politics in 1936. Vargas, with the support of the army, easily prevailed, and soon afterward he instituted the authoritarian Estado Novo. The populist experiment in Rio, however, had a lasting effect: it demonstrated to Vargas and other politicians that urban voters constituted a large new element in electoral calculus, one most effectively recruited by the populist methods developed by Pedro Ernesto. In the closing years of World War II, Vargas himself decided to create a populist movement based on his Labor Ministry and its program. Although a crude and obvious approach, Vargas' Brazilian Labor Party (the PTB) effectively extended populist politics to São Paulo and other cities after 1945. This chapter concentrates on the city of Rio between 1925 and 1945, examining the origins and development of Brazilian populism. It concludes with the transition from one-city multiclass populism to the national movements of the post-war period.

Conditions had been excellent in the 1920s for the emergence of urban politics in Rio de Janeiro. By then the city contained well over a million persons, and local politics had begun to heat up with frustration over unrepresentative government. The city had lost influence in national elections due to the predominance of the big states in presidential successions, and due also to the enfranchisement of rural "literates," which gave *coronéis* the balance of local power. The new urban politics—expansive, reform-minded, and based on interest group representation—contained the seeds of populism. Colorful and effective politicians arose to challenge the government and to give voice to working- and middle-class discontent. In the end practitioners of the new politics were unable to defeat the incumbent system of municipal politics, which delivered votes through a network of *chefes* and *cabos* (precinct bosses), yet the urban reformism they pioneered served the important role of stimulating democratic recruitment in the city and contributing to the late 1920s atmosphere of crisis that sparked major reforms in the 1930s.

The impact of the new urban politics was clear in voter turnouts. In 1926 only 28,000 persons cast ballots in Rio, or about 10 percent of those eligible to vote (Table 2). Soon, however, active recruitment among union members and middle-class citizens pushed the total up rapidly. The expansion of labor voters was easy to understand, for repression in the early 1920s had left the union movement with few other means of expression.[2] These groups registered and got to the polls impressive numbers of new voters, sparking a period of intense debate among leftists over labor's future role in society. Worker solidarity revived along with the new interest in politics, and several labor parties were formed in the late 1920s.

The 1920s middle-class vote emerged in an entirely different way. Although the middle class constituted the core of Rio's electorate, disenchantment with rural fraud and big-state manipulation resulted in high rates of abstention. But beginning in 1927, teachers and students spearheaded a drive to register middle class citizens, under the banner of the new Democratic Party (PD). The PD was classically reformist, directing most of its attention to the need for democratic procedures and programs for the poor (the so-called social question). In hindsight, it can be seen that middle-class reformism sought to restore much of what had been the colonial tradition of Brazilian cities, in which all persons had a place, citizens regularly voted, and the municipality had wide-ranging responsibilities for the well-being of the lower class. The PD did not have sufficient votes to elect candidates in the 1920s, so its leaders posed as a force for what they termed the "moralization" of politics. Eventually, of course, they could combine efforts with other oppo-

Table 2. Vote Turnouts in Rio de Janeiro, 1926—1945

Year	Votes	Offices
1926	28,000	president, councilmen
1927	39,000	senator, deputies
1928	42,000	councilmen
1930	64,000	president, senator, deputies
1933	70,000	constitutional delegates
1934	110,000	deputies, councilmen (indirectly president and senators)
1945	482,000	president, constitutional delegates

sition parties, particularly with the Democratic Party of Sao Paulo, begun in 1926.[4]

Despite low turnouts in Rio elections, competition for public office was always intense because the possibilities for advancement were great. To make names for themselves, candidates often adopted bizarre and even radical stances, so such exotic (for Brazil) ideologies as communism, positivism, and maximalism could be found. The bedrock of Rio politics still consisted of patronage, however, and few politicians had been able to rise to office on broad issues alone. No matter what his program or ideology, a candidate had been obliged to work with neighborhood leaders known as *cabos eleitorais*. Politicians whose only campaign method was the exchange of patronage for votes were chefes, or bosses, but a newer breed in the 1920s tried to break away from that practice. Their foremost characteristic was vocal opposition to whatever government was in power, a stance bound to be popular with the disenchanted local citizens. They preached reform as the only remedy for the evils of an unresponsive regime.[5]

The most famous of these new politicians were Maurício de Lacerda, Adolfo Bergamini, and João Baptista de Azevedo Lima, all quasi-socialists. Because they opposed the government and had limited patronage available to them, these reformers needed constantly to renew and enlarge their followings. This necessitated a popular image, constant contact with the electorate, good oratorical abilities, and a keen sense of current events. From the soapbox they provided editorial interpretation of the daily news, serving as the public conscience, so to speak. Because of these characteristics, the reformers experimented with the elements of populism without quite achieving the winning combination. Probably their greatest failing was not taking over the means of registering voters, which remained in the hands of cabos, union officials, and PD volunteers. So although the reformers experimented with an expanding labor–middle-class coalition, they did not succeed in taking control of city politics by 1930.[6]

The reformers' principal contribution to 1930s populism was discrediting the old regime and thereby creating pressure for change. Crisis is too strong a term for the presidential election of 1930, but it is appropriate for the growing manifestation of philosophical grievances against the new urbanism of the republican politicians. The press in Rio, sympathetic to the PD, hastened the process of eroding the regime's legitimacy. The upshot was the successful revolt of the losing candidate, Getúlio Vargas, and his subsequent characterization of the movement as a "revolution." During Vargas' installation as provisional president following the coup, Adolfo Bergamini became mayor of the capital and many of the reformers took city positions. Reform and multiclass participation were thus important local outcomes of the revolution of 1930, irrespective of Vargas' own intentions.[7]

Disintegration of national political forms and structures marked the years 1931 and 1932, culminating in São Paulo's unsuccessful revolt against Vargas. Much to the surprise of Rio's reformers, a group of *tenentes,* organized into the Club 3 de Outubro, took over governance of the capital in September 1931 and assumed an informal role as politico-military advisers to the president. By early 1932 the tenentes published a major reform plan, which incorporated most proposals from the 1920s and thus went far beyond the tentative stance of the reform politicians. The president of the Club, Pedro Ernesto Baptista, had been appointed mayor of Rio, a position he used to forge Brazil's first populist movement.[8]

Pedro Ernesto was a Pernambucano who had settled in Rio after completing his medical training in the capital's leading charity hospital. He built a surgical clinic in the 1920s that became the best in Brazil and made him wealthy. He became involved in politics through participation in the *tenente* movement, which he aided with medical services and other forms of support. For his role as tenente collaborator, Pedro Ernesto was chosen to be the Rio coordinator for the 1930 revolution. Soon after the revolution, he helped found the Club 3 de Outubro, of which he became president in April 1931. It was in this capacity that he was able to seize the government of Rio.

Pedro Ernesto's political apprenticeship had been unusual in the extreme, and perhaps for this reason Vargas chose him in 1932 to help turn the tenente movement into the vanguard of a party that would give the county a new constitution and elect Vargas to a regular term of office. With the backing of several federal agencies and his own tenente following, Pedro Ernesto formed the Autonomist Party to accomplish these tasks.[9] From the beginning, the party was unique in Brazilian experience. Using contacts in the bureaucracy, it quickly composed a middle class following by registering civil servants. Pedro Ernesto brought the old-line chefes and cabos into the party by promising them jobs and future legislative posts. He encouraged women and 18-year-olds (enfranchised in 1932) to join the party and take part in politics. Finally, in 1933 and 1934 Pedro Ernesto sent recruiters into working-class neighborhoods and hillside shantytowns (favelas) to register tens of thousands of new voters. A sample of new voters demonstrated the lower class origins of the new recruits: 51 percent were unskilled workers and 57 percent were migrants. He forged for the first time an expansive movement that sought to represent heterogeneous social strata for electoral purposes. [10]

Pedro Ernesto was able to tap such diverse constituencies because of his growing charismatic authority among the people. His image was a blend of tenente reformer and *médico bondoso* (good-hearted doctor). Other tenentes who joined him added to the appeal of the party, as did popular artists, feminists, and a priest (Padre Olympio de Melo) who had worked in the slums. The newly available medium of the radio greatly enhanced the mayor's ability to reach out to the people, and he was among the first to experiment with its political potential. Because the new stations had begun to broadcast popular music and humor programs, the radio itself was gaining a mass audience at the same time it attracted politicians as users. It would be difficult to explain Pedro Ernesto's popularity without the radio. By creating an attractive image for himself and the party, and by using the radio, Pedro Ernesto gained such authority that he could create and mold public opinion. That was the basis of his charisma, or the masses' recognition of his exceptional qualities.

The Autonomist party explicitly sought to broaden the mayor's popularity by stressing his role in expanding city services. The Autonomist party had, from the very start, adopted major portions of the tenente program for social reform: education, public health, and welfare. Pedro Ernesto argued that previous administrations had addressed only physical problems in the city, choosing to ignore such glaring social problems as illiteracy, disease, indigence, unemployment, and slum housing. The Autonomists would redress such neglect by building schools and hospitals as well as by delivering other services to the city's poor.[11] The mayor was aided in these efforts by a sharp increase in revenues in 1933 and 1935, which derived from federal aid and general recovery from the Depression. This attention to the social question set post-1930 governments off from their predecessors, and it became a major feature of Brazilian populism.

Educational reformer Anísio Teixeira was appointed director of schools, in which post he introduced progressive methods adapted from his studies in the United States. A central educational institute trained teachers and administrators in the new philosophy, and the city undertook the construction of twenty-eight new schools, largely in lower class neighborhoods. Enrollments rose 25 percent in two years, and attrition rates declined. To crown the system Teixeira created the University of the Federal District by bringing under one administration various independent *faculdades* and expanding their curricula. Teixeira enjoyed remarkable success and became one of the country's foremost educators and intellectuals.[12]

Pedro Ernesto personally directed a program of public health, oriented by his experience as a doctor in clinics and charity hospitals. The city built five new hospitals, largely in poor neighborhoods, for treating the population. Small health centers and support facilities were also provided, and by the end of the decade most of the city's public health system was already functioning. The delivery of medical services rose substantially, enhancing the mayor's image as *médico bondoso*.[13] Finally, a social service institute was created under the direction of Pedro Ernesto, which among other things coordinated united charity efforts in the city.

The mayor's populist appeal among the lower classes was based largely on innovation in the area of social welfare programs. But the mayor's populism was multiclass, and he drew support from the upper and middle classes. Some members of the elite joined him because they saw his style as an effective way to stem lower class agitation. Others benefited from city purchases and building contracts, or used the mayor for access to the president. The opening of gambling casinos for tourists was popular among the elite, as was the inauguration of the annual Municipal Theater Balls as part of the Carnival celebrations. The middle class benefited greatly from the expansion of social services, which created over a thousand well-paying professional jobs. The city hired 800 new teachers, for example, and hundreds of doctors, nurses, and medical personnel. The priority given these programs brought greater prestige and stability to the middle class and was consonant with a parallel expansion of federal jobs in the city. So sharp was the growth in salaries that it sparked an early recovery from the Depression and a real estate boom, both of which benefited the middle class. Finally, both the upper and the middle class saw the importance of "doing something" about poverty and labor unrest, if only to protect their own standing.

The masses, however, represented the largest potential for electoral recruitment. The social programs, therefore, were directed toward incorporating the poor and *favelados* into the life of the city, making them participating citizens. The city made many improvements in favelas and provided subsidies to the Samba Schools, the principal attraction of Carnival. Carnival was, in fact, a highly symbolic time for the mayor, when people of all walks of life and all races could join together in good-hearted revelry. That message was also contained in a cultural awakening underway in the 1930s. Rather than look down upon the lower class as an embarrassment, intellectuals and artists sought to discover in the "people" the true soul of the culture. Gilberto Freyre's book, *The Masters and the Slaves* (1933), set the tone for a general revision in attitudes toward the Indian and black. It came to be recognized that they had contributed culturally and materially to Brazil's progress, and the result was a hybrid civilization better adapted to the tropics than any of its parent cultures. The novels of the 1920s and 1930s also explored the life of the lower class. Di Cavalcanti's paintings of mulattas became famous, as did Portinari's of workers. While not as striking as Mexican mural art, Brazilian painting in Rio and São Paulo during the 1930s made the lower class a major subject. Finally, in the field of music Villa-Lobos took themes from folklore and the peasantry for his compositions.[14] These and many other intellectual and artistic currents of the 1930s reinforced the populist movement and its strategy of incorporating the lower class into the urban masses. Indeed many of the aforementioned persons were employed by the city or the University of the Federal District to take their messages to the people.

How successful was this improvised political movement in winning elections? In the 1933 voting for constitutional delegates, the Autonomist Party won six of the ten seats, an impressive victory given the inexperience of the mayor and most of his party leaders. As is evident in Table 2, voter registration continued apace. Even with entirely new voter rolls some 10 percent more persons voted than had in the hotly contested 1930 presidential race. An even better test of the populist movement came in October 1934, when voters chose congressmen and city councilmen by direct ballot. Also at stake were the city's two senate seats and the mayoralty, which would be determined by the Council in early 1935. Due to Autonomist recruitment of new voters, the turnout showed a stunning 57 percent rise over the previous year. Mass politics were rapidly becoming a reality in Rio. The Autonomists captured eight of the ten congressional seats and twenty of the twenty-two Council places, which meant they controlled the selection of the mayor and senators as well.[15] Another twist was to put Pedro Ernesto's name at the top of the ballots, effectively identifying the new populist mayor with the "people's" party. The 1934 Rio election was a major breakthrough in urban politics, one watched by politicians from other large cities.

The importance of the 1934 Autonomist victory was especially great because the opposition parties were themselves innovative, not old-style patronage groups. On the one hand, the 1920s reformers had banded together with business leaders to create the Economist Party, which ran a professional and well-financed campaign on behalf of its candidates. This group promised sound economic management by respectable community leaders, and it charged Pedro Ernesto with sloppy if not illegal spending practices. The Economists only placed two candidates in Congress.[16] On the other hand, a variety of labor-socialist parties, which had been attempting to gain office since the late 1920s, also found themselves blocked by the Autonomist juggernaut. The mayor's popularity had penetrated the rank and file of the city's unions to such an extent that labor leaders were unable to aid these parties. The upshot was great pessimism among politicians on the right as well as the left, for they preferred corporatist representation by sector rather than an unpredictable but highly effective populism. Communist leader Luís Carlos Prestes, in fact, privately labeled Pedro Ernesto as the principal obstacle to a labor-intellectual alliance in Brazilian politics.[17] Populism had put a new set of rules into operation.

During 1935 Pedro Ernesto's popularity continued to grow, and the mayor decided to pitch his appeal to the left in an effort to preempt the union movement from communist leadership. Vargas encouraged the mayor in this direction, despite his private conviction that a corporatist-authoritarian regime was desirable. Vargas' style was tentative and indecisive in these years, and it is plausible that had Pedro Ernesto forged a national center-left movement

Vargas would have taken its leadership. The two men had worked closely together for several years, and Vargas had always supported the populist movement in Rio. Pedro Ernesto made a bid for leadership of the biggest labor unions in the city, which would be incorporated into the Autonomist party. In several strikes and in a highly publicized debate over petroleum prices, the mayor posed as a man of the people defending the interests of the common citizen against the monopolists. The petroleum episode was especially popular, because it dealt with a public utility wholly owned by foreigners.[18]

Pedro Ernesto's shift to the left was accompanied by more explicit discussion of income redistribution and state intervention. Several redistributive schemes had surfaced in earlier years, but they had been defeated by upper-class opposition. The elite approved of social programs but did not wish to be taxed heavily to finance them. In April 1935 the mayor came close to recommending a more forthright approach to the problem of poverty. While refusing to give an ideological label to his administration, he nonetheless endorsed two principles:

> The first is that perfection of the means of production has made possible, by increasing the social wealth, a more equitable distribution of goods, compatible with the needs of the modern worker. The second is that the state can no longer maintain an attitude of mere spectator or policeman of human progress, but rather must be a regulator of the life of the community during this phase of its historical evolution. . . . [We will press for] the progressive socialization of those [public] services that most affect the collective welfare of the people.[19]

This stance had been embodied in the tenente program of early 1932, but this was the first time a nationally-known politician had spoken up in favor of redistribution. Later the concept would become intimately linked to populism by Vargas's trabalhismo (to be discussed below), and it was quite similar to the social justice promised by Cárdenas, Perón, Ibáñez, and other Latin American populists.

Pedro Ernesto's populist experiment was nearly shattered, however, by the November 1935 communist uprising in several Brazilian cities. Ordered by Moscow and closely monitored by the police, the revolts were not a serious threat to Vargas's regime. However, they gave the army high command an excuse to demand more repressive powers, and Vargas a reason for deciding that the time had come for a rightward shift. From then until the November 1937 Estado Novo coup, Vargas governed with growing reliance on the police and with special authority under state of war powers conceded by Congress.[20] Immediately after the revolts, army commanders clamored for Pedro Ernesto's arrest, alleging that he had associated with the conspirators. Simultaneously critics of the city's educational program forced the resignation of Anísio Teixeira and many other progressive administrators. That effectively ended the social reform phase of the movement.

Pedro Ernesto now realized that Vargas intended to remove him, so he rebuilt the Autonomist party and shifted back to centrist ground. He continued to enjoy enormous popularity, but Vargas's now obvious intentions made the mayor's position difficult. The latter decided to counterattack with continued expansion of the party through lower-class recruitment and alliances with anti-Vargas parties in other states. Pro-Pedro Ernesto newspapers in Rio began criticizing the president, who was due to step down in less than two years. A confrontation between populism and authoritarianism became inevitable.[21]

The period between 1930 and 1936 had seen a marked transformation in the Brazilian state, which went from a liberal, laissez-faire model to an interventionist corporate system. This change occasioned growing use of police powers to quell opposition, and it thereby altered the tenor of political discourse. Previously politics had been an activity of the elite with little concern for public opinion or the well-being of the masses. The revolution of 1930 and the Depression brought attempts to ameliorate the hardships of the masses through social programs, but also efforts to control working-class agitation. Populism was the foremost manifestation of the former enterprise, and police repression of the latter. The federal police, under the direction of Filinto Muller, broadened their activities to encompass undesirable political and social behavior. It is in this sense that populism and authoritarianism may be seen as the "soft" and "hard" sides of growing state intervention in Brazilian society during the 1930s.[22]

Populism and authoritarianism were not, however, compatible, for the one stood for political participation while the other restricted it. In 1936 the two strains of governance created a couter-point or a dialectic concerning the degree of participation or repression required in Brazil. For some time the authoritarian line remained dominant over the populist, until in the post-War era populism emerged triumphant. A curious aspect of the counter-point was that each needed the other to justify its own approach to politics. Populists maintained a militant stance in defense of the rights of the masses, which were threatened by the police, the army, the oligarchy, and the old-style politicians. The authoritarians, by the same token, continually decried the dangers of mass mobiliza-tion by demagogues, whom they portrayed as irresponsible oppor-tunists who profited from the ignorance of their followers. The opening strains of this counterpoint, which echoes through Brazil-ian politics today, date back to the mid-1930s.[23]

In April 1936 Vargas instructed police chief Muller to arrest Pedro Ernesto for alleged complicity in the communist uprisings. The evidence presented by the government was flimsy, and the case was ultimately dismissed in 1937; but in the months following the mayor's imprisonment the authoritarian system was consolidated in Rio and elsewhere. Padre Olympio de Melo, who became interim mayor, was soon replaced by the former Economist leader, Hen-rique Dodsworth. The functions of the these two mayors were largely administrative, for political activity disappeared. The Coun-cil did not convene after 1937, and no elections were held for the next ten years. The police ran the city, while federal authorities imposed corporate rule on urban society. Populist recruitment was of course ended.[24]

One exception to the repressive trend of the late 1930s occurred: José Américo de Almeida, putative official candidate in the 1937 presidential campaign, recognized Vargas' desire to become dicta-tor, and he attempted to mount a populist movement along the lines of Pedro Ernesto's in 1935. If he could build overwhelming support in the cities, he might force Vargas to abandon secret plans for a military coup. Ironically, José Américo misunderstood the populist strategy and made a mockery of his campaign. He champi-oned the poor in a way that threatened the wealthy, and he failed to generate charisma or a sense of the "people." In short order he forfeited any chance of blocking Vargas' takeover, and indeed he contributed to it by raising the spectre of class antagonism. Massive demonstrations for Pedro Ernesto (released in September) were explicitly used to convince the army high command of the need for an authoritarian regime. The coup occurred nearly as scheduled on 11 November 1937.

Although the authoritarian theme was dominant during the Estado Novo, the populist line was not inaudible. Vargas himself now embraced social reform as his own banner, especially labor and social security legislation. The Ministry of Labor pressed for the incorporation of factory workers into the social security system, and it managed to institute a minimum wage and a labor code by 1942. Simultaneously, the Department of Press and Publicity (DIP) became a major source of propaganda, stressing over the airwaves and in printed media the benefits Vargas had given the masses. This new image constituted Vargas's first flirtation with populism.[25]

Labor had all along been in the back of Vargas's mind. Even before taking power, Vargas had believed in the need for federal regulation of industrial relations to avoid labor conflict. One of the earliest attempts at such regulation was called the Getúlio Vargas Law.[26] After 1930 Vargas's concern was to prevent communist or radical influence among union members, and his early policies in this regard differed little from those of his predecessors. It had been the populist coalition in Rio that had proven the political potential of labor. First, Pedro Ernesto and the Ministry of Labor had managed the election of forty "class representatives" to Congress, most of them labor leaders supportive of the government. Moreover, Pedro Ernesto's ability to recruit working-class votes and to stem radical labor organization had further demonstrated the potential of mass politics. So after 1936 Vargas increasingly posed as the benefactor of the working class, the image which would become his source of charisma in the 1940s.[27]

Alexandre Marcondes Filho became the chief architect of Vargas's populism in the early 1940s. A Paulista lawyer who for three years doubled as Minister of Labor and of Justice, Marcondes took up his chief's new theme, which was dubbed *trabalhismo,* or laborism. He also endowed the Labor Ministry with many attributes of an official party, including the *Labor Ministry Bulletin* (circulation 100,000) and a radio station. During these years Marcondes personally made over 200 radio talks. He forged close relations with DIP directors, whose programs publicized labor advances. It is probable that Marcondes even drafted Labor Day speeches for Vargas. In 1943 a plan was readied for using labor carnets to qualify voters after the war, which made it imperative that as many workers as possible be registered with the Ministry. So from 1942 on, an embryo of the labor party was nurtured in the Labor Ministry.[28]

The reasons for not creating a party before 1945 merit some discussion. The Constitution of 1937 had authorized the government to create an official party, but Vargas had declined to do so. He had instituted the Estado Novo in part to gain freedom to make economic policy, and the existence of an official party would have compromised that power. Vargas preferred the civil service bureaucracy, especially that of the Labor Ministry. Another advantage of the latter was its broad jurisdiction over workers, employers, professionals, and even civil servants, all of whom were supposed to be registered in order to work. That made its constituency eminently multiclass. Finally, it was not difficult to find Ministry employees willing to work overtime developing a labor following, and many of them were later elected to Congress. So Vargas created the nucleus of a labor party within the ministry, avoiding the cost or risk of actually creating a party.

By March 1945 it became imperative to prepare for elections, which Vargas had promised upon termination of the war. Marcondes was instructed to charter the Brazilian Labor Party (PTB), along the lines of the British Labor Party. From then on Marcondes spent most of his time managing the creation of the PTB, and he was relieved of his duties as Minister of Justice. Most of the officials of the new PTB were Ministry employees, and government resources were increasingly devoted to what was essentially electoral campaigning. Voter registration by place of employment went into effect, which greatly aided the Ministry in expanding the urban electorate.[29] Vargas treated the PTB as his own personal vehicle, which turned out to be a wise decision.

The PTB was unquestionably a populist party, for leaders defined its constituency as broadly as possible. Marcondes said,

> The party is for the "Brazilian worker," regardless of his class or creed . . . for those who live from their toil, be they manual laborers, technicians, intellectuals, workers, clerks, bank employees, engineers, doctors, lawyers or any others.

He went on, "The beauty of the movement is its [attempt] to aggregate politically all those who until now have not participated in political life. . . ."[30] It also met other criteria of a populist movement: it expanded its electoral following and promoted the leader's charismatic authority, in this case Vargas' image as father of the poor and benefactor of the working man. Here was an approach that had only one precedent in Brazilian politics—the Autonomist Party.

The parallels between Pedro Ernesto's and Vargas's populist movements were too close to be accidental, so it must be concluded that Vargas (consciously or not) imitated the former's pioneer politics. Much of the popularity of each was based on a paternalistic image as man of the people concerned with the welfare of the masses. They both recruited voters from all sectors of society, stressing social integration and class harmony. They both utilized newly developed publicity media,which permitted them to reach less sophisticated voters than in the past. They both sponsored progressive reforms: Pedro Ernesto's in health and education; Vargas's in labor legislation. Such programs came to be adopted by all populists, who promised economic growth with social justice.

The sources of Vargas's post-1945 program need closer analysis. The PTB platform adopted in August closely resembled those of the Autonomist Party and the tenente Club 3 de Outubro. Of course several of the early 1930s proposals had already been adopted by the Labor Ministry (which was staffed by some former tenentes), and they were lauded by the PTB: for example union recognition, minimum wage, social security, and strike mediation. In addition, virtually every other PTB plank could be found in the earlier tenente or Autonomist programs. Prominent examples were more equitable distribution of income, land reform, homestead programs, stimulation of industry, nationalization of transportation and public utilities, profit-sharing, and vocational training. It is worth recalling, too, Pedro Ernesto's campaign for equitable income distribution and petroleum price regulation in 1935, both of which became prime issues for the PTB after 1950.[31]

Two points need stressing, then, at this juncture. First, Vargas was not a populist until he formed the PTB in 1945, although some preparatory elements go back to the late 1930s. The Vargas reputation as a Latin American populist is based entirely on the last ten years of his political career. In the preceding decades he had been a politician from the traditional mold, albeit an outstanding one. Second, Vargas's populist approach drew heavily on the experimental Autonomist Party of Pedro Ernesto, which in turn synthesized tenentismo, middle class reformism, labor advocacy, and social welfare programs.

Because at the national level Vargas needed to deal with rural as well as urban politics, he kept his labor constituency separate from the traditional political networks in the states. For the purpose of dealing with the latter, Vargas had the Minister of Justice form the Social Democratic Party (PSD), which managed the patronage that had sustained rural politics for two generations. This was the first overt act designed to forge a multiclass following, though of course that strategy had been implicit in Vargas's policies for some time.

The creation of the PTB and the PSD turned out to be a stroke of genius, but the rest of Vargas's politics in 1945 were an abject failure, leading to his ouster by the army in late October. The best interpretation of his failure seems to be that he mismanaged the unfamiliar elements of populism. When it became clear in early 1945 that Vargas was creating a populist movement, opponents criticized him roundly. Symptomatically, he received more advice, publicly and privately, than at any other time in his career.[32] The PTB was interpreted as being a tool for continuing in office, which of course it was. Others denounced the way Vargas released leftist political prisoners, extracting from them a commitment to support his populistic "We want Vargas" campaigns. To some, it was especially offensive that Communist leader Luís Carlos Prestes would embrace reelection of Vargas, the man who had kept him in prison for ten years. Therefore, Vargas's first essay with populism was badly mismanaged, and to a great extent it backfired.

A good example of the contradictions committed by Vargas was his stance on economic nationalism. Since 1944 his speeches had broached such issues as the "economic emancipation of the country" and the desire to "combat economic colonialism."[33] Labor Ministry propaganda stated that Vargas would protect the working man from unfair monopolies, providing him with dignity, just wages, and benefits appropriate to a modern society. In June 1945 the Justice Ministry drafted an Antitrust Law ostensibly to make good the promises of protection against big business. It required all corporate entities to be approved by the government, which would break up monopolies and assure a competitive marketplace. Nevertheless the law was not enforced nor even defended in public, due largely to opposition by influential businessmen and the United States government.[34] This constituted a betrayal of his promises to the working class and an indicator of Vargas's unsure grip of populist politics.

In reponse to Vargas's vacillating stand on economic nationalism, a group of radicals in the PTB submitted an alternative program shortly before the coup. The self- styled "youth wing," drawing on Harold Laski and other European writers, called for reform socialism and a ten-year development plan, complete with targets. Under this plan more sectors of the economy would be subject to nationalization. In addition, the federal government, through special development banks, would provide massive injections of capital in order to direct the private sector toward industrialization. Wages would be raised in order to broaden the internal market for domestic manufactures.[35] This more radical program in fact greatly influenced the PTB after Vargas's reelection in 1950, charting a gradual leftward drift for populism. That Vargas was unable to reconcile these elements in 1945 showed a faulty grasp of populist methods.

Another major contradiction was Vargas's maintenance of police repression through most of 1945, in the face of mounting pressure for a return to broader freedoms. Indeed the men in charge of the Federal Police, though perhaps not as hated as Muller, who had been dismissed in 1942, were nonetheless symbols of totalitarianism. For example, Coriolano de Góes (July 1944-March 1945) was infamous for his bloody suppression of student demonstrations in São Paulo. Students used his name to dub the police the Góestapo. Even censorship continued until February 1945, contrary to the populist image Vargas was cultivating. In hindsight, it can be seen that Vargas mistakenly allowed both lines of the populist-authoritarian counterpoint to overlap.

As soon as he was deposed, Vargas regained his composure and handled populist strategy skillfully. His farewell speech and later statements stressed *trabalhismo,* and he acknowledged paternity of the PTB. He said, "The workers, the humble, whom I have never forgotten in sentiment nor deed—the people, that is, will understand my actions." He also said that the PTB was the "heir and the continuation of the revolution of 1930," and he urged the people to join its ranks. Regarding philosophy, the ties with 1930 were genuine, in view of the influence of the tenente movement on the formation of the PTB. Finally, Vargas wrote to a former tenente and PTB leader, "I always favored the workers with my policies, and I will continue to do so. We must strengthen the PTB so that it may survive and fight."[36] Vargas for the most part sought a conciliatory stance, hoping thereby to maintain favor among as many sectors of the electorate as possible.

Vargas demonstrated restraint in the tense negotiations between the PTB and PSD candidate, General Eurico Dutra, over the former's support. Vargas had all along withheld PTB backing in order to assure his control over the labor vote, as well as to maintain credibility with the left. Vindictively Vargas considered having his own name head all PTB presidential ballots, a ploy used for populistic ends by Pedro Ernesto in 1934. However, last minute bargaining between party representatives produced a deal whereby the PTB gave support to Dutra in exchange for a share of the spoils. Specifically, Dutra promised to consult the PTB on selection of the Minister of Labor; to give cabinet and other appointive posts to the PTB proportional to its share of the votes; to implement all labor legislation then on the books; and to respect the PTB program.[37] Had most PTB votes gone to the opposition candidate (a former tenente), Dutra would have lost the election. It was to Vargas's advantage, however, to have a mediocre man in the presidency, as it was to maintain friendly ties between the PSD and the PTB. Conciliation of diverse voting sectors was, of course, a general characteristic of Latin American populist movements, and Vargas's restraint in the weeks after being deposed revealed strengthening grasp of populist strategy.

The 1945 and 1947 elections demonstrated Vargas's successes and failures in creating his own populist movements. Overall, the PTB won 10 percent of the vote in each contest. Like its sponsor agency, the Ministry of Labor, the PTB barely existed outside Rio and São Paulo, where it received two-thirds of its ballots.[38] Those two states contained, however, the only metropolitan areas that could foster voting among the workers. With the gradual spread of the Labor Ministry and the PTB to other cities in the 1940s and 1950s, large numbers of newly enfranchised persons registered with the PTB. Therefore the PTB was Vargas's voter mobilization party, similar to Pedro Ernesto's Autonomist Party. Since the PTB was the only national party to grow significantly—it tripled in size by 1962—it became the wild card of electoral politics and of congressional coalitions.

The PTB had to compete with other new parties, of course, many of which were populist in character. Luís Carlos Prestes's Brazilian Communist Party (PCB), for example, displayed attributes of a populist movement during its brief legal phase (1945−47). Prestes used his senate seat to generate publicity for the party and to establish relations with other urban parties. He avoided ideological militancy and sought to make the PCB into "a party of integration with national society." His position stressed nationalism and antiimperialism, which gave it considerable overlap with other center-left parties, including the PTB. Indeed for two years the PCB and PTB sparred for leadership of the working class vote, but before any conclusive trends were established the government outlawed the PCB and dismissed its representatives from Congress. The PTB was, of course, the principal beneficiary of this move.[39]

Another Vargas rival was Adhemar de Barros, elected governor of São Paulo in 1947 over the PTB candidate. Adhemar ran a patronage machine and blatantly campaigned on the slogan, "He steals but he gets things done." He also anticipated the need for a charismatic image earlier than Vargas, so that by 1944 he was posing as a man of the people in São Paulo. Unable to defeat Adhemar, Vargas finally made a deal with him in 1950, promising him the vice-presidency and Rio's two senatorial seats in exchange for electoral support. Adhemar mistakenly believed that he would be able to succeed Vargas, but even before the next elections he had lost the governship to another Paulista populist, Jânio Quadros, one of the new breed of politicians. But Adhemar did not fade from the scene, representing as he did an alternative to Vargas's populism.[40]

In Rio another young politician arose to challenge the Vargas legacy, Carlos Lacerda, who had been active in mid-1930s leftist organization. From the front pages of several newspapers Lacerda launched a campaign on behalf of the urban poor who lived in favelas. The spread of shantytowns had accelerated alarmingly since the early 1940s, largely due to income and housing policies unfavorable to the working class. Lacerda's crusade, called the "Battle of Rio," blamed the government for doing nothing to aid the poor, a claim reminiscent of the early Autonomist campaign.[41] He made an impressive name for himself as a maverick politician in the 1950s, and he managed to capture the Rio governorship in 1960. An assassination attempt on Lacerda's life in 1954 precipitated the events that led to Vargas's suicide. Symbolically, it took a populist to kill a populist, and the rivalries engendered were indeed intense. Vargas, it seemed, had adopted populism too late to use it as effectively as many younger, bolder politicians did.

During the postwar period populism moved into a new phase,

one which increasingly stressed class interest and redistribution of income. This occurred for two reasons: first, because the working-class electorate was large enough to support its own candidates, who made direct appeals based on class interest; and second, because policymakers found themselves unable to devise development plans beneficial to all sectors of society. The problems of political economy faced by Vargas, Kubitschek, and Goulart were truly formidable, and each was forced to make critical decisions regarding shares of income, public investment, profits, and nationalization. Thus, issues which had remained largely in the realm of ideas and promises in the 1930s and 1940s became inescapable choices after 1950, the consequences of which altered the socio-economic order.[42] The easy phase of populism was over; the difficult phase had begun. Postponing or hedging decisions was possible only by violating fiscal norms and engendering inflation, which itself became an ever-growing problem. Such dilemmas had stymied Vargas in 1954, Kubitschek in 1958, and Goulart in 1964. By the 1960s the very governance of the country became nearly impossible by the existing rules of the game. The military finally stepped in and changed the rules for an extended time.

Postwar populists in Brazil have been accused of betraying the masses, because they promised more for the working class than they delivered, and because they did not help the country break out of its dependency relationship to the industrial countries.[43] Regardless of the many failings of the populists as leaders, it is mistaken to blame them for not doing something they never meant to do; that is, carry out a militant working-class mobilization, perhaps even a social revolution. Moreover, such a criticism overlooks the fact that the later populists had a harder time fulfilling promises of reform. It was a quantum leap from early populism in the 1930s, when the Depression had accomplished considerable socioeconomic leveling, and when parties rarely amassed a million votes—to the 1950s, when sectoral differentiation had become pronounced, urbanization far advanced, and international pressures sharper.

The whole logic of the populists was to represent "all the people" and to deliver economic growth with social justice. To have done otherwise would have violated the rules as developed in the earlier phase. One can lament the unwillingness of the system to reward labor more, but to attribute the failure to the populists misplaces the blame. Populists were always of the system and could not threaten it by siding exclusively with the masses against the middle class and bourgeoisie. They hoped to reform the system, make it better perhaps, but never overthrow it. When it appeared that Goulart—trapped in the worst politicoeconomic dilemma of the postwar period—would undertake far-reaching structural changes, most sectors of society mobilized against him for having violated the rules of the game.

This examination of the rise of urban politics and of early populism helps explain the subsequent phase of Brazil's political history, especially the parodoxes and crises of the populists who followed Getúlio Vargas. Yet such considerations go beyond the scope of this chapter, whose primary concern has been the period between 1925 and 1945. The concluding section will summarize and analyze that period.

The imposition of a new urban ethos in early twentieth century Brazil, part of an ongoing metropolitan revolution, caused a strong reaction in Rio by the 1920s. More than ever before, it seemed, the city needed an interventionist government to handle the problems of modern industrial society. The generation of the Republic, however, intentionally abandoned the poor and unfit, rewarding instead those who excelled in business. The growing protest in Rio took the form of reformist, expansive electoral mobilization, which pointed the way toward mass politics and populism.

The revolution of 1930 drew upon urban reform currents, despite its overall character as a regionalist revolt; indeed it created the conditions for Brazil's first populist movement. Looking back on the 1930s, it is easy to imagine other outcomes had an urban politics not gained vigor in preceding years. Fascist tendencies such as arose in Argentina and Chile, for example, were not absent and might have been acceptable to rural elites. For a time, too, it seemed possible to recreate the *ancien régime,* a hyperfederalist system favoring the large states of the south. As it turned out, however, Vargas was forced to rely on the tenentes for a crucial year between 1931–32, at which time he became committed to a body of reforms loosely called *tenentismo.* The president of the tenente group, Pedro Ernesto, became mayor of Rio and by 1934 had forged an effective populist party. For the next few years Pedro Ernesto and other urban leaders helped Vargas solidify and legitimate the revolutionary regime.

Alternative forms of governance reappeared in 1935 to challenge the urban and populist innovations in Rio. Gradually a dialectic evolved that pitted participatory politics against corporatist ones. For a time the latter tendency prevailed, and Pedro Ernesto's movement disappeared. The cities continued to grow, however, and Brazil's role in World War II obliged a return to electoral politics. From among the alternatives available, Vargas chose the populism developed in Rio in the mid-1930s; he began building such a party within the Ministry of Labor. By 1945 the PTB emerged fullblown with some 10 percent of the national electorate. Vargas's intention, then, was to capture as much of the working class vote as he could through the party and then to fold that into a broader national coalition. The PTB was nonetheless the vanguard and fastest growing element in his populist movement.

Pedro Ernesto's populism had been relatively simply to build and sustain, with the constellation of forces in the 1930s. It was not yet capable of national projection, which would fall to Vargas in the late 1940s. The important conclusions to be made are that Vargas drew upon a proven populist experiment in Rio, which in turn emerged from the new urban politics of the late 1920s. Also, the core populist "mandate" remained little changed from the 1930s until the 1960s; that is, to restore the colonial urban tradition of interventionist government, one which would represent the people and promote the well-being of all.

NOTES

1. Most of the material on the 1920s is based on newspaper and interview research and is extracted from my *Urban Politics in Brazil: The Rise of Populism, 1925–1945* (Pittsburgh: University of Pittsburgh Press, 1981).

2. On the early labor movement, see especially Boris Fausto, *Trabalho urbano e conflito social (1890–1920)* (São Paulo: DIFEL, 1976); Sheldon L. Maram, "Labor and the Left in Brazil, 1890–1921; A Movement Aborted," *Hispanic American Historical Review* 57 (1977): 254–72; Paulo Sérgio Pinheiro, *Política e trabalho no Brazil (dos anos vinte a 1930)* (Rio: Paz e Terra, 1975); José Albertino Rodrigues, *Sindicato e desenvolvimento no Brazil* (São Paulo: Difusão Européia do Livro, 1968); and Leóncio Rodrigues, *Conflito industrial e sindicalismo no Brazil* (São Paulo: Difusão Européia do Livro, 1966).

3. The flavor of this debate is best captured by Everardo Dias, *Historia das lutas sociais no Brazil* (São Paulo: Editora Edaglit, 1962); and John W. F. Dulles, *Anarchists and Communists in Brazil, 1900–1935* (Austin: University of Texas Press, 1973).

4. *Jornal do Brasil,* 18 May 1927, pp. 7–8; 25 May 1927, pp. 7–13.

5. Conniff, *Urban Politics in Brazil,* chapter 4.

6. Much can be gleaned from such sources as Maurício de Lacerda, *Entre duas revoluções* (Rio: Leite Ribeiro, 1927); João Baptista de Azevedo Lima, *Reminiscências de um carcomido* (Rio: Leo Editores, 1958); Evaristo de Moraes, *Minhas prisões e outros assumptos contemporâneos* (Rio: by author, 1927); and Ernesta von Weber, *Bergamini* (Rio: Editora Moderna, 1931). It is important to note that Vargas and the reformers failed to win the support of organized labor in the 1930 election.

7. The best surveys of the revolution are: Alexandre José Barbosa Lima Sobrinho, *A verdade sobre a revolução de outubro* (São Paulo: Gráfico-Editora Unitas, 1933); and Jordan M. Young, *The Brazilian Revolution of 1930 and the Aftermath* (New Brunswick, N.J.: Rutgers University Press, 1967). Details on Rio's role in the revolt are given in Conniff, *Urban Politics in Brazil,* chapter 5.

8. Michael L. Conniff, "The Tenentes in Power: A New Perspective on the Brazilian Revolution of 1930," *Journal of Latin American Studies* 10 (1978):61–82.

9. *Jornal do Comércio,* 5 March 1933, p. 16; *New York Times,* 26 March 1933, sec. 4, p. 8. Several unsuccessful attempts were made in late 1932 to create a national tenente party, which led to the formation of the Autonomist Party in March 1933.

10. Most of the information on electoral recruitment is from the press and interviews, covered in Conniff, *Urban Politics in Brazil,* chapter 6. The breakdown of registrations is a sample drawn from the *Boletim eleitoral,* 1 June-31 September 1935, n=385. Unskilled were industrial and construction workers (*operários*) and store clerks (*comerciários*). Recruitment was greatly aided by the 1932 electoral law, which enfranchised women and 18-year-olds, instituted the secret ballot under federal supervision, and permitted registration in the workplace. All of these changes dramatically enhanced the power of urban voters.

11. Conniff, *Urban Politics in Brazil,* chapter 7.

12. These reform programs are partially covered in studies by and about Anísio Teixeira; see Charles F. O'Neil, "The Search for Order and Progress: Brazilian Mass Education, 1915–1935" (Ph.D. diss, Univ. of Texas, 1974); Wanda Pompeu Geribello, *Anísio Teixeira: análise e sistematização de sua obra* (São Paulo: Atlas, 1977); Anísio Teixeira, *Educação pública, administração e desenvolvimento* (Rio: Departamento de Educação, 1935).

13. J. P. Fontenelle, *A saúde pública no Rio de Janeiro, D.F., 1935-1936* (Rio: n.p., 1937).

14. A general survey of Brazilian culture in this period is Fernando de Azevedo, *Brazilian Culture: An Introduction to the Study of Culture in Brazil,* trans. William Rex Crawford (New York: Macmillan Co., 1950).

15. *Boletim eleitoral,* 27 February 1935, pp. 568–75.

16. *O Globo,* 12 November 1932, pp. 1–2; *Jornal do Comércio,* 13 April 1933, p. 4; *Jornal do Brail,* 30 June 1934, p. 7; 22 June 1933, p. 7; 2 October 1934, p. 9; 27 July 1933, p. 8.

17. *Jornal de Brasil,* 2 May 1933, p. 10; 1 July 1933, p. 8; 20 April 1934, p. 7; *O Radical,* March and April 1933, passim; *A Vanguarda,* September 1934, passim. Prestes's comment, discovered by police in his secret correspondence, is reproduced in Mário Bulhões Pedreira, *Razões de defesa do Dr. Pedro Ernesto Baptista* (Rio: n.p., 1937), p. 194.

18. Freedoms guaranteed to unions under the 1934 Constitution gave rise to greater labor activity, including strikes. In 1934 twelve full-scale strikes occurred, and industrial conflict remained high in 1935. The petroleum episode is documented in the two volume file, Processo 257 (563.631), of the Conselho Federal de Comércio Exterior, located in the presidential papers (PR-13) of the Arquivo Nacional.

19. Partido Autonomista do Distrito Federal, *Ao povo carioca e à opinião pública,* 2 vols. (Rio: Imprensa Nacional, 1935), 1: 209–14.

20. The revolts and their aftermath are documented in Robert M. Levine, *The Vargas Regime: The Critical Years, 1934–1938* (New York: Columbia University Press, 1970),

chapter 5; Thomas E. Skidmore, "Failure in Brazil: From Popular Front to Armed Revolt," *Journal of Contemporary History* 5 (1970):137−57; Hélio Silva, *1935: a revolta vermelha* (Rio: Civilização Brasileira, 1969).

21. Conniff, *Urban Politics in Brazil,* chapter 8.

22. See the framework proposed in Aspásia Alcântara de Camargo, "Autoritarismo e populismo, bipolaridade no sistema político brasileiro," *DADOS* 12 (1976):22−45. For a somewhat different treatment, see Alistair Hennessy, "Fascism and Populism in Latin America," in *Fascism: A Reader's Guide, Analyses, Interpretations, Bibliography,* ed. Walter Laquer (London: Wildwood House, 1976), pp. 255−94.

23. This analysis does not hold with the so-called corporatist interpretation of Brazilian politics, which has been widely diffused in recent years. According to that theory, Brazilian society (and Hispanic-American too) contains a built-in bias toward organization into corporate structures commanded from the top. Because populism does not fit such a predisposition, it is usually "explained" as an aberration or a means to incorporate uninitiated masses and rural migrants into the system. In that theory populism is *ipso facto* manipulative and insidious, because it takes away individual freedom while claiming to increase it. This view does not fit Brazilian populism during the period at hand, for it misrepresents the motives of both followers and leaders.

24. On the concept of corporatism and its application to labor relations and the state during this period, see Kenneth P. Erickson, *The Brazilian Corporative State and Working Class Politics* (Berkeley and Los Angeles: University of California Press, 1977), especially chapters 3−4.

25. Virtually no work has been done on the development or content of propaganda in the period under study. A contemporary assessment is Walter R. Sharp, "Methods of Opinion Control in Present-Day Brazil," *Public Opinion Quarterly* 5 (1941): 3−16. Other information has been extracted from memoirs, interviews, and archives.

26. This law, sponsored by Vargas while a member of the Chamber of Deputies in 1928, is explained in *O Globo,* 12 July 1928, p. 12; 8 January 1929, p. 2; *Jornal do Brasil,* 21 July 1928, p. 6.

27. For a discussion of Vargas's "mystique," see Edgard Carone, *O Estado Novo (1937-1945)* (Rio: DIFEL, 1977), pp. 166−69.

28. Late 1945 speech by Marcondes, in the Marcondes papers, AMF 45.11(?).OOpi, in Rio's Centro de Pesquisa e Documentação em História Contemporânea (CPDOC). Printed documentation is available for this period in Hélio Silva, *1945: porque depuseram Vargas* (Rio: Civilização Brasileira, 1977) and Edgard Carone, *A Terceira República (1937-1945)* (São Paulo and Rio: DIFEL, 1976).

29. On the PTB, see Silva, *1945,* pp. 171−73; the ex officio registration system, first used in 1933, is discussed in Maria do Carmo Campello de Souza, *Estado e partidos políticos no Brasil (1930-1964)* (Sao Paulo: Alfa-Omega, 1976), pp. 121−24.

30. Marcondes press release, September-October 1945, AMF 45.09/10.00 pi.

31. The Autonomist platform is in *Jornal do Comércio,* 4 March 1933, p. 16; that of the tenentes in Club 3 de Outubro, "Esboco do programa revolucionário de reconstrução política e social do Brasil," in Assembléia Nacional Constituinte, *Anais da . . .* (Rio, 1933−34), III, 187−245. The PTB program is reprinted in Carone, *Terceira República,* pp. 451−59 and commented in Marcondes's speech, AMF 45.11(?).00 pi.

32. The secret intelligence reports to Vargas, located in his papers in CPDOC, were dated from September 1944 to January 1945. Obviously a good many more oral reports were given to him.

33. Getúlio Vargas, *A nova política do Brasil* (Rio: José Olympio, 1938–47), 10:288; 11:38.

34. Affonso Henriques, *Ascensao e queda de Getulio Vargas,* vol. 2: *Vargas e o Estado Novo* (Rio: Distribuidora Record, 1966), pp. 335–38.

35. João Leaes Sobrinho to Marcondes Filho, AMF 45.10.27' and "Manifesto-Programa da Mocidade Trabalhista," AMF PTB 1945, remitted with foregoing document.

36. Vargas' resignation speech, AGV 45.10.30; speech AGV 45.11.10; Vargas to Napoleão Alencastro Guimarães, AGV 45.11.10-11.

37. Dutra to PTB leaders, AGV 45.11.22; Napoleão Alencastro Guimarães to Vargas, AGV 45.11.19; Fernando Nobre Filho to Fernando Costa, 5 January 1946, AMF 46.07.25.

38. The Federal District (later Guanabara state) vote is taken to be part of the Rio de Janeiro State vote. In 1975 the city and state were merged. A convenient summary and interpretation of postwar election returns is Charles Daugherty, James Rowe, and Ronald Schneider, eds., *Brazil: Election Factbook Number 2* (Washington, D.C.: Institute for the comparative Study of Political Systems, 1965). A curious aspect of the PTB growth was the rise of a small-town PTB vote in Rio Grande do Sul, in addition to the party's original urban labor base. This latter element remained the majority and set doctrine for the party, however.

39. Francisco C. Weffort, "Origens do sindicalismo populista no Brasil (a conjunctura do após-guerra)," *Estudos CEBRAP* 4 (1973):65−105; Ronald H. Chilcote, *The Brazilian Communist Party: Conflict and Integration* (New York: Oxford University Press, 1974), pp. 50−51; Silva, *1945*, pp. 147−49, 188−210.

40. Although no good biography of Adhemar exists, much may be obtained from Henriques, *Getúlio Vargas,* 2: chapters 30−31; and Mario Beni, *Adhemar* (São Paulo: Grafikor, [1973−74?]), pp. 173−81.

41. This fascinating episode is recounted by Luciano Parisse, *Favelas do Rio de Janeiro: evolução-sentido* (Rio: CENPHA, 1969), pp. 113−20.

42. See for example the analysis by Thomas E. Skidmore, "A Case Study in Comparative Public Policy: The Economic Dimensions of Populism in Argentina and Brazil," *New Scholar* 7 (1979): 129−66.

43. The most forthright statement of such a view is Kenneth P. Erickson, "Populism and Political Control of the Working Class in Brazil," in *Ideology and Social Change in Latin America,* ed. June Nash, Juan E. Corradi, and Hobart Spalding, Jr. (New York: Gordon and Breach, 1977), pp. 200−36.

5

The Late Populism of Luis Echeverría

Jorge Basurto,
Instituto de
Investigaciones Sociales

A little-studied concept among Mexican political scientists is that which sees the Mexican Revolution as populist, or to be more precise, which regards as populist the regimes that emerged after the Revolution had become secure in about 1920. The official interpretation obviously opposes such a view, since it holds that the Mexican Revolution was one in which the popular masses, and especially the peasants, spontaneously rose up against the misery, oppression, and lack of democracy under the Porfiriato (1876–1910). All the governments emanating from the "revolutionary family" (according to the official view) have sought to correct those injustices—that is to say, the revolutionary period broke with the past.

Nevertheless, recent studies have pointed out the populist characteristics of the revolutionary regimes, beginning with Alvaro Obregón (1920–24)[1] and running through Lázaro Cárdenas (1934–40).[2] After 1940 certain populist episodes may be seen, especially under Adolfo López Mateos (1958–64) and Luis Echeverría Alvarez (1970–76). During this period it was common to exalt the memory of General Cárdenas and his populism (even though it was not called that), and the official line held that

93

Echeverría's accomplishments would rival those of Cárdenas himself.

This chapter examines Echeverría's administration in an attempt to show that it may be regarded as populist precisely because it sought to follow Cárdenas's example. It will also be shown, however, that the stabilizing effects of thirty years of measured development would no longer permit a repetition of the Cárdenas experience.

THE STABILIZING DEVELOPMENT

General Cárdenas' administration, which is regarded as populist, led to the strengthening of the bourgeoisie,[3] even though it produced some important—even structural—reforms in the countryside. After Cárdenas, the bourgeoisie was able to alter the nationalist model of development (which had envisioned greater shares of the benefits for the masses) by putting a higher priority on economic growth, irrespective of which sectors of the society owned capital and accumulated profits. Therefore, the process of capital accumulation and profit concentration greatly accelerated, along with the penetration of foreign capital, which was given every assurance of being able to repatriate its profits.

As a result, since 1940 the savings rate has been relatively high. Industrialization has also proceeded rapidly, through import substitution, which gave tariff protection, subsidies (such as cheap PEMEX oil), tax benefits, and other incentives to national producers. The structure of industry underwent a qualitative change, in which large capital-intensive businesses with high technology predominated.

However, because this process occurred within the capitalist framework, investors sought those markets which offered the greatest profit, irrespective of the internal necessities of the country. That is, the new industry moved preferentially into luxury consumer durables such as automobiles, refrigerators, and the like, where higher profits existed. Traditional industries (food, tobacco, textiles, shoes, and clothing) continued to exist, of course, and measured by value added or labor force they were still dominant; but they tended to be small- and medium-sized plants that were frequently bought out by large businesses. Much the same has occurred in retail commerce, where heavy capital investments created chains of department stores that achieved lower prices through high volume; thus medium and small retailers in the big cities gradually declined.

In both these sectors—industry and commerce—two new elements were present, government and foreign owners, both of which constituted the bourgeoisie, along with traditional landowning and business elites. Yet the new elements played a quite different role in the economy. Indeed, public ownership in the economy grew rapidly until it accounted for about half of the capital stock, especially in petroleum (where it held a monopoly), electric power, communications and transport, telephones, and other utilities. But public investment preferred those sectors regarded as *less* profitable, leaving the others for private enterprise. Thus state enterprises produced only three percent of manufacturing output. Because the government controlled sectors critical for economic growth, it had an inordinate influence on private investment and general development. Private enterprise then became a dependent variable of public investment, waiting to see how the government would act before making its own decisions. In effect, shortages of private funds were made up for by the government, which provided infrastructure and even low-cost inputs for private businesses.

The foregoing was essentially the structure of the mixed economy that the Mexican government shaped after 1940, and it was clearly different from a pure capitalist economy. But what made the Mexican state typically capitalist was its acceptance of the principal that the state should improve investment conditions and capital accumulation.

This coincidence of interests between the public and private sectors gave the bourgeoisie a decisive influence in the state, and it fostered a political economy favorable to private enterprise. That is why managers constantly circulated between business and government: businessmen were appointed to important posts in government and vice versa. The growing importance of direct foreign investment was another factor that influenced Mexican politics and impeded any radical changes, as will be seen below.

Moreover, the inequality of income distribution between labor and capital reached unusual levels in comparison with other Latin American countries. First, industrialization proceeded by ignoring the rural and peasant markets, which were not profitable; and second, wages in manufacturing were kept permanently low in normal times and even lower when inflation occurred, while simultaneously profits grew inordinately. This was especially true in older labor intensive industries where profits were a function of wage contention rather than of productivity in general.

At this point another element must be introduced: the control the government exercised over the workers through unions that were managed by bureaucratic leaders more responsive to the government than to their constituents. This mechanism was important for achieving stabilizing development, since it was responsible for the contention of wages; but it resulted in a decline or at least a stagnation in the standard of living for workers and peasants. Obviously some strata, especially among the highly skilled workers and in capital intensive enterprises, benefited from development. Yet the existence of so-called labor elites did not disprove the overall fact that the standard of living of the working class was declining.

During the period of stabilizing development a middle class emerged, made up of the public and private bureaucracies, professionals, and students, a class which received little attention because it identified most closely with the bourgeoisie. Nevertheless its standard of living was not satisfactory.

Under these conditions the development model had exhausted its potential by the mid-1960s, giving rise to frustration and protest among the middle and lower strata: doctors in 1965; students in 1966 and (with considerable middle class support) in 1968, when they were forcefully repressed by the government; and guerrilla movements among workers and land invasions by peasants after 1970. A high official in the Echeverría government later explained the situation, saying that "the problems compounded in magnitude and complexity, due to inertia on the part of the dominant class and to their mistaken conception of development."[4]

These facts were manifestations of a crisis nurtured during the years of stabilizing development and which opened up latent divisions within the revolutionary family. On one side were those who approved of the existing development model, and on the other those who, like Muñoz Ledo, criticized it and demanded change, a return to "Cardenismo." The first were linked closely to the more conservative sectors of the national bourgeoisie and foreign capital; the second maintained ties with the progressive intelligentsia (from which many came) in hopes of winning the support of the nationalist bourgeoisie.

By the end of the 1960s, then, an economic crisis clearly existed, whose indicators were sketched by economist Ifigenia Martínez de Navarrete: scarce governmental resources and curtailed programs; low capital formation in public enterprises and weakening of the public sector, which contributed to a rise in the federal deficit from 741 million pesos in 1958 to 10.2 billion in 1972; a growing deficit in the balance of payments current account; a trade deficit; reduced governmental revenues; rising supply of labor and resultant unemployment; and a weak internal market due to unequal income distribution.[5] In addition, a rise in foreign indebtedness made Mexico highly dependent upon U.S. financial sources, and increased foreign domination of the economy by multinational corporations had the effect of decapitalizing the economy, since they reinvested little and remitted abroad most of their enormous profits. Finally, a low growth rate in the agricultural sector since 1966 had stimulated rural migration to the cities.

The political system had for its part created a state that was supposed to be an infallible arbiter among the social classes and to monopolize political activity. Yet its authority was brought into question by some of the very members of the bureaucracy and checkmated by sectors of the opposition. The fracturing of that model was evidenced by the student movement of 1968 and the larger number of votes (over one million) received by the communist candidate in the 1970 presidential election.[6]

THE LUIS ECHEVERRÍA PROGRAM

Although as we have seen the causes of the economic crisis of the late 1960s had been taking shape during the thirty years of the stabilizing development, many persons still believed that the social malaise derived merely from the maldistribution of income and rigidities in the political system. Thus the candidate nominated by the power holders devised a reform platform that would adjust these two aspects of the system. In his inaugural address, Echeverría noted the problems and designated solutions: "Grave deficiencies and injustices continue, which could jeopardize our accomplishments: excessive concentration of income and marginalization of large groups threaten the harmony of development." He went on to state the need to raise the standard of living of the people, stressing the situation of the peasantry and Indian groups. He ended promising to enforce "minimum wage and profit-sharing laws," as well as

97

to prevent price rises in basic commodities, which "the popular classes deeply resent."

As for investment, President Echeverría favored autonomous capitalization, which would reduce Mexico's reliance on foreign capital. The country would not be hostile to outside investment, as long as it served to complement Mexican capital. He stressed the efficacy of the mixed economic regime the country had developed, asserting that constitutional law "presupposed that public investment would be sufficiently strong to direct growth." That is, he implied that the state would channel investments into necessary areas, which would eventually alter the productive structure of the country. State investment policies (which amounted to a plan) would tend to decentralize productive activities so as to avoid excessive concentration of the benefits of modernization in a few locations. He offered government collaboration to the private industrial sector, warning however that he would revise the protectionist system in effect to stimulate productivity, withdrawing support from inefficient enterprises. Moreover, he mentioned the need to achieve a balance in external payments by increasing exports of manufactured goods, in which the private sectors would play a leading role. In summary, the president attempted to engage the bourgeoisie in a basic revision of the development model.[7]

President Echeverría's intent was to rescue the autonomy of the state vis-à-vis the social classes, especially the bourgeoisie and foreign capital, restoring to the state its role in guiding the development process, which would in turn require strengthening the state itself.[8] Nevertheless, to put this program into practice it was necessary to adopt measures that would encroach on vested interests. In particular he needed to build up a sociopolitical base with which to sustain his administration, because the preceding one had destroyed the old alliance with the popular sectors. The only portions remaining loyal were the government party bosses, who themselves had fallen into disrepute. In this situation, without some change the only way to preserve control over the working masses and peasants would have been to continue the repression instituted by Díaz Ordaz (1964–70).

It should be remembered that the means of controlling the masses had been created during the Cárdenas mobilization and that they had been used later to maintain an internal peace. Only in moments of crisis did governments avail themselves of force to contain the masses. But in 1970 it was clear that the systems of control were themselves totally discredited and had to be overhauled or replaced. Therefore, President Echeverría attempted to set in motion a *new* mass mobilization, on four different levels:

1. Mobilize the working class through the traditional unions, dominated by the state-selected bureaucrats, in order to bring about a change in leadership by means of active member participation. The result would be a new, younger union leadership which would be respected by the rank and file.
2. Take advantage of several union federations headed by discontented leaders and bring them under government influence. Apparently this was an important aspect, since some of the discontented leaders were long-time followers of Cárdenas and still favored a populist program of economic rewards and government support for nationalist sectors of the bourgeoisie. This wing of the working class favored strengthening the nationalist sector within the ranks of government; its outstanding spokesman was the electricians' representative, Rafael Galván, who lost influence with Díaz Ordaz precisely for taking part in the 1960s nationalist protests.
3. Rekindle in the peasantry the hope of carrying through a total agrarian reform, removing the obstacles that had been set up during the period of stabilizing development, especially the regional bureaucracy and the caciques. In this case, it was hoped to renew the leadership of the ejidos, the agrarian leagues, and the National Peasant Confederation.
4. Incorporate the middle classes into the Mexican political model, classes which had been largely forgotten since the 1940s. They made their voices heard during the student protests of 1968 with a vigor which surprised even the party bosses, who had come to expect apathy and conservatism from the middle classes.

On another front, general political reforms were envisioned, including the democratization of the party, whose image had completely deteriorated. According to presidential plans, constitutional liberties would be respected absolutely and the government would permit the formation of new political groups that could revive the national scene. Moreover, a channel of communication to the progressive sectors was needed, especially to the intellectuals, whose voices had been muffled by the Díaz Ordaz administration.

THE MOBILIZATION

The Workers. The structure of the labor movement was the product of the mass mobilization undertaken by Cárdenas beginning in December 1934, which had led to the unification of labor in one confederation with leftist (if not Marxist-Leninist) and nationalist tendencies, under the leadership of Vicente Lombardo Toledano. The Workers Confederation of Mexico (CTM) was incorporated into the state shortly after its creation in 1936 by means of enlisting its members in the official party, the Party of the Mexican Revolution (PRM). Since then, wages and benefits have been largely dictated by the government, since no one ever questioned the original decision to convert the CTM into the labor wing of the PRM.

Nevertheless, the stabilizing development required avoidance of conflict, that is, labor demands which the government or the bourgeoisie regarded as excessive. Since the intent was to accelerate the process of capital accumulation and industrialization, largely through private enterprise, restriction of wage demands and benefits in general was essential, along with maintenance of stable prices. At first the approach worked well, but on occasion (for example, at the end of World War II and during the Korean and Viet Nam wars) inflationary pressures caused workers to break with the government and to repudiate subservient leaders in the official union movement; at these times great explosions of discontent occurred.

When Luis Echeverría took over, the country was on the verge of another explosion, and the activities of the labor leaders were no longer seen as legitimate either by the bureaucracy itself or (what was worse) by the rank and file. Corruption in the labor hierarchy was limitless and scandalous, and its ties both to government and to the bourgeoisie were obvious. So discredited had labor leadership become that the government itself decided to overhaul the sector by means of rank and file mobilization. This would, from all appearances, have the eventual goal of replacing the CTM with some other organization, such as the Revolutionary Confederation of Workers and Peasants (CROC), which was given open encouragement by the government, even over the CTM. As a last resort, Echeverría's intention was to replace all of the CTM leaders (if he couldn't replace the organization itself) with dissidents such as Demetrio Vallejo or Rafael Galván.

Thus, Echeverría launched a campaign of agitation among the workers, urging them to participate actively in union affairs, to attend meetings at which union business was deliberated, to express themselves freely without fear of reprisals, to "fight in league with their companions to assure healthy and independent unions, and to demand respect for their rights as members; giving them a guarantee that the government would not interfere in their local affairs."[9]

Prominent members of the presidential team played important parts in this labor mobilization scheme, men like Porfirio Muñoz Ledo, Secretary of Labor and Social Welfare, and Jesús Reyes Heroles, president of the official party (now renamed PRI). The former, echoing the president's own exhortations, assured the rank and file that Echeverría's policy of dialogue would be carried right into the heart of the union movement in order to guarantee union democracy, "so that ideological consistency would prevail and the social struggle continue."[10] Reyes Heroles stressed that the independence of unions would be respected.[11]

Given the state of the union movement as consolidated in the thirty years following Cárdenas's administration (in which for example direct and secret voting did not exist), Echeverría's words were a frontal assault on the labor bureaucracy as subordinated to the official party. They had two immediate and practical effects: first, a reaction among the labor leaders who were clearly threatened and who believed that their traditional alliance was being eliminated by the president; and second, a genuine effervescence among the rank and file. The latter tendency often manifested itself as open rebellion on the part of those who, having escaped repression by Díaz Ordaz, had formed a timid but independent labor movement. This movement, as we will see, was composed of two currents which joined together, unions that maintained a populist stance and criticized "deviation by the revolutionary governments," but which wished to strengthen them through popular bases; and an alliance of nationalist sectors in the government with radical, socialist, and communist groups who wished to change the system itself.

The first movement, representing populist organizations, was headed by Rafael Galván, general secretary of the Electrical Workers Union (STERM). His arguments stressed the need to reinforce nationalist groups within the government, with the long-range goal of strengthening the state itself so that it could lead a program of income redistribution, antiimperialism, industrial modernization, and defense against rightist elements.[12] The second group drew upon older unions as well as a few formed in response to Echeverría's pronouncements, such as the university workers and teachers union, which had been the principal support of the Communist ticket in the 1970 election. The program of this group was radical and its approach militant. Christian-Democratic organizations, such as the Authentic Labor Front (FAT), also belonged to this independent current.

Moreover, within the ranks of official unions some dissident action occurred, which occasionally led to their separation and realignment with the independent unions, such as in the case of workers in the Volkswagen and Nissan industries. These groups' experience proved advantageous, for after withdrawing from the CTM they achieved substantial economic gains.

The Peasants. The goal of land reform went back to the 1915 Veracruz Decrees, one of which (6 January 1915) obliged the revolutionary governments to undertake land distribution. Yet these objectives remained unattained until 1935, when massive land distribution began under Cárdenas: 18 million hectares were distributed to 800,000 families. Then after 1940 land reform lapsed again, so that with rapid population growth and little assistance for the ejidos, rural tension mounted. During the years of stabilizing development, in fact, rural unemployment grew considerably—the most conservative estimates suggest that 3.3 million peasants needed land [13] and the underemployment affected some 60 percent of the labor force, or 4 million out of a total of 5.7 million.[14] According to a survey conducted by the Bank of Mexico in 1965, 76 percent of the families in which the head was an agricultural worker had monthly per capita incomes of 59 pesos or less (at the time the peso equalled 8 cents). The entire rural labor force received 8 percent of the agricultural income, despite the fact that they represented half of the economically active population.

Thus the situation in rural Mexico could not have been worse, and as a result Luis Echeverría gave it special attention. In his presidential campaign he stated the need to solve agrarian problems through a program of rural industrialization. He also proposed reorganization of production utilizing cooperatives, alterations in the legal structure of ejidos, and renewed distribution of land. [15] In the meantime Echeverría began making weekly visits to the countryside to listen to the problems of the peasants and to urge them to take the initiative in solving them, either using pressure on the appropriate authorities, or by reporting abuses and violations of the law. The weekly visitations produced genuine agitation, whose results were seen later and were not quite what Echeverría desired. If fact, they provoked land invasions, a sign that the peaceful means suggested had not produced results. Indeed in the course of his visits Echeverría did not solve anything: he listened, promised to study the problem, and then delegated responsibility to subordinates who accomplished nothing, either due to negligence or the impenetrable web of special interests.[16] Thus, although the trips to the countryside might have enhanced Echeverría's image (showing that the charismatic nature of the presidency continued), they had no practical effect. As Salvatore Bizzarro suggested, given the inefficiency of the governmental bureaucracy, the only way to solve problems would be for the president to "rush out to the country giving orders on the site, which would be an inconvenient way for any governeent to conduct business."[17]

The Middle Classes. Populism often utilized socialist language to mobilize the masses. In the case of Mexico, that language was used largely because the revolutionary regimes emerged from a tradition of armed peasant and worker movements, which demanded socialization. The official calendar is still full of celebrations in honor of Zapata and the Casa del Obrero Mundial, as well as the precursors of the Revolution, the strikers of Cananea and Rio Blanco.

Nevertheless, such language did not work for the middle classes, who did not identify with the workers and peasants. Rather their aspirations were to attain an upper-class life style, for they were exposed to and manipulated by bourgeois ideology as purveyed in the mass media, especially television. Therefore the phraseology of "revolution" did not move these middle sectors, who responded more readily to liberal bourgeois language.

Paradoxically the ideology of caudillos and presidents always took into account the importance of the middle classes, since in the United States and Europe these sectors were a sign of prosperity.[18]

Hence official policy always tended to satisfy the needs of the middle strata.

From the political point of view, the middle classes had a special place reserved for them in the PRI: the National Confederation of Popular Organizations (CNOP). The efficacy of the CNOP has been questionable, because part of its base was ex officio: they became members of the party by the simple fact of occupying a place in the bureaucracy. Thus most of the time they failed to participate in the party, and in addition the CNOP was by its nature the most susceptible to control by the higher echelons of the bureaucracy. For that reason, its actions were negligible, despite the fact that it was the most favored in the distribution of public jobs.

The middle classes broadened considerably due to the necessities of economic development and as a result of it. In addition, during the 1960s the middle class underwent a change in mentality—whereas in the earlier generation middle-class youths believed in the traditional values of society (family, religion, morality, and so forth), the later one abandoned them as a result of liberalization of customs, such as in sexual relations, leaving home, and autonomy of behavior, among others.

Coincidentally the corruption at every level of the bureaucracy, as well as the latter's notorious inefficiency, greatly discredited the government and produced generalized discontent. Such sentiments were most pronounced among the middle classes, whose malaise grew because most of the burden of federal taxes fell on their shoulders.

Therefore, it is not surprising that the middle classes became protagonists in the student-popular demonstrations of 1968, nor that Luis Echeverría should have tried to integrate them into the mobilization in favor of his government. The universities, a principal habitat of the middle class, saw their federal subsidies rise substantially. A large number of intellectuals were called upon to collaborate with the government, at very attractive salaries. At the same time the bureaucracy saw its work week reduced to five days. The leaders of the official party attempted to attract the middle classes: for example, during the meeting of the national council of the PRI, its president Jesús Reyes Heroles spoke of winning over these new bases of supprt "by means of a healthy politicization . . . as much in the urban developed sectors as among the politically marginal." But he did not want to give up the existing support, that is workers and peasants.[19]

The mobilization of workers, peasants, and the middle classes led inevitably to the creation of a Popular Alliance—an expression used mainly by President Echverría, by his secretary of labor, Porfirio Muñoz Ledo, and by the president of PRI, Jesús Reyes Heroles. By Popular Alliance they meant a reconciliation of the interests of labor with those of the nation, in favor of the reform program of the government.[20] When government officials spoke of the "general interests of the nation," they naturally implied economic development according to the model in which private enterprise played a preponderant part. For that reason, capital was assumed to be a part of the Alliance, which is how businessmen saw it. According to a business spokesman, "We support and fight for a national unity in which each of the parts recognizes the efforts of the others, treats them with respect, and does nothing to the other's detriment."[21] However, the government should favor small and medium-sized producers, and national enterprise, joining with them if necessary to take advantage of their experience and talent.[22] And depending upon the nationalist position of the administration, it would attempt to put limits on foreign capital, especially that of the multinational corporations.

POPULISM ON THE MARCH

The nationalist reform campaign of Luis Echeverría failed, largely because it was founded on false premises. The chief executive believed that the presidentialist system conferred him with omnipotence and that this authority would be reinforced by the mass mobilization, especially with regard to his negotiations with the bourgeoisie and more conservative elements of the bureaucracy. However, thirty years of stabilizing development had shifted the balance of power away from the presidency, the opposite of what had occurred in 1934, when Cárdenas achieved a renewal of his power with a similar mobilization. In fact, economic power and bureaucratic organization had grown so much by 1970 that the state had lost its old autonomy. The political system had become so corrupt that it was dependent upon money, especially since most politicians were simultaneously big businessmen or simply millionaires.

Under these circumstances, threatened social groups were on guard and organized effective defenses. The first sign of this collusion of interests was the episode of 10 June 1971, when paramilitary groups from the lower class, trained and supported by the Mexico City municipal authorities (in the hands of some of the most reactionary and corrupt members of the revolutionary family) attacked a peaceful student demonstration.

From that point on, presidential action underwent a change: the weekly trips to the countryside ceased; the exhortations to democratize unions ended; and proposed laws were given to business groups for comment prior to submission to the legislature, a pre-1970 usage that Echeverría had tried to end. Yet in the following years some important legislative packages were passed to protect the economic well-being of the masses. For example, the Tripartite National Commission, composed of government, union, and business representatives, was created to discuss common problems. In addition the Ministry of Labor instituted annual increases in the minimum wage and more frequent labor contract renewals (all of which had been on a biannual cycle) in order to compensate workers for rises in the cost of living.

As the same time confrontations were provoked between the chief executive and the business sector, one of which is worth noting. Unions had requested a 35 percent raise from employers, but the latter refused to discuss the request or even to attend bargaining sessions ordered by the Ministry of Labor. As a result a general strike was scheduled for 20 September 1974.[23] The official union bosses took that stance to provoke the president into attacking them in his State of the Union message to Congress. But Echeverría instead gave his full support to labor, saying that he had from the beginning

> repudiated the economic model that favored concentration of income and strengthening of small privileged groups. In times of stress, labor policy gains special urgency. Rather than maintain apparent equilibria in individual cases, we must promote equity among the social classes.[24]

When employers warned that any wage increases would actually erode workers' income by contributing to inflation,[25] Echeverría rejected their logic, saying that "to hold back necessary reforms for fear of inflation would be to hand over the future of the country to the [wealthy] few for their personal benefit." Therefore he would not permit inflation to fall solely on "those sectors which generate national wealth and barely enjoy its benefits." Turning from his prepared text, the president rebuked business representatives in the Chamber for raising prices at the mere request of a wage increase. "Those who could not wait to raise prices now cite grave economic reasons for insisting that workers wait."[26]

Finally, after a series of separate meetings between the labor authorities, unions, and employers, it was agreed to raise wages 22 percent for workers who earned less that 5,000 pesos, and to give the rest monthly raises of 1,100 pesos. [27]

Meanwhile, business and political groups that had been powerful under presidents Alemán and Díaz Ordaz, and which had close ties to foreign capital, were joined by official unions and major landowners in a campaign to resist Echeverría and to sabotage the economy. In 1976 they provoked a capital flight and a run on the peso by buying dollars. They also ceased making long-term loans, which brought the savings rate down, despite the fact that market demand was strong.[28] Likewise U.S. tariff increases on Mexican exports contributed to the decline of the economy and of the government itself.

Thus relations between Echeverría, capitalists, and political groups deteriorated. A "crisis of confidence" was said to exist, whereby the new sources of support did not come forward. In fact, the president ran into many obstacles in his attempts to restructure the official labor movement, as was evident in the actions of Fidel Velázquez, secretary general of the CTM. For example, during the PRI national council meeting, which dealt with democratization of the party, Velázquez allied himself with conservative leaders. And even after some of the top positions had changed hands, the party remained as unresponsive as before. Leaving the meeting, Velázquez confirmed as much by claiming that his group had won a great victory. Later, when confronted by heavy opposition, the old-line CTM leader threatened to use all of the means at his command, constitutional and otherwise, to destroy his antagonists. He could count on the backing of conservative sectors in the PRI, as well as more powerful business groups that in the course of the stabilizing development had forged mutual ties with the CTM. In other words, the labor bosses could augment their own power by allying with the bourgeoisie when their common interests were threatened. At this level, then, the state was challenged by its own progeny, the union bureaucracy, demonstrating the impossibility of altering the now-ankylose structures. This constituted the failure of the Echeverría campaign, and the president himself soon recognized defeat, realizing that he would have to join forces with them rather than try to overthrow them.[29]

Inflation played an important part in the president's change in attitude toward the official union movement, especially in 1972 and 1973. The government's usually efficient control over the working class through the CTM began to falter, expecially as the buying power of workers' paychecks eroded. Union bosses were challenged by the rank and file, who started their own movements outside the official hierarchy. These movements might be demands for higher wages already agreed to by the government and employers, or they might be aimed at replacing the union leadership itself in an attempt to gain independence from government controls.

This situation was doubly dangerous, since it could severely weaken the powers of containment of the official unions and fracture the corporative structure of the state itself. In these circumstances, the official hierarchy was obliged to become more radical, in essence to take up the banners of the dissident labor leaders, in order not to lose control of the movement itself. Thus the official unions found it necessary to challenge the bourgeoisie, which remained opposed to any and all increases in wages and benefits. In this way the official hierarchy came to occupy roughly the same position as Echeverría. Moreover, they had to compete with the independent unions, many of which were bringing home far better contracts than the official unions. The independents became more attractive as workers suffered the impact of inflation.

On the other hand Echeverría's retreat from his original position supporting union democratization, together with certain repressive actions against labor crusaders, prevented a permanent alliance between the government and the independent union movements, either the populist or radical ones.

For their part, the peasants quickly perceived that the president's promises would not be honored, because the network of entrenched interests—caciques and bureaucrats in the agrarian banks—stopped the rural mobilization. Such a movement would of course have neutralized their power and carried out the original intent of the agrarian laws. Instead, then, the pressure erupted in land invasions and violence that tarnished Echeverría's image. In the last days of his administration he carried out some unexpected and sensationalist land distributions, which did not solve any problems and indeed created others. In fact, these acts gave rise to rumors that the bourgeoisie was about to lead a coup d'etat.

The populist campaign also failed to generate support among the middle classes, which were seriously hit by inflation. They were especially receptive to antigovernment propaganda, often in the form of rumors. All Echeverría's efforts to recruit students and intellectuals (efforts that occasionally included outright bribery) failed, because leaders insisted on knowing beforehand the results of an investigation into the repressions of 1968 and 1971. Some in fact knew the results already. When Echeverría did not comply, he suffered the worst ostracism a public official can experience: he was practically driven from the university campus by multitudes of students, among them extremists of both the left and the right.

The nationalist group within the bourgeoisie, formed during Cárdenas's administration and which at first gave Echeverría considerable support, also soon left the populist camp. It was too severely affected by the crisis, because it was composed of small- and medium-sized businesses whose costs rose rapidly with general inflation. With contraction of government credit, several of these businesses went bankrupt, because they lacked sufficient internal capitalization. Moreover, some were ruined by the emergency wage increases. These businessmen were told that the unexpectedly radical stance of the union bosses was instigated by the president's office and was not the result of a challenge by independent union leaders. [It should be noted that while small businesses suffered due to inflation and wage hikes, the large companies reaped even higher profits, as can be seen in table 3.]

Finally, with regard to the political machinery, Echeverría was able to accomplish a few changes, but only in the upper echelons of the party. The president of PRI, Manuel Sánchez Vite, a member of the most conservative groups and a close ally of the CTM bosses, was replaced by Reyes Heroles. The mayor of Mexico City, Alfonso Martínez Domínguez, who was tied to the Monterrey group, was removed when it became known that he was the ringleader of the massacre of 10 June. The governor of the state of Nuevo León,

Table 3. Sales and Profits [losses] by Economic Sector (millions of pesos)

Sector	Sales		Profits	
	1970	1976	1970	1976
Mining	3,646	10,878	332	485
Food, beverages, tobacco	4,705	13,578	230	[31]
Steel	1,603	3,377	[115]	24
Metallurgy	401	1,207	51	114
Metal products	236	558	17	16
Automobiles	1,247	3,498	64	[55]
Textiles, clothing	163	276	9	1
Chemicals	2,078	5,908	236	220
Paper, cellulose	1,241	3,959	138	239
Construction	662	2,758	79	26
Commerce	1,804	5,453	132	400
Services	2,547	9,970	261	1,142
Electronics	1,353	3,950	94	114
TOTALS	21,689	65,191	1,529	2,695

Source: Coordenación General del Sistema Nacional de Información, *Boletín mensual de información económica,* vol. 1, no. 5 (1977).

drawn from the rightist National Action Party (PAN), was forced to resign. But little or no change took place at the lower levels of the party, that is, change which might have affected its power bases.

The campaign of Luis Echeverría, based upon the populist model of Lázaro Cárdenas, encountered the same obstacles as had its predecessor of the 1930s, yet it lacked the solid popular bases of the earlier one and had to confront an economically more powerful bourgeoisie and a more entrenched bureaucracy. The results in terms of structural change and improvements for the masses were scanty or even null. Nevertheless, not all the blame should fall on the president or on the flaws in his program. Over the coming years new evidence will come to light to help us judge the 1970–76 presidency with greater clarity.

Notes

1. Arnaldo Córdoba, *La ideología de la Revolución Mexicana* (Mexico: Ediciones ERA, 1973).

2. Jorge Basurto, "Populismo y movilización de masas durante el régimen cardenista," *Revista mexicana de sociología* 31 (1969): 853–92.

3. Ibid.

4. Porfirio Muñoz Ledo, "El sistema político mexicano," *El Día,* 24 July 1976.

5. *El Día,* 14 May 1974.

6. Without admitting as much, the official tabulation recognized this number of votes under the rubric, "unregistered candidates."

7. Speech by President Echeverría, *Excélsior,* 2 December 1970.

8. Julio Labastida, "Nacionalismo reformista en México," *Cuadernos políticos* 3 (1975).

9. *Excélsior,* 3 February 1971.

10. Ibid., 6 January 1974.

11. Ibid., 13 January 1974.

12. "Demandemos medidas efectivas contra la carestía," *Excélsior,* 7 June 1974.

13. Rodolfo Stavanhagen, "Aspectos sociales de la estructura agraria en México," in *Neolatifundismo y explotación* (Mexico: Editorial Nuestro Tiempo, 1976), p. 49.

14. Juvencio Wing, "El subempleo rural en México," cited by Arturo Bonilla, "Un problema que se agrava: la subocupación rural," in *Neolatifundismo y explotación,* p. 129.

15. Cf. the new Agrarian Reform Law and the Water Rights Law.

16. One of Echeverría's closest collaborators, Alfredo B. Bonfil, perished in an airplane accident provoked by representatives of those interests.

17. Salvatore Bizzaro, "Mexico Under Echeverría," *Current History,* May 1974, p. 224.

18. Córdova, *Ideología de la Revolución.*

19. *Excélsior,* 13 January 1974.

20. Ibid., 28 September 1973 and 13 January 1974; *El Día,* 24 July 1976.

21. *Excélsior,* 14 January 1974.

22. Ibid., 17 April 1974, cited by Labastida, "Nacionalismo reformista."

23. *Excélsior,* 31 August 1974.

24. Ibid., 2 September 1974.

25. Ibid., 14 September 1974. A business spokesman calculated that the increase would cost his company 33 million pesos a year, which would have to be recuperated through higher prices.

26. See Note 24.

27. *Excélsior,* 14 September 1974. Negotiations between Muñoz Ledo and businessmen were so tense that talks were nearly suspended. Finally, employers agreed to a compromise when it became known that the CTM would be authorized to call a general strike the next day.

28. *Análisis económico* (Mexican edition of *Business Trends*), 9 April 1973.

29. Echeverría's speech at the opening of the 9th CTM Congress contained the following: "The workers affiliated with the CTM will give their votes to those who have served the cause with absolute loyalty, to those who possess a spirit of dedication and unbreakable fervor for workers' interests, [to those] who perform their duties with serenity, experience, and strength of convictions . . ." *Excélsior,* 22 April 1974.

6

Populism in Peru: APRA, The Formative Years

Steve Stein
State University of New York, Stony Brook

Under the undisputed leadership of its founder, Víctor Raúl Haya de la Torre, APRA (the Alianza Popular Revolucionaria Americana) has evolved into the most significant political force in modern Peru. It seems destined in the 1980s to capture the presidency, even without Haya and despite the long-standing opposition of the military. Paradoxically, this prospective success follows a half-century of virtual exclusion from the presidency and extended periods of illegality. This chapter will examine the origins and early growth of APRA, attempting to isolate the principal elements responsible for its emergence and endurance. In the process it should become clear why APRA is one of Latin America's most famous populist movements.

APRA, founded in Mexico in 1924, began to participate actively in Peruvian politics in 1930, in preparation for Haya de la Torre's candidacy in the 1931 presidential election. But the true beginnings of APRA date back to 1919, when Haya de la Torre first became associated with influential sectors of Lima's industrial proletariat. Indeed, the story of the birth and development of APRA is the story of the careful nurturing of mutual loyalty over a ten-year period between the future Aprista leader and the urban labor groups that would later constitute the mass base of his populist movement.

A prerequisite for the growth of APRA into a significant political force was the existence of a mass that could be mobilized by the leaders of the future party. Such a popular mass began to emerge in Peru's capital city during World War I and the 1920s, and its appearance is evident from the urban growth in that period. Lima's population rose 117 percent, from 173,000 to 376,000 between the 1908 and 1931 censuses, for an annual growth rate of 3.4 percent. Approximately one-third of the increase came before 1919, and the remaining two-thirds occurred in the 1920s. Even more significant in terms of the appearance of a political mass was the high proportion of that growth attributable to working class expansion. Dramatic changes in Lima's employment structure between the pre-World War I days and 1931 showed that not only had the capital become an enlarged metropolis, but moreover it had become something of a working class city. Overall employment in working class jobs increased 186 percent between 1908 and 1931, with particularly high rates of growth in construction workers (182 percent), market vendors (316 percent), domestic servants (310 percent), peddlers (an astounding 1,333 percent from 1920 to 1931) and textile workers (319 percent).[1] It was from among these textile workers, Lima's incipient industrial proletariat, that APRA derived much of its early popular support. Indeed, the birth of APRA resulted from Haya de la Torre's first formal contact with labor organizations in the textile sector in January of 1919. Against a background of increasing worker discontent touched off by a noticeable deterioration in the living conditions of the urban masses during the inflation-ridden war years, the capital's labor organizations went on strike for an eight-hour working day and an increase in hourly wages. The first to walk off their jobs were the textile workers, and they were soon joined by bakers, tanners, shoemakers, public transport workers, and printers. Haya was brought into the conflict when the protesting workers sought to blunt the intransigence and repressive actions of the goverment by involving university students. The strikers reasoned that students, coming from so-called privileged backgrounds, might carry more weight in official circles and would presumably be immune to the more extreme forms of repression.

Out of Haya's initial experience with important sectors of Lima's working classes came those patterns of interaction between leader and followers that ultimately formed the cement of the Aprista movement. Quickly asserting himself as the head of the three-man student delegation, Haya de la Torre became the chief negotiator for the strikers, in other words, the intermediary between labor and government. Traveling back and forth between the union headquarters and the Ministry of Development, Haya's presence came to dominate the strike meetings. Not only did he bring the news of changes in the government's position, but Haya was also responsible for formulating the workers' position in the negotiations. His lively progress reports made him the center of attention at strike meetings. And at several points during the conflict Haya reinforced the workers' admiration for him by standing up to government troops and daring them to kill students. After three days of almost nonstop negotiating, Haya de la Torre announced that the workers had won their fight for the eight-hour day. By personally presenting the eight-hour decree to the strikers, Haya consummated his identification with the eight-hour victory and with the cause of the workingman. In the space of thirty-six hours, Víctor Raúl Haya de la Torre had risen to a position of considerable prominence, in fact of leadership, vis à vis much of the capital's labor force.

It might seem strange that an individual of Haya de la Torre's middle-class background would have assumed the championship of labor's cause in 1919. Haya was born in the northern provincial city of Trujillo in 1895 to a family that, particularly on the maternal side, had close connections to various sectors of Peru's economic and political elites. He attended the Seminario de San Carlos, the preferred educational institution of the local elite. When the young Haya arrived in Lima in 1917 to take courses at the University of San Marcos, he had numerous useful contacts with individuals in the "establishment" through his family connections. Haya described the impact upon him of his initial experiences in the capital:

> At that time I was a little *criollo* brat, sick to my bones with that epidemic frivolity—the plague of the people of high status . . . . Because of this I arrived in Lima thinking about the immense honor of seeing myself in the classrooms in contact with certain personages who were so frequently mentioned in the press.[2]

Various factors seem to have contributed to Haya's transformation from a "sickly criollo" to a determined representative of labor. The same year he came to Lima the future Aprista leader visited for the first time the old Inca and colonial town of Cuzco, where he claimed to have become cured for good of his "criollo" frivolity after seeing suffering worse than anything he had previously imagined. Another important stimulus for Haya's "social awareness" appears to have been the ideas of Peru's leading nonconformist intellectual, Manuel González Prada. Like many of his fellow students, Haya avidly read and discussed González Prada's works. Particularly taken by González Prada's essay on the intellectual's role as the guide of the workingman, Haya began to see himself as able to "instruct the masses in order to transform the most humble worker into a conscious collaborator."[3]

A final clue to Haya de la Torre's interest in representing labor on the occasion of the eight-hour movement may be found in his youthful experiences in Trujillo. From his early years Haya admits that he had a passion for political organization and an interest in social movements. His childhood games were, in fact, devoted to these central interests. As he recalled:

> We had some very spacious rooms to play in, and we created a republic there. We had a president, we had cabinet ministers, deputies. We had politics. And there we practiced. And we were twelve-year-old kids. And we practiced at reproducing the life of the country with spools of thread. All my brothers, I got them into the game. I used to receive very nice toys; locomotives, trains. But I was not interested in these things. What interested me was to have an organized setup, like a country. . . . When I recall this, you can see how early I had a political imagination. It was quite noteworthy, because we imitated life, but we assured a life of order. Now I tell myself, how I've always had this thing about organizing. We directed political campaigns.[4]

For Haya, participation in the eight-hour movement was vitally important in determining what direction his penchant for leadership and political organization would ultimately take. Haya recently summarized the significance of his first active participation in a labor cause: "I took advantage of the eight-hour strike to forge ties with the workers."[5] And ensuing events reflected his considerable success in that endeavor. The extent of Haya's ascendency with the labor groups that participated in the eight-hour movement was evident the day after the end of the strike, when he presided over the birth of the Federación de Trabajadores de Tejidos del Perú (Federation of Peruvian Textile Workers), an organization that in the next decade would constitute the most powerful force in the Peruvian labor movement.

Haya relinquished the presidency of the Federación Textil immediately after its foundation, but in the coming months he made a concerted effort to maintain and strengthen the ties he had forged with labor in the critical days of January. He remained in contact with many of the union leaders whom he had met during the eight-hour strike, and he soon began to offer classes in psychology to a group of them. Those classes were the precursor of the "Universidad Popular González Prada," a school for workers manned by university students that would serve more than any other institution to strengthen and widen Haya's contacts with labor throughout the 1920s.

At every step of the way leading to the eventual establishment of the Universidad Popular in January 1921, Haya's personal leadership was the decisive element. He encouraged the labor leaders with whom he had worked in the eight-hour movement and the formation of the Federación Textil to spread the idea of a popular university among their peers. He carried out a kind of "whistle stop" campaign: from atop a horse-drawn carriage Haya spoke daily to union meetings, to groups at factories, entreating workers to use their free hours to advance themselves culturally in the classrooms of the Universidad Popular instead of squandering their time and money in taverns and bordellos. At the same time, Haya de la Torre worked within the Student Federation to gain the backing of the university community. Elected president of the Federation in October 1919, due largely to his prominence in the eight-hour movement, he was able to convince a considerable number of his fellow students to become teachers at the projected workers' school.

It was from among this group of university student-professors of the Universidad Popular that the nucleus of Aprista Party leadership later emerged. Many of these youths had middle- and upper-class backgrounds similar to that of Haya de la Torre and were often motivated by the same kinds of social and political concerns. The first indication of the emergence of an anti-status quo and socially concerned faction among the nation's youth coincided with the initiation of the University Reform movement in Peru. These students' protests against a conservative university geared to the education of a social and political elite were part of a larger repudiation of the older generation. World War I, the promise of the Wilsonian Doctrine and the Peace of Versailles, the Mexican and Russian Revolutions—all produced in certain segments of the student population an awareness of great social evils while at the same time encouraging them to see themselves as missionaries of social and political reform in Peru. Like Haya, they were also touched by the teachings of Manuel González Prada whose oft-repeated phrase—*los viejos a la tumba y los jóvenes a la obra* (the aged to the tomb and the youth to work)—had become a rallying cry for those who advocated youthful self-affirmation. Their awareness of the social question was further increased by the appearance of urban workers in ever larger numbers and a growing labor movement.

The student activists and industrial laborers—the two eventual pillars of Aprismo—came together in an institutional context in the Universidad Popular. From the beginning Haya de la Torre was the dominant force of the school. In addition to being Rector, he taught courses, appointed professors, developed the curriculum, planned special social and cultural activities, and personally signed the identification card of each matriculated student. Operating at night, the Universidad Popular placed a heavy emphasis on practical education, with classes on hygiene, anatomy, arithmetic, grammar, and geography. The school sponsored sporting events, hikes into the countryside, and musical programs. Medical school students who donated their time to the Universidad Popular established popular clinics, diagnosed illnesses, and prescribed remedies. Workers and their families were urged to attend numerous dances and other social events organized by the school.

Most of the leadership of Lima's organized labor force studied at the Universidad Popular at some time between 1921 and its closing by the government in 1924. Men who conducted the major unions in this period and who would direct labor in the 1930s and 1940s shared a common experience in the classrooms of Haya's school. The constant contact between university students and labor leaders in the Universidad Popular led to the generation of deep ties of friendship between these two groups. These laborers, who had received little or no formal education before entering the workers' school, gave the student-professors credit for "bringing the rays of learning to our dark minds."[6] Haya de la Torre was singled out for special praise. Called *El Maestro*, the soul of the Universidad Popular, and *el compañero Rector*, Haya was particularly looked up to because he had seemingly abandoned the aristocratic world of the University of San Marcos for the world of proletarian Lima.

The bonds of friendship and personal loyalty established in the Universidad Popular were the most important elements in the emergence of a coalition of university students and workers between 1921 and 1923 that ultimately took the form of the Aprista party. In the classrooms of the Universidad Popular, professors from middle and upper social strata and their worker-students became acquainted for the first time. A visible solidarity between these two groups—a reciprocal trust—grew out of their common educational experience. The *frente de obreros manuales e intelectuales* (front of manual and intellectual workers), Haya's favorite title for the Aprista movement, was the offspring of the workers' school he formed in 1921. And in the particular case of Haya de la Torre, doubtless many of the techniques that he used as a populist leader in attracting urban laborers to his cause were first learned in the Universidad Popular.

In May 1923 Haya's manual and intellectual worker front faced its first critical test, a test that would contribute significantly to the shaping of its trajectory in coming years. Early in that month President Augusto Leguía made known his plan to consecrate Peru to the Sacred Heart of Jesus, purportedly to gain clerical backing for his imminent re-election attempt. Shortly after the news of the consecration became public, Haya as the head of the Universidad Popular began to work secretly against the maneuver. On the afternoon of 23 May 1923 the protest was officially launched with a public meeting in the assembly hall of the University of San Marcos. Crowded with students and workers, the session began with the election of Haya de la Torre. Then, with Haya at its head, an ardent multitude numbering approximately 5,000 people erupted from San Marcos to carry their indignation into the streets of Lima. Unable to contain the protestors, the troops charged them with swords drawn. Fire from soldiers' rifles echoed in the streets. Soon the word was passed from group to group that Salmón Ponce, a trolley car motorman, and Alarcón Vidalón, a university student, had been killed by the onrushing troops. When groups of demonstrators succeeded in reaching Lima's central square, Haya de la Torre, with gestures reminiscent of the eight-hour movement, faced the menacing soldiers and harangued the crowd. Pointing to the troops he declared, "The man who murders students and workers is not among you, soldiers. You are acting under a reign of terror." And then turning toward the Presidential Palace he shouted: "The real villain is the tyrant hiding there!"[7]

The events of 23 May, the aggressive spirit of the San Marcos assembly, the violent encounters with government troops, the deaths of a worker and a student, Haya's bellicose speech—all brought added cohesion to the protest. On 24 May, in a sensational move, a group of protestors with Haya in the lead, stole the cadavers of Ponce and Vidalón from the city morgue and carried them to the University. The next morning a crowd estimated at 30,000 attended their funeral at which Haya de la Torre was the principal orator. That same day the Archbishop of Lima announced the suspension of the consecration effort. The protest movement was victorious.

The events of May signified much more than the victory of a multiclass campaign of dissent against the political-religious strategy of the government. In the longer view, the consecration protest cemented the concord between university students and workers later to be translated politically into the Aprista movement. In individual terms the most direct beneficiary of the sentiments produced by by the consecration protest was Haya de la Torre. Acknowledged as the undisputed "soul of the movement," Haya was a national hero, and more importantly, in the eyes of the Lima proletariat, "the responsible guide of the working class of which he had already become *Maestro*."[8]

The movement of 23 May signaled a profound transformation within the ranks of Lima's organized labor force: the departure of labor from apolitical traditions to the acceptance and even advocacy of politics as a necessary activity for the betterment of daily existence. With some hindsight it may be said that the politicization of these workers was imminent from the instant that they joined the Universidad Popular. The anthem of these workers' school, for example, which exhorted, "Awaken slaves! Already the rays of a new sun are bright in the East. . . . The more ignorant the worker, the more impossible it will be for him to conquer his liberation," expressed the necessity of taking concrete actions to gain personal advancement. But it was the unity of the Sacred Heart protest and its aftermath of repression against the movement's most prominent leaders by the government that convinced workers their fight was with the rulers of the state, and hence a political fight.

During the months following the 23 May protest, various prominent labor leaders approached Haya de la Torre about the creation of a formal political entity. But their plans were cut short by Haya's imprisonment and subsequent deportation in October 1923. In succeeding months and years the government went on to make the Universidad Popular and Lima's labor unions two of its principal targets for repression. One by one the locales of the Popular University were forcibly closed down, and both professors of the workers' school and labor leaders were imprisoned or deported. These actions were directed at the most prominent members of Haya's nascent student-worker movement.

While this repression and Haya's seven-and-a-half year exile certainly delayed efforts in Peru to convert the student-worker alliance into a formal party, they did not ultimately proscribe the emergence of APRA. On the contrary, in some ways these acts probably improved APRA's chances of success. With Haya's exile in 1923, for example, the legend of the eternally persecuted leader was born. From that year on, the "martyr" image constituted a vital element of Haya de la Torre's political style. Most importantly, the events of these years deepened the attachment, now political in nature, between Haya de la Torre and Lima's industrial workers. As Haya observed in a 1970 interview, when referring to the Sacred Heart protest and the ensuing period of repression:

> With the 23 May movement and with my exile, my relations with the workers were strongly reinforced. That is the base. This solidarity appeared at that time because we all contributed, we all fought, and afterwards, we all suffered repression.[9]

Seeing themselves as the victims of the same outrages as the rector of the Universidad Popular, urban workers identified themselves more closely with him and announced their intention of carrying on his fight while anxiously awaiting his return. The name of Haya, while prominent in the labor press before 1923, came to dominate the pages of working class publications after his deportation. He was even recalled in songs written after his exile and sung at meetings of worker groups during the years of persecution.

The repression had transformed a relatively amorphous student-worker alliance into an incipient political party and had secured for Haya de la Torre the leadership of that party by strengthening the ingredient of personal loyalty in his relationship with the members of the Lima proletariat. When in 1924 Haya officially founded the Aprista movement during his residence in Mexico City, the most influential members of the Lima proletarian community promptly declared their adherence to the new organization. Seven years later, many of these same men formed the backbone of Haya's popular support in the 1931 presidential campaign.

APRA did not take the form of a national political party until 1930. But in the preceding decade Aprismo manifested all of the elements that would distinguish it during its first presidential campaign in 1931. The movement appeared in the form of a political coalition between separate socioeconomic groups: the middle-and upper-class leadership with its core of ex-Universidad Popular instructors; and their proletarian supporters who belonged in most cases to the ranks of organized industrial labor in Lima. Víctor Raúl Haya de la Torre was the nexus between these different strata of Peruvian society.

The political joining of *la juventud del brazo y del cerebro* (the youth of muscle and the youth of brains), as Haya enjoyed referring to his creation, was necessary, according to the Apristas, because of the "ignorance that predominates in our working classes." Given this relatively negative view of the capacity of the Peruvian working class for self-government, the balance of power between the two factions of Aprismo regarding decision-making was predictably unequal. The Aprista leaders reasoned that, since the workers lacked the consciousness and ability necessary for independent political action, the running of the party and eventually the ruling of the nation would be left to the middle-and upper-class intellectuals who were best prepared for governing. These men would be the specialists, the political technicians who would direct the management of the state with the interests and the defense of the masses in mind.

The uneven division of power within this vertical mold was accepted and even advanced by the proletarian members of the Aprista coalition as well as by their upper-and middle-class leaders. From the days of the Universidad Popular, the workers had considered that the University students were "the best prepared to bring us light. . . . We always need a shepherd.''[10] And in the 1931 campaign, this group continued to insist on the guidance of former university students instead of men from their own socioeconomic level. The most prominent Aprista labor leader, Arturo Sabroso, described the workers' view of party and national leadership:

> A government totally made up of people from the proletariat was never considered as a possibility. Precisely when we became convinced of this a few fellow workers said, fine, we will join the party, but fifty percent workers and fifty percent intellectuals in everything: deputies, senators, everything. Others of us reasoned that no, impossible to have half workers. In a parliamentary block you have to have professional men, technicians, doctors, engineers, economists, lawyers, professors, workers, and employees. For study and consultation on many problems you need experts in their fields. This will assure that all the studies can be more effectively carried out. It is not a question of demagoguery. This is being realistic.[11]

At the top of this hierarchical framework was Haya de la Torre. Accorded the title of *Jefe máximo* (highest chief), his right to the position of supreme interpreter and director of the "vague and imprecise desires of the multitude"[12] was disputed by no one who still called himself an Aprista. No other individual could aspire to the ultimate direction of the party. That position belonged to Haya by right, as he was considered "the creator of the doctrine and its principal instrument and (deserved to lead) for having done what he has done."[13]

The Aprista leader and his followers considered themselves members of a single large family in which parents were to be respected and emulated by their children. They also referred to themselves repeatedly as a great brotherhood in which party members were treated as individuals and not just as votes. Notwithstanding this emphasis on the brotherliness of the party in general and of Haya as the "older brother" in particular, the Apristas bestowed on their leader all the attributes of a political patriarch. Haya himself warmed to his fatherly role. He viewed the working class contingent of his party as a child: "A child lives, a child feels pain, a child protests because of the pain; nevertheless, a child is not capable of guiding himself."[14] In a 1970 interview, Haya outlined the nature and origins of his paternalism by comparing in ideal terms the leader-follower relationship in Aprismo to the social relations that characterized the traditional *casa grande* or seigniorial house in his native city of Trujillo:

> In Trujillo there existed the very highest nobility. . . . These ties are very strange because they come from the family. Aristocratic ties were conserved in Trujillo. . . . I was nurtured in this aristocratic tradition. . . .One inherited this like a kind of code of conduct. This aristocracy was closer to the people. It was an old tradition. They treated the people very well. In Trujillo good treatment of the servants is traditional. The families that lived in what were called the *casas grandes* obeyed this rule. That the children wait on the servants on their birthdays, that they do all these things; be the godfather of their marriages, all this sort of thing. . . .And you have to go up to each one of the servants and greet them and kiss them. . . .It's a different spirit. And we who come from the North, for example, with the blacks, very affectionate, and everything. At the same time there was always something very cordial with the people. That is APRA! The Aprista masses have seen in their leaders people who had come from the aristocracy. . . .We were educated in that school. . . .People who don't know the inner workings of the Party don't understand these things...we were born of this stock. . . .In a country which was not an industrialized or bourgeois country, still a patriarchal country, these ties meant much. And APRA owes its success in its first years to this fact.[15]

Considering the source and substance of the alliance between the socioeconomic groups that made up APRA, the party involved an approach to politics and social change that posited a beneficent minority at the top directing the less favored majority toward what was good for them. This approach was evident in statements of Haya and in the whole evolution of the APRA movement. The Popular Universities, for example, represented the establishment of a series of vertical, patron-client relationships through which intellectual elites held the masses in dependent relationships by providing such nonmaterial benefits as education. Later these same relationships would be used to create the kind of mobilizable mass following necessary for the successful launching of a populist party. Cooperation between the different strata was the watchword of that party. Class distinctions were replaced by identifications with the person-to-person relations of trust, dependency and obedience between a charismatic, upper-middle-class leader and his mass following. As it emerged on the political stage in 1930–31, Aprismo did not represent, as many terrified members of the elites thought at the time, the beginning of the class struggle in Peru or even an attempt at structural change; instead it was an effort on the part of certain sectors of the urban masses to gain more desirable life styles by tying themselves to a man whom they considered their protector and benefactor. Ten years of intimate contact with those followers had gained for Haya de la Torre the highest position of leadership.

The precedents of the 1920s were closely followed in APRA's presidential bid of 1931. Adherence to the lessons of the early years was clearly evident in the most important elements of the party's campaign: an obsession with elaborate and tight organization; the production of a complex ideology; and the preeminence of Haya's paternalistic political style.

The Aprista's deep concern with elaborate organization became a trademark of their campaign for the presidency in 1931. Haya himself was the most decided advocate of a well-planned party organization. In the early political games of his childhood he had demonstrated an overriding interest in bringing order to his imaginary republic. Later, in the Popular University, APRA's founder stressed time and again that discipline was an indispensable ingredient in any enterprise devoted to the accomplishment of social change. His penchant for order became even greater during his exile years, when he was deeply impressed by the methodical operation and rigid stratification of European fascist and communist parties. For Haya, vigilance against any sign of internal division in his movement became a top priority for the building of a smoothly functioning political machine.

Spurred on by Haya's insistence on organization, the Aprista leadership group in Lima began feverishly to build organizations to recruit followers from the ranks of the urban proletariat. They spawned a large number of working-class branches bearing a myriad of titles including committees, subcommittees, cells, juntas, federations, and unions. These organizations were in most cases first set up and then closely coordinated by the central core of middle-and upper-class party leaders who repeatedly insisted upon the necessity of discipline, arguing that political success was possible only through strict obedience to the dictates of party. Individual followers were permitted to make suggestions about policy in the formative stages but once policy had been determined, no dissent was tolerated. Given their faithful compliance to a central chain of command, the Apristas' characterization of themselves as a civilian political army was not inappropriate. Every Aprista organization, from the National Executive Committee to the smallest local cell, had a disciplinary commission that was charged with maintaining central control.

The orderly party meetings and mass demonstrations that immensely impressed the friends and foes of APRA constituted tangible evidence of the movement's control over followers—both individual, and collectively. Advance preparations for large public meetings included exhaustive attention to the smallest of details. Special commissions supervised the manufacture of banners, the choice of speakers, and the rehearsal of cheers and songs. Only standards and signs approved by the party's disciplinary commission were allowed to be carried. Only approved speakers could individually voice their support for APRA. Special committees carefully planned the routes marchers would take, and appropriate maps appeared in the party newspaper, *La Tribuna,* on the day of the demonstration. APRA directives even stipulated that a distance of 30 meters be kept between groups of 2,000 demonstrators in order to facilitate cross traffic. The demonstrators began by marching through the streets from various geographic points in Lima to a central meeting place, usually a public plaza. There, amidst a veritable sea of party flags, the crowd joined in a series of rehearsed unison shouts of: "A . . .! PRA . . .! A . . .! PRA . . .!" They intoned numerous Aprista songs and formally initiated each rally with the singing of both the Aprista hymn, the *Marsellesa Aprista,* and the national anthem. These preparations all led up to the dramatic entrance of Haya de la Torre. Preceded by shouts of "Víctor Raúl! Víctor Raúl!" Haya suddenly stepped onto the speakers' platform, and with his left arm extended in the air, greeted the crowd with the Aprista salute. Surprise, an instant of silence, and then an enormous ovation. Preliminary speeches by middle class and labor leaders, punctured by songs and shouts. Haya's address, the highpoint of the event. More songs, more unison shouts, and the end of the rally with Haya's followers slowly filing away.

At these public gatherings as well as in their official platform, APRA's top leaders demonstrated a deep concern for the creation and diffusion of a complex set of ideological tenets. Their continued insistence on the importance of Aprista doctrine plus the very volume of newspaper and magazine articles and pamphlets written during and after the campaign has led to an exaggerated emphasis on the importance of political ideology in APRA, particularly when considering its effect on mass participation. Specific Aprista doctrinal statements, nearly always encased in relatively sophisticated language, had little direct effect on the mobilization of a working class following in 1931. Discussions about the impact of imperialism on international and national politics or about the subtleties of Marxist-Leninist thought generally confused mass audiences rather than convinced them of the rightness of party precepts. Aware of the limited interest exhibited by the popular masses in his movement's ideology, Haya urged those who did not understand the doctrine to "feel" it.[16] And some years later Haya's second in command, Manuel Seoane, supported this view by affirming: "Therefore, we could almost say that we are less interested in how an Aprista *thinks* than knowing how an Aprista *feels.*"[17]

While working-class Apristas may have failed to understand many of their party's doctrinal statements, the ideology as an undifferentiated whole did, nevertheless, have an indirect impact on mass mobilization. Above all, it gave individual Apristas a sense of political identity, of something concrete beyond the figure of the candidate to adhere to. Despite the difficulty the party's working class members might have experienced in reciting specific arguments about Peru's relationship to imperialist powers or about how the "Aprista State" differed from the Bolshevist State, they knew that those arguments existed and that they had been fashioned by a competent set of leadership figures. Indeed, the grandiloquent tone and complexity of APRA's ideological language reinforced the confidence of the rank and file in the party leaders who possessed a high degree of intelligence. Men with the ability to create and manipulate such an ideology were judged to be superior individuals who could not only direct Peru's destiny but also effectively interpret the world around them.

In attempting to win the support of the working class, APRA leaders cast their campaign as a moral crusade, eschewing ideology as well as bread-and-butter issues. After 1931 they strove to provide their followers with a system of values and behavior that touched on every aspect of their lives. The conception of APRA as a moral-cultural force was strongly reminiscent of the morals campaigns during the days of the Popular University. And the idea that there existed an almost familial bond between APRA's moral revolutionaries suggested an important facet of the initial development of the movement in the 1920s. In 1931, as previously, that bond was designed to make the individual Aprista "enjoy the gratification of feeling oneself a member of a vast and intimate family of men"[18]while also functioning to preclude any serious threats to the unity of the party. The moralistic and familistic fervor in APRA led many outside observers to believe that the loyalty of Apristas to their party far surpassed all other loyalties including those, for instance, to the nation, to a geographical region, or to a particular city. Haya de la Torre's description of the degree of solidarity that existed in APRA at the time of the 1931 election supports this belief: "We proved ourselves to each other with our sincerity . . . and with this indestructible bonds of solidarity were established. There was no way to doubt one another . . . . It was an emotional thing, a mystical thing, a creed."[19]

Haya may be faulted for exaggeration in his portrayal of the "indestructibility" of the Aprista bond, but his overall choice of words does not seem excessive to describe the movement at the time of the 1931 campaign. The explicitly religious overtones of the idea of a "mystical credo" are eminently appropriate to characterize a party that repeatedly called itself "the new religion" and which had exhibited religious overtones since the Popular University days. Apristas now identifiied their movement as a "religious" organization every time they sang the words of the party hymn, the *Marsellesa Aprista:*

> Peruanos, abrazad la nueva religión
> LA ALIANZA POPULAR
> conquistará la ansiada redención![20]

> Peruvians, embrace the new religion
> THE POPULAR ALLIANCE will conquer
> our longed-for redemption!

The heavy reliance on the themes and language of the New Testament to symbolize Aprismo in party tracts and speeches indicates that the movement was represented as a brand of political Catholicism to its membership. Aprista spokesmen described their organization as a communion of true believers, joined by a messianic faith, and engaged in the sacred mission of purifying the nation and driving out the evil political pharisees that had ruled in the past. *Solo el Aprismo salvará al Perú* (only Aprismo will save Peru) became the party salute to be used every time two or more Apristas met.

Apparently the use of religious rhetoric had a significant impact on Aprista followers, who began to refer to themselves as the dedicated "disciples" of a predestined, Christ-like Haya de la Torre. APRA's political religiosity grew out of several factors, not the least of which was the influence of the movement's *Jefe máximo.* A seminary student in his youth, Haya infused all of his major ventures with a mystical tone. He classified his participation in the University Reform movement as service for a missionary cause. He fashioned the Popular Universities, which he called "lay temples," along lines similar to the neighborhood church that brought people together socially, culturally, and spiritually. In addition to Haya's personal imprint of religiosity on Aprismo, the repression of the original student-worker front suggested that the movement was a persecuted sect with an evolution akin to that of early Christianity. The party's maintenance of this religious tone is one key to its resilience over the years, despite persecutions and apparent radical deviations in ideology; from the outset APRA developed into much more than a simple political party.

The Apristas' fervent faith in their party resulted in large part from Haya de la Torre's effective projection of himself as a man of extraordinary personal qualities and abilities. Haya had been the vital cornerstone of the Aprista movement since its initial development as a worker-student alliance in the 1920s, and his dominance in the 1931 campaign was simply the logical expression in electoral politics of well-established tendencies. The Aprista leadership declared that Haya de la Torre alone meant the salvation of the fatherland. His return to the country in 1931 was called a special Peruvian Easter, one which marked the rebirth on the nation. He was, according to party advocates, the Apristas' "Supreme Guide" and the living incarnation of the APRA program.

Haya de la Torre's exalted image in the campaign was the product of his skillful combination of specific personality traits into a coherent political style. The major elements of that style had been developed well before the election. Not unexpectedly, the Aprista leader built his political image for the 1931 presidential race through the dramatization of his past actions in the 1919 eight-hour strike, the Consecration protest, and the Popular University. From the constant recounting of these episodes, two major personality characteristics emerged to consitute the basis of his political style: Haya the hero and Haya the educator. To emphasize the heroic Haya, the APRA camp reminded voters of his resolute confrontation of govenment troops in 1919 and 1923. And party spokesmen added that the bitter reward for this brave and devoted man who had created APRA was his lonely yet instructive exile from Peru. Apristas underscored these specific incidents of Haya's valor to depict their *Jefe máximo* as preeminently a man of action, a person of concrete accomplishments, ready to jump into the breach at any time to better the situation of his followers.

The single most frequently cited past achievement of the Aprista leader in the campaign was his creation of the Popular University. And in the explicity political APRA school of 1931, Haya was no less the *maestro* than he had been eight years earlier. Through his style of political oratory and his repeated emphasis on his personal educational mission, the *Jefe máximo* revealed his continuing identification with the role of master teacher of the working classes. Haya's lengthy and often complicated speeches resembled class-room lectures in which he marshalled evidence and logic to convince his listeners of the rectitude of his position.

Whether the hero or the teacher, Haya during the campaign was ever the patriarch. The paternalistic posture was hardly new to the leader in 1931. Indeed, the only notable differences between "the father of the workers" in the 1920s and the "father of APRA" in the campaign were that in the latter period his "children" had grown in numbers far beyond a small group of union leaders, and in the electoral context there were political stakes to be won. Paternal affection and paternal authority constituted central features of Haya's style. Numerous observers remarked about the Aprista leader's extraordinary personal warmth, his contagious smile, his generally pleasing disposition, and his prodigious memory for people and events of the past. Many of his person-to-person conver-sations with members of the Aprista faithful during the campaign revolved around the intimate problems of their daily lives, and Haya

always seemed ready with sympathetic understanding and perti-
nent advice. The physical manifestation of Haya's personal warmth
in the form of long handshakes, pats on the back, and above all fond
embraces was a salient feature of these individual encounters. The
Aprista leader's predilection for physical expression became an
integral part of his paternalistic style. But all was not fatherly
benevolence from the Aprista patriarch. Aprista literature portrayed
Haya as a stern disciplinarian, equally quick to reproach bad conduct as he was to reward good actions. The coexistence of kindness
and severity made for a dynamic counterpoint in the appeal of Haya.
At the same time he maintained an intimate relationship with his
followers, he was also able to set himself apart as a powerful and
specially gifted leader.

The impact of Haya de la Torre's political style was particularly
notable in APRA's fight to capture working-class votes. The Aprista
campaign abounded with references made by Haya himself and by
other party notables to the Aprista leader's long history of collaboration with urban labor groups, collaboration which, it was promised, would result in the use of the power of the state to improve
the conditions of the proletariat. Most important, Haya made the
renewal of the ties of personal loyalty between himself and the
capital's union leaders—ties forged from the eight-hour strike on-
wards—a top priority of his campaign. Labor leaders were invited
to frequent face-to-face meetings with Haya, who was always quick
to recall with affection specific instances of his past contacts with
these individuals.

Haya was eminently successful at using his ties with Lima union
leaders to gain the organized labor vote in the 1931 election. he
was also able to secure much urban middle sector support. His
popularity among these groups was not, however, sufficient in
terms of votes to offset the winning margin of his populist opponent, Luis M. Sánchez Cerro, who won the backing of Lima's more
numerous *lumpenproletariat* population plus the support of the
upper class electorate.

For Haya de la Torre, electoral defeat and subsequent years of
persecution marked the beginning not the end of a political career.
The Aprista leader was never to be president of Peru, yet he became
the head of the nation's most important twentieth century political
organization. Haya was prevented from personally competing for
the presidency again until 1962 by a rabidly anti-Aprista military,

whose violent opposition to him had largely originated in APRA's 1932 Trujillo massacre of Army officers and was fed thereafter by certain oligarchical sectors that feared the consequences of APRA rule. Notwithstanding his proscription from competing formally for high office, in the period between 1933 and the 1960s the *Jefe máximo* of APRA took advantage of the lack of stiff competition to gain a strong hold over the working-class vote in Peru for his political movement. Only in the last decade—particularly after the rise of the military Revolutionary Government in 1968—did Haya's popularity among his proletarian following begin to show signs of decay. Nevertheless, he and his tightly organized party retained enough of a political following to win the largest number of votes in the 1978 elections for a Constituent Congress. Over fifty years after his entry into politics Víctor Raúl Haya de la Torre showed his political staying power by becoming the President of that Congress, and just before he died in 1979, he placed his signature on Peru's new constitution.

While this study has concentrated on the formative years of Peru's and one of Latin America's first important populist movements, the political patterns established during those years continued to be a major cornerstone not only of APRA but of a large variety of other populist movements in Latin America. A few concluding remarks summarizing those populist patterns exemplified by the Aprista case would seem to be in order.

Aprismo was a vertical movement united by relationships of personal loyalty between leader and followers. It differed appreciably from class or interest-based horizontal movements that consolidate around specific issues or an ideology. Unlike these generally horizontal organizations whose members usually come from the same strata, APRA cut across class and status lines to include individuals from various levels of Peruvian society. A primary element in the adherence of mass supporters to the populist party was the accessibility it provided to links with men above them on the social pyramid. For the working-class populist, such links seemed to afford a route to men with power who could help supply a degree of material welfare. For most such followers, though, Peru's urban mass society of the early 1930s precluded the direct receipt of immediate rewards from those in power. But that reality did not seriously detract from the populist image of personalized, "family" government, of government which, if unable to provide directly for all, still symbolized a generous force sympathetic to the suffering poor.

The political clientelism inherent in this early populist movement paralleled in many ways the patron-client relationships that have permeated Peruvian and Latin American social life since colonial times. Like the archetypical dyadic contract between the rural *hacendado* and the peon, the political tie between populist leader and follower was an individualistic, decidedly personal association between men from distinct social strata. Basic to the relationship was the reciprocal exchange of services and/or goods between those involved. For the political patrons, the exchange meant support in the streets and at the voting booth. From the masses' point of view, populist clientelism developed as a realistic effort on their part to improve their standard of living or simply to cope with a difficult, often threatening environment by forging ties to those who possessed greater power over the resources of the state.

While the varieties of patronage remained important under populism, the dominant presence of a charismatic leader constituted the primary source of political cohesion. The formation of Aprismo, its campaign style, its rhetoric, its very reason for existence seemed to hinge upon providing a springboard for the rise of its chief to political power. Central to the successful mass recruitment carried out by APRA was the effective glorification of the special personal qualities of Haya de la Torre. Accounts of past accomplishments, testimonials to present capabilities, and the personal appearances of the candidate ended in the communication of the image of a big-hearted, affectionate, and above all protective father figure possessed of an extraordinary ability to understand intimately the needs of his followers.

For the members of the Lima working class, the importance of these personal ties to the powerful increased enormously in times of adversity or crisis. The powerless perceived even in normal times that they disposed of scarce resources with which to confront their environment, and crisis situations acted to make available resources even more scarce. Accordingly, the lower classes sought bonds of dependency with political patrons. Such a crisis situation was touched off in Peru by the Great Depression. In part the enthusiastic mass response to APRA occurred because the deepening impoverishment of the urban proletariat impelled them to see in the populist leader a powerful and apparently generous patron figure with whom it was possible to forge valuable ties of personal dependence, at least on the symbolic level. Also, in a time of general confusion and distress arising from the effects of rapid social change, political crisis, and economic hardship, the paternalistic populist presented an attractive image of strength and direction. Hence, the Depression did not radicalize the Peruvian working classes; instead it induced them to respond to the populist alternative as the most faithful political embodiment of patrimonial social relations.

Notes

1. Excellent social data on demographic changes in early twentieth century Lima are available in Peru, Dirección de Salubridad Pública, *Censo de la Provincia de Lima (26 de junio de 1908)*, 2 vols. (Lima, 1915); Peru, Ministerio de Hacienda, *Resumen del censo de las Provincias de Lima y Callao levantado el 17 de diciembre de 1920* (Lima, 1927); and Peru, *Censo de las Provincias de Lima y Callao levantado el 13 de noviembre de 1931* (Lima, 1932).

2. Víctor Raúl Haya de la Torre, "Mis recuerdos de González Prada," *Repertorio americano* (San Jose, Costa Rica), vol. 15, no. 6 (13 January 1927), 84–85.

3. Some of González Prada's most suggestive writings in this regard include "Propaganda y ataque," in his *Páginas libres* (Lima, 1966), vol. 2, especially pp. 154 and 158–59, and *Horas de lucha* (Lima, 196?), especially pp. 47–51 and 70.

4. Víctor Raúl Haya de la Torre, interview with the author, 20 May 1971.

5. Víctor Raúl Haya de la Torre, interview with the author, 12 December 1970.

6. *El Obrero textil,* vol. 3, no. 42 (January 1923), 3.

7. Quoted by Luis Alberto Sánchez, *Haya de la Torre y el Apra* (Santiago, Chile, 1955), p. 124.

8. *El Tiempo* (Lima), 6 July 1924, p. 3.

9. Víctor Raúl Haya de la Torre, interview with the author, 12 December 1970.

10. *La protesta* (Lima), vol. 9, no. 95 (May 1921), 2.

11. Arturo Sabroso Montoya, interview with the author, 29 January 1971.

12. Partido Aprista Peruano, *El proceso de Haya de la Torre* (Lima, 1969), p. 16.

13. Luis Alberto Sánchez, *Testimonio personal* (Lima, 1969), vol. 3, p. 970.

14. Víctor Raúl Haya de la Torre, *El plan del Aprismo* (Lima, 1931), p. 12.

15. Víctor Raúl Haya de la Torre, interview with the author, 12 December 1970.

16. Haya de la Torre, *Plan del Aprismo,* p. 34.

17. Published in *Radiografía de Haya de la Torre* (Lima, 1946), p. 20.

18. Ibid.

19. Víctor Raúl Haya de la Torre, interview with the author, 12 December 1970.

20. In *Cancionero aprista* (Lima 193?), p.2.

7

Populism in Venezuela, 1935–48: Betancourt and the Acción Democrática

Steven Ellner
Universidad del Oriente, Venezuela

Populism in Venezuela originated in the aftermath of the student rebellion against the authoritarian regime of Juan Vicente Gómez in 1928. Venezuela was then in a petroleum boom that was converting the country into the world's largest supplier. A by-product of the modernization made possible by oil revenue was a changed social order. A small working class began to emerge, one which at the time of Gómez's death in December 1935 included 47,000 workers engaged in manufacturing—many of whom were artisans—and 25,000 oil workers out of a total population of four million. Despite the limited size of the working class, many of the discontented students—who themselves were a new urban elite—became convinced after the events of 1928 that workers were ready to be recruited to socialist causes. Venezuelan populism, then, arose from the disjuncture between intellectual desires for change and labor union backwardness.

Rómulo Betancourt, a member of the "generation of '28" and soon to become one of Latin America's outstanding populists, understood Venezuela's transitional condition. Although a believer in Marxism, Betancourt preferred to delay the struggle for socialism until after the advent of industrialization and democracy. Although the industrial working class should be the vehicle for socialist transformation, he pointed out, such a sector was minuscule in Venezuela. Therefore the Left should subordinate its ultimate Marxist objectives to a "minimum program" of democratic and economic reforms. Betancourt invoked Lenin's dictum that in countries whose economies were dominated by foreign capital, the establishment of a "national bourgeois" government committed to industrialization had to precede the socialist revolution. For Betancourt, however, the essential feature of this initial bourgeois stage was democracy, whereas for Lenin it had been antiimperialism. In a letter to Raúl Leoni dated August 1935, Betancourt explained why the Left should commit itself to the struggle for democratic government:

> It is not advisable for us to say that we, as communists, see bourgeois democracy as a farce. The backward masses, kept from being able to educate themselves, harbor illusions regarding the democratic system . . . . In this situation we cannot say to them: bourgeois democracy is a means to fool you; we fight not for it but for Soviet power.[1]

Betancourt also questioned the viability of a working class party in a country like Venezuela where the workers were few in number and weak politically. Such an organization, he predicted, with its narrow political base, would be annihilated in the first wave of political repression. Instead, Betancourt proposed a multiclass party whose cadres could represent the interests of a variety of social groups, including the national bourgeoisie. Within the party the adherents of socialist doctrine would constitute a Marxist faction. These militants, relying on their tight organization and discipline, would "push the party to the radical left" when the nation's political climate became favorable to revolutionary change.[2]

Pragmatic considerations underlay Betancourt's opposition to raising the socialist banner. He warned that while the oligarchy and imperialists might reluctantly tolerate a reformist movement, they would move instinctively to crush any group advocating socialism.

His thesis diverged from that of orthodox Marxists, who wanted to propagate socialist theory despite the improbability of putting it into practice. Betancourt labeled Venezuelan Communists dogmatists for importing dogmas from nations whose socioeconomic and political development was far in advance of Venezuela's.[3]

In short, the young Betancourt subordinated ideology to pragmatic considerations based on a particular set of conditions. This predominantly Venezuelan orientation led Betancourt and his followers to consider themselves nationalists and to spurn the internationalist creed of orthodox Marxism. Thus, even though imbued with Marxist rhetoric, the *betancourtistas* displayed three characteristics that were trademarks of Latin American populism: nationalism, advocacy of a multiclass party, and commitment to electoral expansion.

The year 1936 brought democratic liberties under Gómez's handpicked successor, General Eleazar López Contreras. The Left, comprised mostly of *betancourtistas* and orthodox Marxists, attempted to take advantage of the government's new policy of tolerance by creating the Single Party of the Left, known as the Partido Democrático Nacional (PDN). However, this experiment in unity proved disastrous. Not only did the government refuse to legalize the PDN, but it exiled forty-seven prominent leaders. Shortly afterward, the orthodox Marxists, no longer willing to suppress their ideology for the sake of unity, pulled out of the PDN and created the Venezuelan Communist Party (PCV).

These events gave further impetus to Betancourt's populist tendencies. The 1936 democratic reforms followed by repression created in him a profound distrust of traditional politicians, an attitude shared by populist leaders throughout the hemisphere. Betancourt was particularly distrustful of Gómez's former associates (gomecistas), who managed to control the government for the next ten years. The *betancourtistas* therefore stopped collaborating with the *gomecistas*. In fact, after 1936 the Communists' and Betancourt's position vis-à-vis the government became inverted. The Communists in Venezuela, as elsewhere, tried to work with the government against the threat of international fascism. Betancourt, on the other hand, rejected the PCV's premise that the masses had rightfully earned the 1936 reforms through their political activism. Far from demonstrating good intentions, these concessions were designed to mollify the masses, so that when their energies were at low ebb, the government could counterattack with repressive measures. "López's political schooling was in despotism," Betancourt wrote in early 1937, "and as such he identifies with his precursors Cipriano Castro and Juan Vicente Gómez."[4]

Throughout the following decade, Betancourt's political actions were guided by what his 1936 experiences had taught him—that a *gomecista* was incapable of metamorphosing into a democratic leader. On this basis he urged his party to adopt an intransigent position toward López Contreras and his hand-picked successor, Medina Angarita. Betancourt was convinced that both were autocrats masquerading as liberals. Ultimately, the positions of Betancourt and the PCV collided: in October 1945, the Communists took up arms in order to defend the Medina government against a coup d'etat by the *betancourtistas.*

The failure of the Single Party of the Left exacerbated relations between the *betancourtistas* and the Communists. Betancourt feared that the decision of the orthodox Marxists to establish a Communist Party and to publish literature in its name would invite government repression against the entire Left. He was also apprehensive that his own group's ideological identity would be confused with communism. At the time that he helped form Acción Democrática (AD) in 1941, Betancourt, the pragmatist, embraced a heavily charged anti-Communist rhetoric to dramatize the differences between his fledgling party and the PCV. He also cautioned against forming alliances with Communists, even electoral pacts. At first this stand was a minority position within AD, but by 1944 Betancourt swung a majority over to his side. In doing so he often warned against repeating the mistake of 1936, when his followers compromised their indentity by uniting with Communists.[5]

AD's position in World War II clashed with that of the zealously pro-Ally PCV and embittered relations between the two parties within the labor movement. AD advanced the slogan "Venezuela First," which implied that the war was an interimperialist conflict, though the party did show greater preference for the Allied side. Indeed the nationalism of populist movements throughout the hemisphere tended to be translated into neutrality, at least during the early war years. In rejecting the PCV policy against labor stoppages, AD encouraged the workers to take advantage of the war disequilibrium to extract major benefits from the imperialist companies. AD leaders, although discouraging strikes in practice, often threatened walkouts to pressure employers. On occasion they utilized strikes in one or two oil fields to achieve industry-wide improvements.[6]

PCV and AD trade unionists accused each other of putting party loyalties ahead of working-class interests. AD leaders upbraided their Communist rivals for slavishly following party bosses, who, in turn, took their cues from a foreign power. Actually many of these AD leaders considered ideological polemics against Communism a legitimate way to drive the PCV out of the labor movement. They were certain that the vast majority of Venezuelan workers preferred social democracy, with its national orientation and respect for Catholicism over international communism. In order not to confuse the two doctrines, these AD members rejected all forms of organizational collaboration with the Communists.[7]

The AD approach was expressed in the slogan, "To Divide is to Identify," coined in 1944 by Valmore Rodríguez, one of Betancourt's earliest followers. Rodríguez argued that separate AD-PCV labor organizations gave the workers the clearest opportunity to choose between the ideologies for which those two parties stood. The phrase justified the creation of pro-AD parallel unions in order to displace Communist ones, which had temporarily lost their legal status. Parallel unionism became a means for beating out the Communists as the leading political force in organized labor; in fact the same tactics were used by such populists as the Auténticos in Cuba and the Peronistas in Argentina with equal success.[8]

Populist movements in Latin America usually have charismatic leaders, and in this respect Venezuela is no exception. Rómulo Betancourt was well-suited for such a role. Betancourt's very style was populist in that it was easily grasped by common people, while his celebrated humor used heavy doses of slang and folklore. Under Medina, Betancourt took advantage of the extended period in which he could exercise his political rights to establish personal ties with large numbers of Venezuelans. This contact was made possible by extensive travel to the nation's interior, a practice which has since become a standard feature of Venezuelan politics.

In many respects, however, Betancourt's organizational ability was more important than his charisma. This skill enabled Betancourt to outstrip Jóvito Villalba, his main populist competitor, a man with great forensic talent but no organizational ability. For this reason Villalba failed in his effort to vie with Betancourt for leadership of the PDN and was later unable to establish a party that could seriously threaten AD. In contrast, AD early established a solid footing in the nation's interior, under the watchword: "Not a single district, not a single municipality without its party organization." Thus Betancourt's case differs from that of Perón and other populist leaders who developed large followings prior to institutionalizing their mass bases.

During the Trienio period of AD rule, from 1945 to 1948, Acción Democrática's essential populist features became further defined: electoral, reformist, mildly nationalist, and multiclass. The party's democratic commitment was put in temporary doubt by its participation in the 1945 coup. AD soon made clear, however, that its sole objective was to institute direct presidential elections, though it should be noted that the Medina government had been gradually moving in that direction. As it turned out, the 1945 coup was a master stroke for AD. At the time it was a minority party, but when presidential elections were held two years later, AD, at the helm of the government and credited with recently enacted reforms, swept 74 percent of the vote. Indeed the general populace had good reason to support the govenment party. Through the active intervention of the Ministry of Labor under Raúl Leoni, real wages had increased by 39 percent, while an agrarian reform and manifold social welfare benefits had substantially improved the lot of the lower classes. The pace of these reforms was so rapid that, in alienating conservative interest groups, it helped precipitate the right-wing military coup of 1948.[9]

Once in power Betancourt and his followers moderated the fiery brand of nationalism they had embraced in the years prior to the founding of AD. The need to attract foreign capital precluded overwrought antiimperialist rhetoric. Their economic nationalism now focused on import substitution and developmentalist policies, a common trend among postwar reform administrations in Latin America. These governments maintained high tariffs to protect native enterprises that had arisen during World War II. They also took advantage of the accumulation of foreign credits during the war to promote industrial development. In the case of Venezuela, a sharp increment in the international demand for oil had resulted in increased production and prices and a concomitant threefold increase in federal revenues between 1944 and 1948.

Since Gómez's death, government policies to foster economic development, the relative decline of agriculture, and urbanization all contributed to the growth of diverse classes. By the end of the Trienio, business groups, workers, and peasants, highly organized at both national and local levels, had joined the AD ranks, making it a truly multiclass party. The pressures which these groups exerted on Acción Democrática were internalized as competing policy directions, though the appearance of cohesion was usually maintained. AD's precurser parties had been predominantly middle class and their leaders had privately adhered to socialist ideas. The emergence of the broadly-based AD, whose commitment to socialism was less certain, marked the rise of populism in Venezuela. Like all populist movements, AD harbored contradictory tendencies which were not often admitted but which made it possible to accommodate a broad spectrum of the population. At the same time, policy debates over these issues gave party leaders a more subtle grasp of the problems of managing a rapidly developing country. A discussion of five such issues (socialism, the pace of reform, the Cold War, relations with the PCV, and the role of the military) will help reveal the emergence of AD as a genuinely populist movement.[10]

Even before AD's founding in 1941, ambiguity marked the party's political objectives. In hopes of securing government recognition for the projected AD, the *betancourtista* PDN had decided to play down its program of nationalistic socialism. Betancourt later wrote that the battle for legalization had been "full of obstacles" and that "among other things we had to demonstrate that we were ardent defenders of private property." In subsequent years party members remained in doubt as to whether AD's modified program reflected the party's true goals or was a tactical feint to allay the fears of conservatives.[11]

The 1945 coup and the Cold War had a profound impact on Acción Democrática. The outbreak of United States-Soviet hostilities set off a worldwide polarization process that forced nationalist parties like Acción Democrática to choose between two camps. (No Latin American government of the period, with the the exception of Perón's in Argentina, upheld a truly neutral stance.) In addition, now that AD held political power, it had a stake in the maintenance of economic stability. Thus AD labor leaders retreated from their militant stand of the war years. They sternly cautioned workers against overreliance on strikes while exhorting them to win the "battle of production."

The most striking demonstration of AD's *volte-face* was its reassessment of international political figure Nelson Rockefeller. When Rockefeller visited Venezuela for the second time in March 1939, he was caustically denounced in the pro-PDN *Ahora*. Betancourt described him as a "colonialist" who sought to conceal his misanthropy with the hypocritical slogan "For the Good of Mankind." After the 1945 coup, however, the two men struck up a personal friendship. Now characterizing Rockefeller as a benign capitalist, Betancourt attempted to make a showcase of his agricultural enterprises in order to reduce prejudice against foreign investment.[12]

Individual AD leaders held conflicting notions regarding socialism. Betancourt abandoned the socialist convictions he had professed at an earlier date. In fact, his fervent public denunciations of that system convinced fellow party members that he had an aversion to the very word. Other AD members argued for the gradual socialization of the economy, which they considered an undeclared party goal. Nevertheless, they agreed with Betancourt that the word *socialist* had been sufficiently discredited to warrant AD's avoidance of the label.[13] Still other party leaders favored immediate nationalization of public services and other gradualist socialist measures. Their antipathy toward the free enterprise system manifested itself during the Trienio when they argued for strict government supervision of foreign investments. Within party circles, these "left" AD members frequently clashed with those who feared that stringent regulations on investments would discourage capital from abroad.[14]

AD Trienio leaders were in general agreement on the importance of certain economic reforms, particularly those to improve the lot of the working poor. Important differences arose, however, concerning the pace at which these programs should be implemented. Those who favored a gradual, less disruptive aproach tended to emphasize preservation of social peace. They argued that only in an atmosphere of social tranquility could the government carry out its reforms while avoiding reactionary conspiracies. The following principal strategies for the maintenance of social peace were arrived at: (1) organized labor would avoid strikes except in extreme circumstances; (2) the ministry of labor would regularly intervene in labor affairs to "smooth over the rough spots" of industrial relations; (3) the labor movement would commit itself to "winning the battle of production;" (4) the government would prevail upon industry to grant workers significant rewards for increases in production and maintenance of labor discipline; (5) AD would build up the party's mass base before courting confrontation with its enemies.

The desire to avoid confrontations—accepted in principle by AD's entire national leadership—was not fully accepted by the party's lower ranks. The 1945 coup left many local AD union militants euphoric and overconfident. They often resorted to wild-cat strikes, which the AD-controlled Confederación de Trabajadores de Venezuela (CTV) and state labor federations refused to sanction. In *Venezuela: política y petróleo,* Betancourt critized these AD labor militants for "lacking a trade union consciousness . . . trying to outdo the Communists in action and rhetoric." Betancourt attributed such behavior to the nation's weak trade union tradition and the influence of postwar international labor strife.[15]

AD's internal debate over Cold War issues directly involved party labor leaders. One issue in particular, the international rivalry between the American Federation of Labor (AFL) and the leftist Confederación de Trabajadores de América Latina (CTAL), threatened to compromise AD's official posture of nonalignment. Toward the end of World War II, the AFL had begun to challenge the CTAL's influence in the hemispheric labor movement. In the eyes of the AFL, CTAL and especially its president, the Mexican trade unionist Vicente Lombardo Toledano, had become tools of international Communism. The CTV participated in the campaign against the CTAL and at one point the head of the powerful Venezuelan oil workers' federation actually denounced Lombardo as a Russian spy. At the same time the CTV cultivated close ties with the AFL, which in turn used its influence in the State Department to defend Venezuelan interests. However, many AD members expressed reservations about their party's pro-AFL leanings. They feared that their association with the AFL openly allied them with the United States in a Cold War dispute. Furthermore, the AFL's support of hemispheric tariff reductions, a stance sponsored by the U.S. government, violated AD's commitment to import substitution.[16]

The AFL's efforts to dominate the international labor movement came to fruition in January 1948, with the founding of the Confederación Interamericana de Trabajadores (CIT) in Lima, but the

Venezuelan role was complicated by AD debate over affiliation. Originally the AFL had expected the Venezuelans to serve as conference coordinators, but the CTV delegates only participated in observer status. A few days earlier the Venezuelan labor confederation had made its decision not to affiliate with the CIT, stating: "With regard to the attempt at Lima to create another Latin American Worker Confederation with initials different from the CTAL's and in the service of another power [i.e., the United States], we must establish a categorically negative response."[17] Nevertheless, the actual representatives at Lima, led by CTV president Pedro Bernardo Pérez Salinas, held different notions regarding their organization's future role in the CIT. Along with other CTV leaders, they were determined to reverse the confederation's stand against joining the CIT, but they accepted observer status at Lima for two reasons. First, the CTV's charter forbade affiliation with any international labor body which took sides in the Cold War. Second, strong sentiment prevailed within AD for avoiding any form of entanglement in United States-Soviet conflicts. In light of this, Pérez Salinas' group decided to build up support for the CIT within their party before pressing the issue of affiliation.[18]

Different opinions regarding the Venezuelan Communist Party also emerged within Acción Democrática. Betancourt, representing one tendency, considered the Communists a politically insignificant force and denied that AD needed their help in carrying out its reform program. Another current praised the PCV for the qualified support it lent the AD administration. The latter current feared that intransigent opposition of other parties undermined the legitimacy of the political system. They saw the willingness of one party— albeit the PCV—to act as a loyal opposition as an important contribution to Venezuelan democracy. Several of these AD leaders privately proposed a *modus vivendi* to the PCV, whereby both organizations would tone down mutual criticism; in fact, between mid-1936 and early 1948 (when the Communists were expelled from the pro-AD oil workers federation) both parties did avoid harsh attacks on each other. During the last days of the Trienio, party leaders representing this tendency called on the PCV to join them in mobilizing efforts against the anticipated coup.[19]

Throughout the presidency of Rómulo Gallegos in 1948, Acción Democrática felt its hold on political power menaced by right-wing military conspiracies. These plots escalated after the government unsuccessfully attempted to remove Lt. Col. Marcos Pérez Jiménez from his post of chief of staff of the armed forces. The extent of the military threat was revealed when the plotters actually served Gallegos with an ultimatum to reorganize his cabinet.

AD's reaction to this challenge was consistent with its previous behavior. During the Trienio, the AD government had stressed that economic development hinged upon elimination of social conflict and had prided itself on having reduced strikes. Leading AD members made themselves prisoners of this strategy during the crucial months of 1948. They avoided relying on the party's mass support out of fear of galvanizing social tensions. Instead they sought a "solution from above," negotiating with military conspirators who had no interest in preserving Venezuelan democracy. Betancourt, although outside of the government, met with Pérez Jiménez and agreed that both would exile themselves temporarily in order to ease the crisis. This agreement, however, was merely a ruse by the military to disarm AD leaders in the crucial days prior to the coup.[20]

A number of middle- and upper-echelon AD leaders, headed by the governor of Yaracuy, Raúl Ramos Giménez, publicly critized the government's policy toward the conspiracy, and they were in turn censured at the party's 1948 convention. Ramos Giménez called on the administration to inform the Venezuelan public of the full extent of the military threat. The government, he maintained, should take advantage of AD's hegemony in the student, peasant, and worker movements by rallying mass support. Although this ran the risk of provoking a reaction in the armed forces, AD could count on strong backing from certain officers, including relatives of party leaders. Ramos Giménez criticized the November 1948 executive decree on the suspension of constitutional guarantees, which proscribed public gatherings and prohibited the press from publishing news about the conspiracy. He warned that local AD militants would interpret the measure as a call for order, and would thus fail to mobilize mass support on behalf of the administration. During these last days of the Trienio, some members of the Ramos Giménez group urged arming the party's rank and file with weapons acquired from military garrisons during the 1945 coup.[21]

Shortly after issuing their ultimatum to the government, the military conspirators arrested striking workers of the ministry of public works in Caracas's district of Catia. The CTV considered calling a general strike to protest military interference in politics.

The CTV executive committee went to AD headquarters to propose this idea and to ascertain the extent of the military threat. Party Secretary-General Luis Augusto Dubuc not only rejected the strike proposal but denied that the armed forces had presented the administration with an ultimatum. Stressing his opposition to mass mobilization, Dubuc asserted that the military problem was one for politicians to handle, not for "guerrillas."[22]

Throughout this crisis period, President Gallegos attempted to convey the impression of normalcy—he jokingly told visitors that he was wearing his *pantuflos* (bedroom slippers). The November 24 coup, begun at dawn, was thus facetiously dubbed the *"pantuflos* revolt." The military conspirators encountered little resistance to their seizure of power. AD's only defense, a provisional government established in Maracay under Valmore Rodríguez, quickly collapsed; its call for a general strike went unheeded.

AD's multiclass makeup accounted in large part for its timid response to the military crisis. AD trade unionists, on the verge of calling a general strike, were cautioned by the party's more conservative leaders, who favored a political strategy based on reconciliation of class interests. Mass mobilizations would undoubtedly have encouraged the popular classes to demand more rapid implementation of social reforms, thereby upsetting class harmony. In addition, such a course would have required collaboration with the PCV, which was the second largest force in the labor movement and especially strong among the oil workers. For these reasons the AD leadership opted for a solution based on negotiation and compromise. AD trade unionists to this day bitterly recall the "betrayal" of party leaders who refused to take a more audacious approach. Nevertheless, AD's response to the 1948 crisis did not differ from that of Getúlio Vargas in 1954, Juan Domingo Perón in 1955, or many other multiclass populist leaders whose governments succumbed to military coups without calling on the general populace to defend them. [23]

After a decade of clandestine existence under the Pérez Jiménez dictatorship, Acción Democrática returned to power in the presidential election of December 1958. The AD governments of Rómulo Betancourt (1959—64) and Raúl Leoni (1964—69) stood in marked contrast to those of the Trienio. Betancourt now maintained that the radical reforms which AD had implemented or planned during the Trienio were mainly responsible for Gallegos's overthrow in 1948. He insisted that the government play the role of broker between privileged and popular classes without favoring the latter. As president, he regularly consulted the military, the Church, and the Venezuelan business federation (FEDECAMARAS) in order to prevent their disenchantment with the democratic system. AD's positions on key issues in the 1960s (including petroleum exports, land tenure, foreign relations, civil liberties, and educational reform) were to the right of most of the other major parties.

AD's retreat from reformism, however, was not without its casualties, for the party suffered three important defections in the course of seven years: the pro-Castro Movimiento de Izquierda Revolucionaria (MIR) in 1960; the group "ARS" under Raúl Ramos Giménez in 1962; and the Movimiento Electoral del Pueblo (MEP) in 1967. The latter two parties explicitly identified with the 1930 revolutionary nationalism of the PDN and the nascent AD. ARS soon vanished from the political scene, and MEP, after a promising start in the 1968 elections, took up the socialist banner and has since become a rather insignificant political group. Thus AD's rightward drift created an apparent void in Venezuelan politics. No major non-Marxist party in the 1970s advocated the radical reforms and the multiclass recruitment Acción Democrática had pioneered in the 1940s.[24]

In summary, the leaders of Acción Democrática and its precursor parties based their political strategy on what they considered to be an accurate assessment of the socioeconomic and political realities facing Venezuela. In the 1930s they rejected orthodox Marxism as ill-suited for a nation with an embryonic working class. They also delayed raising the banner of socialism in order to avoid a showdown with the nation's conservative classes. Later, the pragmatic PDN leaders modified their party program to facilitate legalization of the AD. Betancourt also utilized the argument known as "territorial determinism," which warned that the United States would never tolerate a forcefully antiimperialist government in the hemisphere. During the Trienio, AD offered the conservative urban classes social harmony and protection of private property in return for significant concessions to nonelite groups; in fact, the AD government did discourage strikes during the postwar period, a time of industrial strife in other Western nations. Acción Democrática's program of radical reforms and its multiclass commitments endowed the governing party with a clearly populist character. However, just as pragmatism induced Betancourt to reject Marxism in favor of populism prior to 1948, the same strategy led him to abandon populism after 1958. During his five-year presidential term he constantly warned that excessively radical reforms would invite a military coup—just as they had during AD's first administration. In the more recent period, the parties of the "system," which include AD, have been ranged against the Marxist left. In this new alignment populism has ceased to play an important role in Venezuelan politics.

Notes

1. *Libro rojo del General López Contreras: 1936,* 3d ed. (Caracas: Catalá Centauro Editores, 1975), p. 201.

2. Ibid., p. 179.

3. Naudy Suárez Figueroa, "El joven Betancourt (II)" *Nueva política* 16 (April-June 1975): 43−49.

4. *Unión Liberal* (Bogotá), 6 April 1937, p.6, Rómulo Betancourt, "Sentido e importancia de una jornada electoral," *Acción Liberal* (Bogotá; July 1937):37−41.

5. *El "Partido Democrático Venezolano" y su proceso: Documentos* (Caracas: Editorial Elite, 1938), pp. 168-172; PDN, "Sobre las proposiciones de pacto que ha hecho el PCV. . ." *Boletín interno* 15 (Caracas; 9 May 1938), Naudy Suárez Figueroa Archive, Caracas; Luis Lander (member of the Central Executive Committee of the PDN), interview, Caracas, 9 June 1976.

6. Ismael Ordaz (vice-president of the oil workers federation, 1946−48), interview, Maracaibo, 5 August 1976.

7. Humberto Hernández (leader of the transportation workers union in the 1930s and 1940s), interview, Caracas, 2 April 1976.

8. Steve Ellner, "La rivalidad sindical entre Acción Democrática y el Partido Comunista de Venezuela. . ." *Nueva política* 28−29 (April-September 1978): 81−82; Augusto Malavé Villalba (secretary general of the CTV, 1947−48), interview, Caracas, 24 August 1976.

9. Venezuela, Banco Central, *Memoria,* 1949, p. 82.

10. Steve Ellner, "The Venezuelan Left in the in the Era of the Popular Front, 1936-45," *Journal of Latin American Studies* 10 (May 1979): 169−84; Moisés Moleiro, *El Partido del pueblo: crónica de un fraude* (Valencia, Ven.: Vadell Hermanos Editores, 1968), p. 126. John Martz mentions AD's conflicting internal tendencies prior to 1948, although he does not elaborate upon them: Martz, *Acción Democrática* (Princeton, New Jersey: Princeton University Press, 1966), p. 175.

11. Betancourt, *Venezuela: política y petróleo* (México: Fondo de Cultura Económica, 1956), p. 133.

12. Betancourt, *Problemas venezolanos* (Santiago, Chile: Editorial Futuro, 1940), p. 48.

13. Ramón Quijada (agrarian secretary of the CTV, 1947−48), interview, Cumaná, 15 October 1977.

14. Luis Lander, "La doctrina venezolana de Acción Democrática," *Cuadernos americanos* (July-August 1950): 24−25; Jesús Angel Paz Galarraga (secretary general of AD in Zulia, 1948), interview, Caracas, 2 September 1976.

15. Betancourt, *Venezuela,* p. 815.

16. Tariff reductions were part of a U.S. proposal known as the Clayton Plan. Fedepetrol, "Informe que presenta el Comité Ejecutivo de la Federación" (Caracas, 1948), Ernesto Silva Telleria Archive, Caracas; Henry Weinberg Berger, "Union Diplomacy: Foreign Policy in Latin America" (Ph.D. dissertation, University of Wisconsin, 1966), pp. 279−80.

17. *El País* (Caracas), 8 January 1948, p. 2.

18. José Vargas, CTV president in 1979, attended the Lima conference and favored affiliation with the CIT. Vargas, interview, Caracas, 18 November 1976; P. B. Pérez Salinas, interview, Caracas 27 November 1975.

19. Valmore Rodríguez, *Bayonetas sobre Venezuela* (Mexico: Editores Beatriz de Silva, 1950), p. 165.

20. Juan B. Fuenmayor[Dubray], *Aves de rapiña sobre Venezuela,* 2d ed. (Caracas, 1972), pp. 72−73; Domingo Alberto Rangel (AD cultural affairs secretary in 1948), interview, Caracas, 27 April 1976.

21. José Marcano (president of the white collar workers union, 1940s), interview, Caracas, 2 June 1976.

22. Pérez Salinas, interview, 27 November 1975; Braulio Jatar Dotti (AD public relations secretary, 1948), interview, Caracas, 2 December 1976.

23. Some historians and AD leaders hold Gallegos mainly responsible for the 24 November coup. They argue that Gallegos lacked political adroitness in handling the conspirators and that he naively trusted his ex-student, Minister of Defense Carlos Delgado Chalbaud, even after there was good reason to doubt him. Robert J. Alexander, for instance, states ". . . lack of political experience and astuteness on the part of novelist- President Rómulo Gallegos was the immediate cause for the downfall of the Acción Democrática regime." *The Venezuelan Democratic Revolution* (New Brunswick, New Jersey: Rutgers University Press, 1964), p. 35. Nevertheless, other AD leaders played important roles in the November events and were also outmanuevered by the conspirators.

24. MIR members at first also identified with the PDN and named their newspaper *Izquierda* after the PDN's official organ. José Rivas Rivas, *Las tres divisiones de Acción Democrática* (Caracas: Pensamiento Vivo, 1968), p. 49.

Part II
COMPARATIVE PERSPECTIVES

Introduction

The second section of this book, emphasizing analogous aspects of populism in non-Latin countries, comprises chapters dealing with Russian and U.S. populism and a concluding essay by Paul Drake. The Russian and U.S. cases were chosen as the most similar to the Latin American experience. Certainly these chapters are not intended as the last word on the respective subjects: each could stand alone but their real value is their contribution to comparative history.

These chapters concentrate on periods after the classic phases of populism had passed, heightening their comparability with the Latin American cases. The most-studied populist movements in Russia and the United States occurred between the 1870s and 1890s, and they were predominantly rural and class-oriented. Blakely's chapter examines the Socialist Revolutionary (S-R) Party during the first years of this century, viewing it as the heir of the classic *narodnic* movement. Ideological dedication to egalitarianism and the mass-based organization provided strong continuities with the earlier phase. Nonetheless, the S-R Party was an urban movement with at least a partial commitment to democratic procedures. The ambiguous mixture of revolutionary and political strategies, as Blakely makes clear, was due to the autocratic setting in which the party arose, an ambiguity that was never overcome. The S-R platform reproduced in the appendix provides especially valuable evidence for comparisons with Latin American populism. It is obvious that European socialism (often stripped of its revolutionary trappings) formed the starting point for many Latin American populists.

Szasz' broad survey of U.S. populism synthesizes the experience of the 1880s and 1890s, laying stress on those features most comparable to Latin American movements. It then moves on to recurring populist phenomena in American life, from the 1930s

153

until the 1970s. The value of this approach is its insight into the ways populism persisted as a style or appeal without an effective mass movement. If, as Wirth and Drake both discuss, populism makes a comeback in Latin America, it might resemble populist resurgences in the United States. As in the preceding chapter, Szasz' study also gives attention to elements found in other case studies: the populist transfer to the urban milieu; its charismatic form of leadership; its search for legitimacy in folkways of the masses; and its attempt to represent "all the people." Perhaps because of its breadth, Szasz' chapter raises some of the most intriguing questions for cross-polity comparisons.

The concluding essay by Paul Drake successfully meets the demands of comparative history, for it sifts the evidence for the broad trends, similarities, parallels, and subtle differences that provide us with a working definition of populism. Drake also took on the task of identifying future research needs and plausible theories, for in no way do we believe this volume to be a definitive work. If the book stimulates debate and divergent research paths, it will have accomplished its goal.

8

The Making of Populist Revolution in Russia, 1900–1907

Allison Blakely
Howard University

The Bolshevik victory in the Russian Revolution and Civil War obscured for decades the importance of the Russian populist parties, which were the overwhelming victors in the only truly democratic, multiparty election in Russian history, held at the end of 1917. The relative neglect of populism by scholars is all the more remarkable since the Russian Marxism out of which bolshevism evolved was originally an offshoot of a populist group of the 1880s.[1] The study of Russian populism is still so undeveloped that there is not yet a consensus regarding its proper definition. Nearly all the recent studies reject the populists' own interpretation of their movement as existing from the 1860s through the revolutionary period.[2] Indeed, at least one has questioned whether it described a real movement when the term populism (*narodnichestvo*) first came to be used in the 1870s; others view the 1870s as the only period when populism did exist; and none but the present author and some Soviet writers have supported the populists' contention that the same movement, admittedly broadly defined, extends well into the twentieth century. Those who deny this continuity overestimate the naiveté of the nineteenth century populists and ignore the validity of the acknowledged debt the twentieth century populists owed their precursors. The approach taken here is that Russian populism as an ideology and a movement showed a marked continuity during the half century from its inception until its suppression under bolshevism. At times it survived only as a shared ideology; when possible it manifested itself as part of the opposition revolutionary movement; and in turn as political parties when that form of organization became current in Russia.[3]

The present essay treats the Russian populists' perception of the dynamics of the revolution they hoped to lead. The essay focuses on the period when the various populist groups which had evolved within Russia and among colonies of Russian emigrés abroad succeeded for the first time in consolidating their resources and forming an empire-wide organization. They completed this by the end of 1902 and thereafter called themselves the Russian Socialist-Revolutionary Party. Out of this rather heterogeneous organization the more radical Socialist-Revolutionary Maximalists and more moderate Popular Socialists split off in 1906. Likewise, in 1917 the large Ukrainian Socialist-Revolutionary Party and the Left Socialist-Revolutionaries were added offspring of this main party. Therefore, although the following concentrates on just part of the history of Russian populism, it details the most representative features.

Given the autocratic nature of tsarist Russia, populism there was necessarily revolutionary. Why it was mainly socialistic will become clear as the discussion progresses. When populism first gained wide public attention in the 1870s it was already both, and it featured two prevalent, rival conceptions of what it would take to make a social revolution, that is , to end autocracy and transform the social order into a collectivist, popular-democratic one. These conceptions looked for either a spontaneous uprising of the masses sparked by an enlightened intelligentsia or a gradual education of the masses through propaganda and literature, which would eventually incite the transformation. The first of these ideas came to be associated mainly with the teachings of Mikhail Bakunin, the second with those of Peter Lavrov. The assassination of Alexander II in 1881 by a band of populists discredited the first conception when no uprising resulted; it also made the second more difficult because of the repression that followed the assassination.

Most adherents to both these schools of thought shared one more assumption; the belief that the peasant commune in Russia provided a ready-made basis for direct transition to a socialist socioeconomic order. This became reinforced when some influential Russian thinkers attempted to adapt the analytical framework of Marxism to the schema just described, thereby satisfying a strong penchant for the "scientific" among the intelligentsia of that period. Eventually the bulk of the radical part of the intelligentsia became divided into those accepting a form of Marxism akin to that of the Western Social Democratic parties and those determined to adapt Marxism to the Russian populist tradition.[4] This showed itself most clearly in lively polemics in periodicals in the 1880s.

By the turn of the century the populist conception of what it would take to bring about a revolution was far more complex than two decades earlier, not only in theory, but in practical questions as well. In the theoretical sphere a full-blown Russian version of scientific socialism emerged, one designed for a society in which the population was more than three-fourths peasant. This theory was elaborated most fully by Viktor Chernov, based on the Russian tradition of N. Mikhailovsky, Lavrov, Bakunin, and looking all the way back to Alexander Herzen. The essential traits of the updated populist revolutionary theory may be summarized under the following three points: (1) consistent with a belief that man acting in consonance with his environment is the main moving force in history, the key element in initiating the revolutionary process is a critically-thinking intelligentsia guided by a morality that demands social equality for all human beings. It is here that Mikhailovsky's influence is most noticeable, as are his differences with Marx on this issue. (2) The toiling masses (peasants and workers) are a revolutionary social force which would explode to induce a social transformation of Russian society once the intelligentsia helped them to become politically conscious. (3) Though claiming also to be Marxists, the populists differed with the Russian Marxists not only with regard to historical materialism and the revolutionary consciousness of the peasantry, but also believed Russia could move directly to socialism without first completing her development of capitalism. The Socialist-Revolutionaries admitted that an intermediate bourgeois-democratic revolution might be necessary en route to the socialist one. However, they denied that capitalism would have to exhaust itself before the socialist revolution could be broached.[5]

In forming a political party at the beginning of the twentieth century, the populists were participating in the most profound societal phenomena of that time in Russia, those growing out of the rapid modernization and rationalization that had finally begun in the 1880s. Thus, in a period when "organization" became a byword, they became more deliberate and scientific in attempting to bring on an armed uprising. They now worked broadly among the military and organized various types of fighting units within the Party in addition to making an unprecedented effort to reach, win over, and organize the peasantry and workers. Their attempt, however grudging, to utilize the new formal legal politics after the tsar's October Manifesto in 1905 was another response to the modernization process.

In order to achieve a significant victory in 1901−07, the Socialist Revolutionary (S-R) Party would have had to succeed in at least one of these two types of endeavor, resulting in a thriving mass organization or at least a viable political party striving toward that. It did not succeed and was reduced to a skeleton by 1908, recovering only in 1917. This is all the more striking in that during the period in question the very kind of revolutionary situation the Party envisioned actually developed beyond what it could have hoped for. The standard Western interpretation of the Party's history has cited weak leadership and organization as the main causes of the Party's dismal performance; the Soviet view is that the fault lay in unsound ideology. A close study of the participants' views of what occurred suggests that both these conclusions miss the full complexity of the situation.

A PROGRAM FOR SOCIAL REVOLUTION

The S-R Party did not formally adopt its program until January 1906. The main reason was probably fear over the potential divisiveness of formal adoption given the tenuous unity in this new Party which contained and applauded diverse opinion. In any case the program's cardinal points had been written by 1903 by the editorial board of the Party's principal newspaper, *Revoliutsionnaia Rossiia* (Revolutionary Russia), mainly Chernov, Gregory Gershuni, and Mikhail Gots. It had been aired in the Party's several periodicals in the intervening years before approval. This program merits special attention here, as it projects Russian populism of this period into clearer relief and also reflects on the questions of leadership and organization.

Since the specific text of the S-R Party program is not known widely among those who do not read Russian, the program is presented nearly in its entirety in the appendix. The following is an outline of its major sections:

I. A complete bill of political and legal rights

II. National Economic Reforms
   A. Progressive taxation, especially income and inheritance
   B. Complete worker protection, including unionization
   C. Collectivization of agricultural land
   D. Cooperative, democratic organization at the grass roots level
   E. Collectivization of the economy without bureaucratization or State Socialism

III. Summary Statement: The S-R Party, waging a direct revolutionary struggle against autocracy, will campaign for the convocation of a Constituent Assembly, based on the above (Sec. I) democratic principles, for liquidation of the autocratic regime and the reconstruction of all contemporary regimes in the spirit of the establishment of free popular government, the necessary personal liberties, and defense of the interests of labor. The Party will defend its program for reconstruction in the Constituent Assembly and will strive to move immediately to the revolutionary period.[6]

Although these demands, especially in section C, were revolutionary and socialist, they were not really very extreme within the context of the political spectrum then emerging. For example, by 1905, all the opposition parties knew that the peasants would eventually have to be given land; the question was how to transfer it. The question of compensation was also a thorny one for the Party, contributing to the splitting off of the faction that formed the Popular Socialist Party. It is worth noting that the last part of the program is liberal-democratic in tone.

That the format, language, and content of this program are a direct outgrowth of nineteenth-century populism is quite obvious when one compares its demands with those advanced by some of the populist organizations of the past, especially those that had combined to form the Party. Good examples, beginning in the 1870s, were "Nasha Programma" [Our Program], which appeared as an article by Lavrov in *Vpered* [Forward]; proclamations of the

Chaikovsky Circle of the early 1870s; the program of the executive committee of Narodnaia Volia [The People's Will], the main populist organization of the late 1870s and early 1880s; and "Nashi Zadachi" [Our Tasks] and the Manifesto, pronouncements of the Northern and Southern Unions of Socialist-Revolutionaries, the strongest populist groups of the 1890s.[7] The foundations of the Party's agrarian policies were worked out initially by the Agrarian Socialist League, an organization formed in Western Europe at the turn of the century which included among its founders Nicholas Chaikovsky and other former members of the Chaikovsky Circle. The League joined the Party in 1902. These early programs and links clearly demonstrate the continuities, both physical and ideological, between the early populist movement and the S-R Party. The latter's concentration on the practical rather than the theoretical showed that it was nonetheless forward- rather than backward-looking. The way in which it was organized further indicated such an orientation.

STRUCTURE AND COMPOSITION OF THE SOCIALIST-REVOLUTIONARY PARTY

The S-R Party considered itself a political organization. Nevertheless, in the period before 1905 such a designation is imprecise, because no constitutional regime existed under which political parties could operate, either in theory or in practice. Thus, the sociologist George Fischer in his work on Russian Liberalism defines politics as "the attempt to influence the distribution of power" and adds that politics hardly existed in Russia prior to 1905. He contends that the Russian government did tolerate two arenas of activity that served as a substitute for institutionalized politics: the press and, after the Great Reforms of Alexander II, local self-government under the zemstvos, or local elected assemblies.[8] To these exceptions might be added other sorts of political dialogue outside the purview of the state. Therefore, to the extent that the S-R Party did carry on those activities, it could be considered a political party, but not in the usual Western sense until the advent of constitutionalism in 1905.

The Party's basic organizational unit was the *kruzhok* (circle), a veritable institution among the intelligentsia since early in the nineteenth century. Whenever possible, opposition and revolutionary *kruzhki* would set up some sort of printing arrangement, sometimes simply a hectograph for printing fliers and sometimes a real press for brochures and periodicals. Discovery of a secret printing press by the government would usually also mean the dispersal of a *kruzhok*. *Kruzhki* existed among all age groups starting from high school age. They were formed among several different social and occupational groups, including students, workers, and soldiers. Among the peasantry the main organizational units promoted by the Party were the peasant *bratstva* (brotherhoods), which were components of a Russia-wide peasants' union created by the Party. In most cases intellectuals initiated the organizations. The usual pattern was for a number of university students to form a study *kruzhok* among themselves; eventually they would undertake some type of social action, which included helping other social groups to form associations having the same aims. A program of study for workers' *kruzhki* published by the Saratov Committee of the S-R Party in 1903 shows that its *kruzhki* were divided into three categories based on the workers' relative political consciousness. Those having the highest level of consciousness would actually belong to the Party.[9] The S-Rs abroad also formed *kruzhki* in the various cities where they resided: Berne, Geneva, Zurich, Berlin, Paris, London, and others at times. One in Paris reportedly specialized in training revolutionaries for work in Russia.[10]

No evidence exists that the S-R Party structure developed according to any one plan, although by the time the program was adopted in 1906 the structure was such that the temporary rules adopted along with the program could convincingly give the appearance of a deliberate scheme. The structure actually grew out of the tradition described and was then fashioned to parallel roughly the administrative divisions of the Russian Empire. It was a pattern not uniquely the S-R Party's, and was common for organizations that were not revolutionary. The Party had a hierarchical system ranging from *kruzhok* to group to committee; committees existed at city, provincial, and regional level. Coordinating all activities was the Party Central Committee. The system was not, however, as neat and symmetrical as this description might suggest. The designation of a given organization as a *kruzhok,* group, or committee was decided by those involved rather than by any set rules. The Central Committee could, however, expel an organization from the Party. Committees in the respective regions (oblasts) formed unions (in this usage meaning alliances), so that by 1907 there were the Northern, Southern, Northwest, Central, Ural, Volga, Ukrainian, Tavrian, Don, Caucasian, Siberian, Far-Eastern, and Turkestani Unions having varying significance and substance. S-R organizations abroad, including one in New York as well as those in Western Europe, were considered to represent an additional oblast.

Organizations at different levels published their own periodicals and had special subordinate units such as militias, various standing committees called bureaus, and respective unions for peasants, workers, soldiers and officers. S-R soldier organizations sometimes also followed the military's organizational pattern; thus there were S-R *voennyi okrug* (military region) committees in some areas. Another type of agency in some locales was the S-R Red Cross, which was an aid society for destitute revolutionaries, especially those imprisoned or in flight. Also, there were special organizations outside of the hierarchical system that were directly responsible to the Central Committee. Examples are the Agrarian Socialist League, the S-R Party Battle Organization (its terrorist arm), and a number of special unions, the most important being the Peasants' Union. Finally, there were a number of organizations totally separate from the S-R Party but associated closely with it, and which in some instances published literature on its presses. Examples are the nonparty All-Russia Peasants' Union, the Railway Workers' Union, and the All-Russian Teachers' Union. The latter was uniquely important because it included the village school teachers, who maintained close touch with the peasantry and who had strong sympathy for the S-R demands.

Regional and local conferences and congresses served as the primary means of coordinating efforts between Party elements, especially prior to the first Party Congress. The evolution of organization often proceeded from the top down (or center outward), with, for example, city committees existing before their local groups and *kruzhki*. Democratic principles were supposed to guide formation and direction of all party organizations. However, in practice police surveillance and constant attrition of key personnel made this impossible before the advent of quasi-legal status in 1905, and difficult even afterward. In areas where the full range of organizations up to regional level did not exist, the highest level present was directly responsible to the Central Committee. Organization at committee level and above was not widespread until 1905–06. Of the fifty-one separate organizations represented at the First Party Congress, thirty-one were city and regional committees, eleven were groups, and the rest were unions, bureaus, and other special organizations. It should be noted that this network of organizations did not just exist on paper; by 1906 it was an impressive reality. Some units were very small; but nevertheless they functioned in nearly every corner of the Russian Empire and responded to Party directives to varying degrees.

It is difficult to estimate the Party's numerical strength, especially during its early period. By all accounts there was a noticeable upswing in Party activity and membership beginning in 1902, a high point was reached in 1906−07; then followed the sharp decline, which would not be counteracted until 1917. Its own estimate in 1906 was around 50,000 members and 300,000 supporters.[11] Any person accepting the Party's program, submitting to its decisions, and participating in one of its organizations was considered a Party member. Contrary to what one might anticipate from such a lax definition, close study of the Party's records shows that individual units did not seem to exaggerate numbers. In fact, what is most striking regarding this question is that during the very period of the Party's most rapid growth its leadership strove to prevent it from becoming a truly massive party, fearing that the broader masses were not yet developed enough in their political consciousness to be constructive members.[12] The Party's general emphasis on quality over quantity of members is obscured by the seemingly open definition of membership, which was itself only a compromise on a much debated issue.

The above estimates are corroborated by the number of S-R deputies and those supporting its program who were elected to the Dumas. A membership of 50,000 plus 300,000 supporters made it the largest populist party in the Empire. The next in size was the Armenian Revolutionary Federation *Dashnaktsutiun,* which claimed a membership of more than 165,000, and which formally adopted the S-R program with minor changes in 1907. Primarily a nationalist party, its membership was like a combination of the members and supporters of the Russian Party. Clearly, these two parties taken together, augmented by a few other minor populist parties, represented the most sizeable part of the radical movement. The S-R Party alone was comparable in size to the combined Social-Democratic Party and larger than either the Menshevik or Bolshevik factions.

A recent study of the Party's composition, using published sources, confirms the analysis based on unpublished archival materials.[13] Using a sample of 1,029 participants in the S-R movement, Maureen Perrie shows that students and other *intelligenty* predominated until 1904; then from 1905 to 1907 all elements of society contributed to the expansion in membership. Worthy of special note is that even during that period workers, students, and minor professionals predominated over peasants, in a party considering itself to be the champion of the peasantry above all. However, this is not so surprising when one considers the criteria the Party used in counting its members and the relatively great ease of organizing workers as compared to peasants. In factories the heavy concentration of worker populations facilitated organizing and sustaining Party ties. In the cities these advantages were further enhanced by many other factors. For example, the presence of students and superior communications facilities made it easier both to reach and to maintain contact with supporters. Reponses to a questionnaire the Party sent out in 1906 to ascertain its strength at all levels indicated that the local committees simply did not have means of providing data on the peasantry. The problem often was that although the given Party committee would be certain that there were peasants organized in their region, the committee was unable to maintain contact because of climate, distance, geography, or lack of personnel. Therefore, in the section of the questionnaire regarding the peasantry they simply stated that they had no reliable data. The practical result of this in the countryside was that militant peasants were less likely to be considered a formal part of the S-R Party, either by themselves or by the authorities. Those isolated from regular contact with the Party would be less likely to possess incriminating propaganda literature.

Another factor which must be considered, one which other studies have cited as well, is that among the Russian masses in the opposition movement there was more of a commitment to the movement in general than to a specific party; and there was considerable mobility between parties. An urban population would be much more responsive to the type of constant activity that could lead to membership in one particular party. From the standpoint of the S-R Party leadership, the education and politicization that could be brought about with urban resources, best of all in university towns, could bring the nonintellectual segment of Party supporters much sooner to a level of sophistication, which would make them acceptable as full-fledged Party members. It should also be reiterated regarding the large proportion of workers in the Party's membership that they were considered to be equally as important as the peasantry as a revolutionary force. Furthermore, since a sizeable part of the factory and urban labor force was still literally half-peasant or recently peasant, it would be a mistake to view the Party's makeup as evidence of failure in its mission to the peasantry.

The intelligentsia remained the Party's main leadership throughout its existence. While some groups were initiated and led without intellectuals, the central leadership remained in their hands, which was consistent with the populist conception of how the revolution would come about. The background of the typical *intelligent* Party member was still very much like that of the populists of earlier decades, some of whom were in the Party, except that in the twentieth century his or her parents were more likely to have been part of the growing middle classes than gentry. He was still usually of upper-class origins, either merchant, civil servant, or gentry. There was also a noticeable number of sons of priests. His revolutionary career usually began while he was a student; and consequently his studies were often not completed. A series of arrests and escapes or releases would now and then punctuate his record of party work. The nonintellectuals, usually of peasant or worker origins, devoted most of their attention to their specific needs as workers or peasants, rather than the Party's. Nevertheless, once associated with the Party in the eye of the police, they experienced the same fate as those more fully involved in the movement.

The Party membership was very young. The median age for the Party in 1905 was probably around twenty-one though that of the top leadership ranged between thirty and forty. A heavy influx of younger members into the S-R ranks occurred after the formation of the Party and then again with the events from 1904 to 1906. The youthful character of the Party gave it tremendous dynamism and appeal in the competition between parties for public allegiance. However, it also created internal strains conducive to factionalism between the older and younger generations. The Party's inclusion of all the nationalities held a similarly dual potential. Both of these matters will be treated in a later section.

POPULIST REVOLUTIONARY TACTICS

To the great detriment of its ideology and its program, the Socialist-Revolutionary Party became best known for its employment of political terror. As a result terror has seldom been viewed within the full context of the Party's activities. In 1902 N. Chaikovsky observed that the tactic of terror arose from powerlessness to bring about immediately an armed uprising; and he dreaded continued use of terror would be certain to perpetuate schisms within the Party. This perceptive comment succinctly describes the S-R Party's tactical dilemma. Its long-term goal was to promote a massive upheaval, and all other activities were supposed to contribute to that end. This included political terror, robberies (the Party used the term "expropriations"), and legal politics.

The depth of the dilemma is shown most clearly in the fact that the Party did not dare attempt a discussion of tactics at its first full congress convened at the end of 1905, and only out of desperation did it call a special congress in 1907 for that purpose. At the root of this dilemma was the enormous emphasis on morality, which had always been a dominant aspect of Russian populism. The S-R's were for the most part reluctant revolutionaries, revolutionaries because they thought they had to be, not because they wanted to be. They thought they had to be because their world outlook rested on their acceptance of social and political equality as a moral imperative for mankind. This, when added to their conviction that man acting in cadence with the march of history is its main moving force, unmistakably demanded personal action given the nature of Russian society. The problem then became one of determining what kinds of action were acceptable without violating their regard for humanity.

Already before the launching of the new Party some local socialist-revolutionary organizations were engaged in sporadic acts of terror. The one which first captured the attention of the revolutionaries and the general public at the turn of the century was the S-R student P. Karpovich's assassination of Minister of Education N.P. Bogolepov on February 14, 1901. Then later that year, simultaneous with the creation of the Party, its Battle Organization was formed. Its main architects and leaders were M. Gots, Gregory Gershuni, Boris Savinkov, and the notorious Evno Azef, who in 1908 was discovered to have been serving all along as a double agent for the secret police.

The Battle Organization's first act was the assassination of Minister of the Interior Sipiagin on April 2, 1902, in St. Petersburg. The rules adopted by the Battle organization explain that its purpose was to struggle against the existing order by removing those of its leaders considered to be the most criminal and most dangerous enemies of freedom. Such acts would not only serve the purpose of self-defense, but also instill fear and create disorganization in governing circles. In addition to performing "executions," the Battle Organization considered its duties to include preparation of armed confrontations with the authorities in order to demonstrate how the theory of revolution could be put into practice. Just as the Agrarian Socialist League was like a projection into the Party of the Chaikovsky Circle, the Battle Organization was a direct descendant of Narodnaia Volia. A good example of the image the Battle Organization hoped to project was presented in *Revoliutsionnaia Rossiia* in May 1903:

> On March 13, on orders from the Governor of Ufa, N.M. Bogdanovich, troops fired into a crowd of striking workers of Zlatoust, pursuing even those who fled. Twenty-eight people were killed outright; nearly 200 were wounded, of whom several score died later. . . . Among those killed and wounded were many innocent bystanders, women and small children. . . . On May 6, on orders from the Battle Organization of the Socialist-Revolutionary Party, the Governor of Ufa, N.M. Bogdanovich, was killed by two of its members.[14]

An explanatory proclamation after an action was considered essential to the accomplishment of is purposes.

The Battle Organization was inherently controversial within the Party. It was given nearly complete autonomy, limited only by the Party program and decisions of the Party Congresses. Ideally it hoped to control all the terrorist activities of the Party's organizations, with all local terrorist units answering to it. However, in practice, partly because of the requirements of conspiratorial techniques, the central organization had difficulty keeping track even of its own members. Local units were usually acting on their own or under the direction of local Party elements. Nevertheless, the Party was highly effective in carrying out terrorist acts, accounting for more than 200 by the end of 1907 and including among its victims Minister of Internal Affairs V. K. Plehve and Grand Duke Sergei Alexandrovich.

However, the practice failed to achieve its objective of arousing the masses, just as Narodnaia Volia had failed to do in 1881 with the assassination of Alexander II. The most common explanation of this failure is that the policy gave the Party a bad name and alienated decent people. But the support shown for the Party in the first two State Dumas as well as its great success in the Constituent Assembly and other elections in 1917 suggest it enjoyed a positive enough image, even after the Azef affair. A more plausible explanation is that the tactic of terror divided the Party internally; and at the same time the *narod* (the people) simply had not yet accepted the S-R Party as its champion. This is not surprising in light of the difficulties in bringing most of the peasantry to an awareness of the Party's existence, let alone what it stood for.

Within the Party the issue went even beyond extensive debate over the morality of political assassinations: a far more controversial dimension was what some called "economic terror." Political terror was defined as that directed at the organized forces of the state, while economic was against individual exploiters and their property. Economic terror was broken down further into agrarian and factory terror. The Party's official policy persistently argued against economic terror, believing it to be counter-productive. It felt factory terror would only harm the industries the revolutionary forces would soon control; and in the more immediate setting it alienated workers who lost jobs or income as a result of factory sabotage. On the subject of agrarian terror the official Party position was more ambivalent. It welcomed the peasants' show of revolutionary ardor, but feared that anarchy would result if it became widely expressed outside the Party's control.

The reason this Party position posed a problem is that a sizeable part of the membership did not accept it. One of the main areas of disagreement between the Party and the Maximalist faction was the latter's insistence on agrarian and factory terror. Perhaps more importantly, many elements remaining in the Party simply ignored the official policy and also urged these types of actions. In some cases regional economic differences also dictated the stand taken by local Party groups.

The practice of expropriations was similarly fraught with ambiguities for the Party. In its broadest sense the problem was how to transfer all property to the *narod* collectively and not individually. Partial expropriation entailed accumulation of property by private individuals and groups. As the Party leadership viewed it, if this type of behavior were allowed in the current period it would make more difficult or prevent socialization later. The main arguments for and against the practice, however, were more practical than theoretical. The issue was perennial and urgent because the Party was always in dire need of money and materials. Hence the appeal to some of bank robberies such as the one the Maximalists executed in 1906 in league with Bolsheviks, netting over a million and a half rubles. In denouncing that feat Gershuni, the most charismatic and one of the most militant of all the S-R's, pointed out that this type of robbery would become impossible now that the banks were alerted; and the tendency would be to attack small, defenseless victims, the *narod.*

The venerable Ekaterina Breshkovskaia, a populist since the 1870s and another of the most dynamic of the S-R's, agreed with Gershuni and pointed out that the hope for the large expropriation would also lull the Party workers into neglect of sound systematic Party work and would cost many good revolutionaries as casualties in unsuccessful expropriation attempts. However, Breshkovskaia, always the protector of the peasantry, tended to support their spontaneous taking of land; and here again the official Party position was ambivalent.[15] On this issue morality was another important concern. It was not clear when it was allowable to steal and when not. Vladimir Mazurin, a member of an S-R group which left the Party over this issue, argued that confiscation of property in the existing society was a revolutionary act. This view was shared only among the Maximalists, with whom Mazurin worked until his execution by the government in 1906. The suggestion was made more than once in Party circles that counterfeit money be produced. But the leadership, already alarmed at the degree of demoralization surrounding expropriations, firmly rejected the notion.

The Party never found relief from this issue during the period under discussion. Since it was one of the points which drove out the Maximalists, the leadership hoped their departure would at least settle the issue within the Party. This proved to be a vain hope since elements of the Party still sympathized with the Maximalists although they did not defect with them. Furthermore, the departure of at least several hundred Maximalists was a significant blow to Party strength because they were some of its most active and effective revolutionaries. The separation of the Maximalists was only the most dramatic manifestation of the impact of the controversies aroused by terror and expropriations. They sorely tested the Party's commitment to the principle of autonomy for local units on local affairs and led to a few groups severing ties on that account. Moreover, these divisions within the Party both reflected and were cast onto the attitudes of the populations with whom it worked, meaning a great disparity in practice and considerable confusion among S-R's in the various parts of the Empire.

Although terror and expropriations gripped the public's attention and shaped its idea of the S-R Party's activities, the Party in fact never lost sight of its ultimate tactic of massive uprising. That it failed to bring one about was not from a lack of effort, although this was not done indiscriminately. The First Congress meeting at the end of 1905 stated that it was inappropriate to call for an uprising at that time although there had been strong agitation during the course of the three attempts at a general strike that year to transform the strikes into uprisings. While consciously exercising such restraint, during the period 1905–07 the Party leadership did make concerted efforts to incite massive revolt on four occasions, which really held hope for results, since they coincided with events placing large amounts of popular sentiment in opposition to the government. These were "Bloody Sunday" in January 1905, the powerful and successful October 1905 general strike movement, and the dissolution of the first two Dumas in 1906 and 1907. The following July 1906 appeal is indicative of the mood of that time:

> Comrades! The last hope of the people for a peaceful course of revolution has been destroyed. On June 9 the tsar dissolved the State Duma by decree. . . . Comrades and citizens. We call you to arms! Let the blood which must be shed fall on the head of the tsar tyrant![16]

This call was not completely detached from reality. It was encouraged by the fact that many significant uprisings among peasants, workers and soldiers were actually taking place. Besides the well-known developments in St. Petersburg and Moscow in 1905, there were widespread disturbances in the historically turbulent Volga area, the Ukraine, the Black Sea Region, Kronstadt and Siberia. In 1906 and 1907 military uprisings in Siberia resulted in shortlived provisional republics in Krasnoiarsk and Chita. These developments were, however, of limited value for S-R purposes because they did not occur simultaneously, achieved little in immediate results, and, most importantly, were neither initiated nor led by the Party.

The fact is that the rapid course of revolutionary developments beginning in 1905 caught the S-R's by surprise. Most of the top leaders were either in prison, Siberian exile, or abroad until late in the year. They were surprised despite the fact that the new developments stemmed from the very types of circumstances the S-R Marxian analysis predicted. The worker unrest which had swelled intermittently since the turn of the century was a reaction to the adverse impact on the Russian economy of the international economic crisis of the time. The formation of a broad oppositional movement from 1904 was most directly a result of the disastrous Russo-Japanese War, which had been initiated by Russian capitalist imperialistic adventures. The additional hardships the war imposed on the peasants and workers, of course, further stirred them into active protest.

Under these cicumstances the masses did not really need the S-R Party nor anyone else to tell them what was wrong in terms of their immediate needs. In general, more moderate counsel seemed to carry less risk, and consequently, it was the liberal part of the opposition movement that enjoyed the widest support. Based on workers from the *zemstvo,* which was primarily a public service institution, and the growing middle class, the liberal opposition crystallized into the Constitutional Democratic Party at the end of 1905. The advent at long last of a significant middle class, which this party reflectd, was another element foreseen in the Marxian paradigm. It was mainly to the combined forces of the liberals and workers that the tsar made his concessions in 1905, not the revolutionaries. In other words, their predicted bourgeois-democratic revolution was commencing, while the S-R's were absolutely unprepared to convert it into a socialistic one.

Fully realizing that they were not on the crest of the revolutionary wave, the S-R Party made every effort to correct that in the course of 1905. They came closest at the end of the year, first by becoming prominent in the newly created Soviets of Workers Deputies, the nonparty brainchild of the Mensheviks. Second, the Socialist-Revolutionaries played an important role in the Moscow uprisings of December 9 to 17, which had greater chances of success than is commonly supposed. There was a remarkably high degree of participation by the general population; by the government's own admission, most of its local troops were too sympathetic to the revolt to be allowed out of their garrisons. Moreover, the revolutionaries had a real chance of controlling the rail supply lines, because of the strong support given them by the Railway Workers Union. The brutality of the government's repression of this revolt further harmed its image, but it also demonstrated the futility of unarmed mass struggle against regular troops, which in this case the government had to bring in from other places.[17]

As a result, during the following two years the Party devoted more special attention to winning military units to its cause. It studied past incidents and attempted to arrive at workable strategy. A 1907 conference of the S-R military organizations reached a set of conclusions that are indicative of the thinking of the Party. It determined that the prerequisites for a successful uprising are:

> 1. a revolutionary garrison located in one of the largest military centers of a given oblast, and a revolutionary proletariat in the same location; 2. a revolutionary peasantry in a region not less than two or three provinces in size surrounding the center of the uprising; 3. propagandized troops at other points in the oblast; 4. ability to handle the police and main rural authorities in the oblast in some fashion; 5. creation of a mood of unrest among the local populations.

The conference also offered guidance on how to create such conditions:

> 1. strengthen military (Party) organizations and concentrate Party organizers in given years (which had already been done at times); 2. strengthen Party organizations in the key oblast, making agreements with the Social-Democrats when possible; 3. organization of special groups for this work, taking workers from hopeless areas and drawing up a special plan of action; 4–5. use of terror, urban militias, and other existing S-R organizations.[18]

During this same period the Party had plans for a school to train leaders for armed uprisings and collected literature on past uprisings, blueprints for making weapons, and so forth.

These plans incorporated the lessons the Party had learned up to 1907. It is important to note, however, that these ideas were becoming most fully formulated at the time when the Party's strength was entering a precipitous decline. Furthermore, reports on the uprisings in which the Party was involved show that there were vital underlying problems left untouched by the proposals. For example, a pervasive problem in the revolts was how to initiate action. All units wanted to wait for a revolt already in progress that they could join. A related question was what type of signal to use. Even national events such as dissolution of the Duma could not serve to launch an uprising for all of Russia because news took weeks to reach some parts of the Empire, the telegraph and railroad notwithstanding. Another impediment was that most pressing issues for peasants and soldiers were local issues, making a simultaneous, national response unlikely. Locally, the signal might be a cannon or gunshot; but available accounts show that only rarely did plans for procurement of weapons and ammunition succeed with the required timing.

Moreover, lack of planning was deliberate. One reason was the fear of drawing up a plan lest it be compromised. Government agents were legion. With Azef among those involved in all important Party decisions during most of this period, the fears were justified. There was also the belief by some that the situation would have to dictate the plan as events developed. Another weakness was the absence of experienced leadership, not surprising given the difficulty of acquiring such experience. On the practical level, there was need for some means of identifying leaders during combat, such as uniforms or badges, and need for strong discipline. Yet, both these ran contrary to the predominant populist desire to erase rank. Some local uprisings in the military failed simply because the revolting troops could not coordinate their firing, while the other side did. Some confrontations featured just shots in the air; but even these are more effective in unison.

The S-R Party recognized that the tsarist officer corps was a pivotal force in this situation, and it had some success in organizing an All-Russia Officers' Union. The government countered here with more special treatment for officers. Whenever possible, it simply transferred dissident officers rather than prosecute them. The officers were also a source of a dispute between the S-R activists and pro−S-R troops about treatment of officers during uprisings. The soldiers and sailors in some instances favored killing them so that they could neither counter the revolt nor testify against unsuccessful mutineers later. However, the Party, because of its insistence on moral purity, refused to allow such killings. This question of morality also preempted expediency in other matter concerning revolts.

The most surprising of all the facets of the Party's approach to armed uprising came to light in 1905−07. The Central Committee found itself repeatedly trying to arrest uprisings that had already started, judging them premature. In 1906, at the peak of the revolutionary surge, Chernov admitted that he feared encouraging a massive armed struggle at a time when the masses were most militant because the Party organization was depleted and weak and would be unable to control the direction of events. Having failed in bringing about a massive uprising, the Party fell back to the idea of partisan struggle in 1907. But while this may have been a step below armed uprising in the minds of the Party leaders, it was still at least one step ahead of the popular consciousness; for it presupposed an acceptance of the notion of a liberation movement and civil war, of which there was no evidence among the people. Meanwhile, the Party attempted to gain a foothold through legal politics that would allow it to survive intact until the time was right for its revolution.

The Socialist-Revolutionary Party backed ever so reluctantly into legal politics, and with good reason. After all, a revolutionary party which became too closely tied to the existing regime or lent legitimacy to its institutions risked losing its credibility. Throughout this early period the Party debated, without resolving, whether it should be conspiratorial, legal, or both. Already in the years before 1905 the Party had shown some willingness and ability to utilize legal means of promoting its cause, with some members publishing carefully worded pieces in the legal press and the Party aiding in the organization of nonpolitical trade unions. A continuation of that was the prominent role of Party members N. Avksent'ev and I. Bunakov-Fondaminsky in the liberal banquet movement of 1904−05 and other S-R's' involvement in the Railway Workers' Union, whose units initiated the successful October strike.

In general the Party showed a willingness to ally with the liberal wing of the oppositional movement as well as other revolutionary parties. Toward that end it called two conferences of all oppositional parties and representatives from the liberal movement in 1904 and 1905. One other way in which the S-R's had recourse to legal channels was through the courts. Because of the nature of the public trials and close press coverage, the S-R defendants often made excellent use of this stage for acquainting the public with what the Party stood for as well as pinpointing the ills of the tsarist regime. Alexander Kerensky, later famous as the main leader of the Provisional Government in 1917, first gained national notoriety as a defense lawyer in a mass trial of S-R Maximalists in 1906.

If before 1905 the Party could debate the relative merits of legal activities, the debate then became irrelevant as the Party was swept along with the tow of events. The concessions wrenched from the tsar temporarily created an environment that would have to be considered revolutionary by any standard. First, in the wake of the protests following Bloody Sunday there was the February promise of a consultative Duma. Then followed a series of related acts, spurred on by the general strike, culminating in the October 17 Manifesto, which in effect promised a consitution for Russia for the first time. On August 27 a law was issued giving autonomy to the universities, which had been closed briefly after student strikes and boycotts. On October 21, after more massive street domonstrations, political amnesty was declared; and on November 24 press censorship was relaxed. The S-R's were literally stunned by these developments and sprang into action only after the enthusiastic response of the public left them no choice but to attempt to take the leading role in exploiting this new world of opportunities. Therefore, they founded new journals, established their presence at the many interminable mass political meetings university autonomy facilitated, and participated in various ways in the burgeoning electoral processes. The Party leaders slowly perceived that this "time of freedoms," as they called October and November 1905, and later intervals when the government was allowing liberal activities, were the most propitious for their illegal as well as legal work.

However, the Party's hesitant attitude toward the Dumas suggests that it still was not prepared to be bound by the full logical consequences of that perception. It did not officially participate in the election campaign for the First Duma, entered the Second only reluctantly, and thereafter boycotted the Dumas. It did this despite its recognition that the Duma held some possibility of constructive legislation, or at least propaganda and organization of the masses. For example, the Trudovik (Laborite) Group in the First Duma, which was virtually a surrogate S-R faction, attempted to introduce a plan to establish local committees that could hold plebiscites regarding land tenure and redistribution. It was only prevented from doing so by the dissolution of the Duma itself. Later, the thirty-eight members of the S-Rs' own faction in the Second Duma, who received thousands of petitions from various parts of Russia, were on the verge of making themselves the nucleus of a similar plebiscite movement when that Duma was dissolved.[19]

In short, uses the Party could make of the Duma were well-known. It provided as well a chance for coalition of oppositional parties within it with a view toward proclaiming a provisional government, such as would occur in 1917. One S-R writing from England in 1906 proposed precisely that plan, reasoning that the army would side with such a body, while it would not with a revolutionary party.[20] In defense of the boycott of the First Duma, Gershuni pointed out that the Party leadership believed that participation in the election campaign would have suggested to the people that the Party was cooperating with the government just at the time the latter was beginning its reactionary retreat from the concessions of 1905; and besides, the mood of the population seemed at first to favor boycott. The Party was correct, he continued, to enter the Second Duma because its constituency had demonstratd with the First that it wanted participation. The Party's strategy in the Duma was very simple: to keep substantive issues on the floor and maneuver so that in the eyes of the people the blame for the inevitable dissolution would rest squarely on the tsar.[21]

Since this scenario was in fact played out as predicted, it is difficult to understand the decision to boycott the later Dumas. It would appear that this choice must have been made either out of despair over shortages of personnel and resources or from an over-estimation of the Party's ability to lead the population in a massive boycott. It seems unthinkable that the Party would deliberately leave its constituency without a party with which to identify in an institution that was clearly going to continue in some form. Whether winning or losing in the Duma, the S-R's had been getting their issues before the public in a positive light.

In boycotting the subsequent Dumas the Party abandoned the arena that had produced the most tangible victory of its life. The land reform projects it promoted in the first two Dumas, through the *Trudovik* Group in the first, had been the main cause of termination of both when it became apparent that there was a high probability they would be approved. Postulating a radical transfer of landownership along socialist lines, these proposals prompted the government, through Prime Minister P. Stolypin, to counter with its own land reform. Stolypin's aimed at building a strong capitalist peasant class that would still remain monarchist. A government proclamation of November 9, 1906 on the tenure and reallocation of peasant allotment-lands allowed a peasant householder to request and receive the lands he held, with or without the consent of the commune. The ultimate significance of this for the populist ideology and for Russia's development is a topic too large to treat here; but what is most important for the present discussion is that this measure showed that the S-R Party had finally exerted real political power.

The Party, nevertheless, considered this encounter a defeat, which is understandable when its total condition at the time is weighed. The sword with which the government opposed the revolution had two edges: conservative reform was one; the other was brutal repression, which became unbounded once the Russo-Japanese War ended. Regarding the Duma, the so-called Fundamental Laws of April 23, 1906 severely restricted its potential to influence or direct government policy, after the October promise had seemed to make it a real legislative assembly. The electoral law of June 3, 1907 served to further insure a docile, conservative body. Another measure symbolic of the times was the employment of what were called "field courts-martial." This policy in effect allowed the government to execute on the spot anyone it chose. This was a severe blow to S-R activities and brought many casualties in spite of the fact that the S-R's had wisely not attempted to answer the brief offer of amnesty. The Party had scored considerable successes during the fleeting legal period by becoming more public and by challenging the government in its own institutions. But this new climate left it no alternative but to go to underground or abroad again.

UNRESOLVED CONTRADICTIONS

Beneath the Party's ambitious organizational efforts, its program, and tactics, swirled an undercurrent of dilemmas that helps explain its weaknesses in all of these areas. The main contradictions may be summarized under the following headings: the gap between the intellectuals and the masses; socialism versus socialism; and socialism versus nationalism.

Time and time again the S-R Party intellectuals encountered a great conceptual and cultural distance between themselves and the masses, those within the Party as well as the rest. The most graphic proof of this separation was the creation of the nonparty All-Russian Peasant's Union in 1905, with hundreds of thousands of members, when the S-R Party had already had peasant unions active in some areas for years as part of its own All-Russian Union. While it is true that in some places S-R's controlled the new Union, it was founded primarily upon peasant initiative and expressly because the S-R Union was not attractive to the bulk of the peasantry.

Another sign of the division between the intellectuals and masses was a hesitancy of peasants, soldiers, and workers to speak up at S-R meetings, yielding to the more educated and articulate.[22] The manifestation of this tendency in practical Party work was that the *intelligenty* avoided giving responsible assignments to the peasants and workers, forestalling their development of needed skills. In moving away from the type of youthful populism of the 1860s which assumed inherent social wisdom in the peasantry, the S-R's had perhaps gone too far. Although they still believed the peasant to be a victim, they now reckoned that his basic instincts had to be guided closely along the path they deemed proper. They at times forgot that the peasant too was maturing as the decades passed. Consequently the S-R's seemed to miss the middle ground where most of the responsible, activist peasantry stood, as represented by the nonpolitical Peasant's Union. The result was, as some Party leaders admitted, that the peasants and workers actually in S-R organizations were those who thought like S-R's and not like peasants and workers generally. Because of this the Party often missed information vital for effective action.

A solution to this problem might have been to have more intellectuals working among the peasantry to bring them around to the Party's position. However, one of the greatest weaknesses of the S-R Party was its shortage of intellectuals in proportion to its enormous constituency. With a largely illiterate peasant and worker constituency, unacquainted with many of the concepts the Party presented, the S-R's needed to maximize personal contact. In remote areas, and some not so remote, there lingered a strong sentiment among some peasants that revolutionaries were trouble-makers who should be taken and thrashed. From all indications, the peasant remained essentially a monarchist, not a republican; he just wanted a good tsar in place of the one reigning.

The shortage of intellectuals who could sway the peasants beyond this mentality would appear to have been an unsolvable problem. There were scarcely enough intellectuals in Russia to provide the ratio of propagandists necessary for any type of immediate results. This statement is not extreme. As an indicator, consider that there were less than 20,000 students in Russia's nine universities; and the 1897 census found just around 25 percent of the population to be literate. Besides, only a minority of intellectuals could be expected to be radical. This situation became still more difficult for the S-R's after the legalization of parties in 1905. Now those having oppositional sentiment—intellectuals and peasants as well—had more choices of affiliation.

With respect to comparative revolutionary attitude, the peasants showed a greater readiness for immediate violent action than the intellectuals, but also a greater tendency to retreat at the first sign of strong measures by the government. They might refuse to pay taxes as long as the matter stayed between village officials, but would capitulate at the first threat to call in the cossacks. The "time of freedoms" induced some of the peasants within the Party to propose at local conferences that the Party be made legal and completely democratic, this against the official Party position. There is some indication, however, that over the decades of the populist experience the peasantry was becoming more militant. Felix Volkhovsky, one of the SR's who had begun his revolutionary activity in the 1870s, noted at a 1908 conference that in the early days it was the intelligentsia that had sought out the peasantry. Now the peasantry was the pursuer, pleading for intellectuals to come among them as orators, propagandists, and organizers. But now the intelligentsia appeared too dejected over setbacks to respond.[23]

To find support for Volkhovsky's observation we need only look to the records of the Second Party Congress, which had met the year before. Deliberately organized at half its appropriate size because of losses from government repression, the Congress had decided to avoid massive membership, because it made conspiratorial work more difficult and invited people who did not have the proper consciousness. Thus, far from making an effort at including the masses within the Party, its leaders decided that for the time being the ties that had been engendered through the Agrarian Socialist League, the Peasants' Union and other such organizations would be as far as the Party should go in establishing formal ties with the masses. This is the clearest sign of all that although it felt the revolutionary process had begun, it viewed its socialist revolution as still far off. Here again, as with the prospect of massive uprising, the Party actually was placing a brake on its own endeavors.

The rivalry between the various socialist parties in Russia is another topic too large to allow more than brief mention here. The main point is, of course, that such rivalry could only hinder the overthrow of autocracy. The rivals of the S-R's were the Social-Democrats, who only at the end of the period under discussion were becoming consistently divided into Bolshevik and Menshevik. An important fact not generally known about the relationship between the S-R's and S-D's is that a number of outstanding cases of cooperation are recorded. The most enthusiastic example was the Ural Union of S-D's and S-R's which flourished for two years until crushed by arrests in 1903. This alliance organized groups and published literature emphasizing the points the two parties held in common without mentioning their differences. This organization was sufficiently strong to draw special denunciations from Lenin in *Iskra* (The Spark).[24] However, despite striking examples of S-R and S-D cooperation, there were far more instances in such events as military uprisings and election campaigns where they harmed each other when working together might have brought a positive outcome for both.

Another frustrating type of struggle among socialists was the schism within the Party, which became pronounced after 1906, but was present throughout its existence to some degree. The major issues have been discussed regarding the Party program and tactics: terrorism, expropriations, and legal politics. Another which might be noted again was friction along generational lines. In some Party organizations the younger and older populists worked at odds, especially as the pace of action increased. The terrorists and Maximalists, for example, tended to be the young members.

The Party reconciled itself to the unavoidability of rivalry with the S-D's. Likewise it accepted the splintering off of its own dissidents of the right and left as an unfortunate, but perhaps cleansing, development. With the problems involving the nationalities, however, it did not know even how to begin to cope. First of all, a crucial fault, which is also closely related to the gap between the masses and intellectuals, was the lack of literature in the non-Russian languages. The Party simply did not have the needed resources to remedy this. Although it was able eventually to publish a small amount in Yiddish, some of the Baltic languages, and some of the Trans-Caucasian, the volume produced was insignificant compared to the demand and need.

The existence of the various national socialist parties, notably those in the Baltic area, Georgia, and Armenia, posed a particularly knotty problem. The main parties included the Bund, the Polish Socialist Party, the Lithuanian Social Democratic Party, the Latvian Social Democratic Worker's Party, the Armenian Revolutionary Federation *Dashnaktsutiun*, the Georgian S-R Federalists, the Ukrainian Socialist Party, and the White Russian *Gromada.* All these and others were among those invited to the conferences of opposi- tional parties mentioned earlier. A majority elected not to attend. These parties more often hindered than helped S-R efforts in their respective areas.

The S-R Party's difficulty in dealing with this problem is illustrated by a vote on resolutions concerning the Jewish question at a 1905 congress. There is ambivalence on nearly every point, including a proposal to aid Jews toward establishing a homeland abroad and another to provide an autonomous parliament for them within Russia.[25] Similarly, though much talk took place in the Party about militancy on the part of ethnic groups, the party was hesitant to promote this where it would be most successful; that is, where there were real national independence movements. The reason was, apparently, the fear of encouraging nationalism. For instance, the Party leaders viewed nationalism in Armenia as bourgeois and inherently divisive. Yet the main Armenian socialist party, the *Dashnaktsutiun,* which was active mainly in Russian and Turkish Armenia, but also had colonies in other countries, could certainly not be ignored with its 165,000 members. As mentioned earlier, this party in effect adopted the S-R Party program in 1907. Even then, however, the issues dividing the nationalists and socialists were not resolved. They were just kept in abeyance. The Armenian party was itself experiencing a schism over this very issue at the time.[26]

What has been described here was a direct prelude to the developments of 1917, although a decade removed. In 1917 there would be S-R's briefly in the government, with Kerensky as Prime

Minister, Chernov as Minister of Agriculture, Avksent'ev and Savinkov heading other ministries, and S-R's elected mayor in several
cities, including G. Shreider and I. Rudnev in Petrograd and Moscow, respectively. Avksent'ev, Breshkovskaia and V. Zenzinov were
among the S-R's who led the All-Russian Soviet of Peasants' Deputies;
and A. Gots was prominent in the Soviet of Workers' Deputies. Later,
at the lone meeting of the Constituent Assembly in January 1918,
Chernov was elected chairman and a younger S-R, M. Vishniak, was
elected secretary. It is debatable whether the Provisional Government was really in power in any meaningful sense. The Soviets were
reluctant to assume the authority their massive following would
have allowed them; and the onset of the Civil War cancelled out the
local electoral triumphs of the S-R's. Thus the full weight of the S-R
Party's potential from these victories was never felt.

In fact, it would seem that the most favorable condition for a
party like the Socialist-Revolutionary is one in which the enemy
regime is weakened but not yet destroyed, a regime that retains
some measure of stability. In a period like 1917, amid the devasta-
tions of World War I and the collapse of autocracy, parties not so
strongly bound by stated moral and tactical principles would have
an advantage. Hence, when they encountered the Gordian Knot
which the peasants' mentality, rival socialist parties, and nationalism
represented for the S-R's, the Bolsheviks handled it in the classical
manner.

Such pragmatic, decisive action could not have been taken by
most of the populists because it violated the very essence of their
beliefs. Even the Left Socialist-Revolutionaries who allied temporarily with the Bolsheviks soon became alienated from them for that
reason. The central role the populists ascribed to the individual in
the historical process had to be guided by fixed moral principles. It
also had to work in consonance with what was seen as the natural
flow of the historical process. It is highly ironic that with this great
preoccupation with timing, the S-R's still remained out of phase
with the events of the initial revolutionary period, 1905–07.
Already aware that men do not make social revolution independent
of supportive historical circumstances, the S-R's now discovered
how difficult it is for men to perceive and direct an imminent social
revolution.

That they failed not only in this but even in surviving as a viable
political party after 1907 should not, however, be taken as an

accurate measurement of the worth of their ideas, organization, and leadership. From what has been presented here, it can be seen that there was substantial organization, and the program was never tried. However, judging from the Party's support in elections and in the Duma, the platform had considerable appeal. It was in the area of tactics that the Party was weakest. Yet, despite its internal problems and external repression the S-R Party hit upon one tactic of great potential by entering the Duma while simultaneously remaining partly underground. Yet by then the Party structure was too weak to pursue this tactic. This was unfortunate for the party because its electoral successes in 1917 suggest that this route could have resolved at last the crucial and delicate problem of how to join, lead, and hold its mass constituency within a framework in which both Party and following would be willing to operate. With that solved the tasks of cementing solidarity betwen socialist factions and satisfying nationalistic aspirations would have become more manageable. While the S-R Party failed in this first bid for power, its experience may prove quite instructive for a better understanding of revolutionary populism. Its concentration on the particular problems of transition from a revolutionary movement to a responsible legal political party and the transformation of a quasifeudal, capitalistic society into a socialistic one holds abiding interest as similar movements continue to emerge in present-day developing societies in Africa, Asia and the Americas.

Russian populism also left a legacy for the new Soviet Union. Suppression of the remnants of the S-R Party in the early 1920s erased neither the filial ties of bolshevism to populism nor certain inherited traits. Lenin's successful borrowing from the S-R platform in 1917 and the alliance of some S-R's with him until July 1918 attest to that kinship's survival well into the twentieth century. The new regime, though avowedly not populist, has borne from its outset a number of populist features, albeit at times in a distorted form. The type of centralized party leadership the populists as well as bolsheviks originally developed exclusively for the revolutionary movement has been institutionalized in the Soviet system and has consolidated itself using a kind of state capitalism rather than its intended communism. Moreover, tactics of expropriation and terror, which the populists used against the state, were adopted by the new state and used against the people. The administrative structure of the Soviet Union is reflective of the strength of the federative principle so strong in populism; but local autonomy exists only in theory.

Applying to the Soviet Union the general characteristics of populism mentioned in the introduction to the present volume, it may be noted that the Soviet government has evinced the urban emphasis characteristic of twentieth century populism. The Soviet system does enjoy multiclass support, another general populist trait. The populist ideal of universal suffrage is also shared by the Soviet regime, although practiced in a form that severely limits its significance. One final common feature, the popular accord for the charismatic leader in populist movements, was carried to its extreme in the so-called cult of personality under Stalin. These divergencies between the lofty aims of bolshevism as a revolutionary movement and bolshevism in power suggest some of the problems with which populism in power would have had to grapple if it had made the transition from opposition movement to governing party.[27]

APPENDIX:
The Socialist Revolutionary Party Program, 1905

The complete implementation of the party program, that is, the expropriation of capitalistic property and reorganization of production and the entire social order on socialistic principles presupposes the complete victory of the working class, organized as a social-revolutionary party, and, if need be, as a provisional revolutionary dictatorship. . . . Before that time, while it is a revolutionary minority, . . . the S-R Party . . . will advocate, support, or force the following measures through its revolutionary struggle:

 I. In the political and legal sphere: recognition of the following inalienable rights of man and citizen: full freedom of conscience, speech, the press, assembly, and association; freedom of travel, of selection of occupation, and of collective refusal to work (freedom to strike); inviolability of person and dwelling; general and equal suffrage for all citizens over twenty years of age, regardless of sex, religion, or nationality, in an electoral system with direct and secret voting; a democratic republic established on these bases, with broad autonomy of regions and communes, both urban and rural; the widest possible application of federative relations between separate nationalities, and recognition of unconditional rights to self-determination; proportional representation; direct popular legislation (referendum and initiative); election and removability at any time and in any jurisdiction of all officials, including deputies and judges; free legal proceedings; introduction of the local native language in all local social and state institutions; establishment of compulsory general secular education, equal for all and financed by the state; in areas with mixed population, the right of each nationality to a share of the budget proportionate to its size, to be designated for cultural-educational aims, and to disburse these funds using the principles of self-government; complete separation of Church and state and the declaration of religion to be the private affair of each individual; abolition of the standing army and its replacement by a people's militia.

II. National Economic Affairs
  A. On questions of the state economy and financial policy, the Party will agitate for introduction of a progressive tax on income and inheritance, with small incomes below a certain level being entirely free from taxation; for abolition of indirect taxes (excluding taxation on luxury items), protective duties and, in general, all taxes falling on labor.
  B. On questions of worker legislation, the S-R Party sets as its goal the protection of the spiritual and physical powers of the working class and countryside and the increase of its ability for further struggle for socialism, to the general interests of which must be subordinated all narrowly-practical, immediate, local, and professional interests of separate strata of the working class. By these means the party will advocate the shortest possible working day consistent with norms stipulated by scientific hygiene (as soon as possible an eight-hour norm for most areas of production, and correspondingly less in those most dangerous and harmful to the health); the establishment of minimum wages according to agreement between organs of self-government and professional unions of worker; state insurance in all of its forms (for accidents, unemployment, retirement, illness and so forth) at the expense of the state and employers and in keeping with self-government by the insured; legislative protection of labor in all spheres of production and com-

merce, consistent with the requirements of scientific hygiene, under the supervision of factory inspectors chosen by the workers (normal working conditions, the state of hygiene of working accommodations, prohibition of overtime work, of work by minors, the prohibition of women's and child labor in cerain periods; sufficient uninterrupted weekly rest, and so forth); professional organization of workers and their progressively widening participation in the establishment of internal organization of labor in industrial enterprises.

C. On questions of the reconstruction of land relationships, the S-R Party will strive to be supported, in the interests of socialism and the struggle against bourgeois property principles, by communal and worker attitudes, the traditions and forms of life of the Russian peasants, in particular by the convictions prevalent among them that the land is nobody's, and that only labor gives the right for its use. In keeping with its own general views on the task of the revolution in the countryside, the party will stand for socialization of land, that is, for taking it off the commodity exchange and converting it from the private property of separate persons or groups to public property in accordance with the following principles: all the lands are placed under management of central and local organs of popular self-government, extending from democratically organized, without class distinctions, rural and urban communes to regional and central institutions (to direct settling and migration, management of lands, and so forth); the right to use the land must be equally granted and on an earned basis, that is, a standard of use must be ensured which is based on investment of real labor, individually or in association; rent, through special taxation, must be applied to social needs; the use of lands possessing more than narrowly local significance (vast forests, fishing areas, and so forth) is to be regulated in compliance with agencies employing the most extensive self-government possible; the mineral wealth remains in the hands of the state; the land becomes public property and cannot be sold; for those who suffer from this turnover of property is acknowledged only the right to public support during the time required of adjusting to new means of existence.

D. On questions of communal, municipal, and zemstvo economy, the party will support: any kind of social service and enterprises (free medical aid, zemstvo-agronomical and food-producing organizations); the organization by zemstvo and regional self-government organs, aided by state resources, of broad credit for the development of the labor economy, primarily on cooperative principles; communalization of water supply, lighting, means of communication, and so forth; the granting to city and rural communes of the broadest rights for taxation of real estate and for its compulsory alienation, especially in the interests of satisfying the housing needs of the working population; communal, zemstvo, as well as state policy favoring development of cooperatives on strict democratic labor principles.

E. In general, the S-R Party will adopt a positive attitude toward all measures having as their goal collectivization of one or another area of the national economy while the bourgeois state still exists, to the extent that democratization of the political structure and correlation of social forces, as well as the very character of the corresponding measures, will give sufficient guarantees against this leading to an increase of the dependence of the working class on the ruling bureaucracy. In the same connection, the S-R Party warns the working class against a "state socialism" which is in part a system of half-measures for lulling the working class to sleep and in part a peculiar form of state capitalism, concentrating various areas of production and trade in the hands of the ruling bureaucracy in support of its fiscal and political goals.

Source: see note 6.

Notes

1. Western and Soviet studies have begun recently to give populism more attention: Oliver Radkey, *The Agrarian Foes of Bolshevism* New York, 1958); Andrej Walicki, *The Controversy Over Capitalism* (Oxford, 1969); Maureen Perrie, *Agrarian Policy of the Russian Socialist-Revolutionary Party* (Cambridge, 1976); Manfred Hildemeier, "Neopopulism and Modernization: The Debate on Theory and Tactics in the Socialist-Revolutionary Party, 1905–14," *Russian Review* 34 (October 1975); 453-75 and *Die Sozialrevolutionäre Partei Russlands: Agrarsozialismus und Modernisierung im Zarenreich* [The Russian Socialist-Revolutionary Party; Agrarian Socialism and Modernization in the Russian Empire] (Cologne-Vienna, 1978); K.V. Gusev, *Partiia Eserov: ot melko-burzhuaznogo revolutsionarizma k kontrrevoliutsii* [The S-R Party from Petty-Bourgeois Revolutionism to

Counterrevolution] (Moscow, 1975); L. Kaptsugovich, *Istoriia politicheskoi gibeli eserov na Urale* [The History of the Political Ruin of the S-R's in the Urals] (Perm, 1975).

2. See, for example, Mark Vishniak, "Opravdenie Narodnichestva" [The Justification of Populism] *Novyi Zhurnal* 30 (1952): 225–42.

3. Richard Pipes, "Narodnichestvo: A Semantic Inquiry," *Slavic Review* 33 (September 1964): 441–58; Richard Wortman, *The Crisis of Russian Populism* (Cambridge, 1967); *Mc Graw Hill Encyclopedia on Russia and the Soviet Union*. The best of the other recent studies have found it convenient to use the term "neopopulist" for the twentieth century.

4. Others remained more like Western liberals. A much smaller part became anarchists.

5. Mikhailovsky outlined his main ideas in "What is Progress?," which first appeared in the journal *Otechestvennyia zapiski* [Notes of the Fatherland] in 1869. Good samples of Chernov's thought are *Zapiski sotsialista-revoliutsionera* [Notes of a Socialist-Revolutionary] (Berlin, 1922) and *Konstruktivnyi sotsializm* [Constructive Socialism] (Prague, 1925).

6. *Protokoly pervogo s'ezda partii sotsialistov-revoliutsionerov* [Minutes of the First Congress of the Socialist-Revolutionary Party] (Paris, 1906).

7. Vladimir Burtsev, *Za sto let (1800-1896) sbornik po istorii politicheskikh i obshchestvennykh dvizhenii v Rosii* [For a Hundred Years (1800-1896) A Collection on the History of Political and Social Movements in Russia] (London, 1897).

8. George Fischer, *Russian Liberalism from Gentry to Intelligentsia* (Cambridge, 1958), pp. 4-5.

9. A. Spirirdovich, *Partiia Sotsialistov-Revoliutsionerov i ee predshestvenniki 1886-1916* [The Socialist Revolutionary Party and its Predecessors] (Petrograd, 1918), Appendix 5.

10. *Obzor vazhneishikh doznanii, proizvodivshikhsia v zhandarmskikh upravleniiakh za 1902 god* [Survey of Inquests Held in the Gendarmes Department in 1902] (Rostov on the Don, 1906).

11. *Rapport du Parti Socialiste Révolutionnaire de Russie au Congrès Socialiste International de Stuttgart* [Report of the Russian Socialist-Revolutionary Party to the Stuttgart Congress of the Socialist International] (August 1907).

12. *Protokoly vtorogo (ekstrennago) s'ezda Partii Sotsialistov-Revoliutsionerov* [Minutes of the Second (Extraordinary) Congress of the Socialist-Revolutionary Party], Archives of the P S-R, International Instituut voor Sociale Geschiedenis, Amsterdam.

13. Maureen Perrie, "The Social Composition and Structure of the Socialist-Revolutionary Party Before 1917," *Soviet Studies* 24 (1972): 223–50.

14. *Revoliutsionnaia Rossiia,* No. 24, 15 May 1903.

15. *Protokoly vtorogo s'ezda,* passim.

16. Archives P S-R, No. 623/II, from the Samara Committee P S-R.

17. P.A. Garvi, *Vospominaniia Sotsial-demokrata* [Memoirs of a Social-Democrat] (New York, 1946), pp. 519–604: Leon Trotsky, *1905,* A. Bostock, trans. (New York, 1971), pp. 234–49.

18. Archives P S-R, Nos. 623 and 791. The conference, which met 2 August 1907 included representatives from the Vyborg, St. Petersburg, Kronstadt and Reval military organizations of the S-R Party.

19. *Rapport présenté par le groupe socialiste-révolutionnaire de la 2(me) Douma au Congrès socialiste International de Stuttgart* [Report Presented to the Socialist International Congress by the Socialist-Revolutionary Group in the II Duma], *Internationale Ouvriere & Socialiste* (Brussels, 1907), pp. 422–73.

20. Letter from F. Rolsovskii, 19 June 1906, Archive of th P S-R, No. 303, Miscellaneous Letters.

21. *Protokoly II s'ezda,* passim.

22. *Protokoly delegatskago soveshchaniia Vserossiiskago Krest'ianskago Soiuza 6-10 Noiabria 1905 v Moskve* [Minutes of the Delegates' Conference of the All-Russian Peasants' Union held 6–10 November 1905 in Moscow].

23. The minutes of this conference, which met 4–10 August 1908 can be found in the Archives P S-R, No. 185.

24. See I. Kaptsugovich, *Istoriia politicheskoi gibeli.*

25. The minutes of this congress, held in Geneva 25–31 September 1905 are in the Archives P S-R, No. 654.

26. *Rapport Présenté au Bureau Socialiste International par le parti socialiste et révolutionnaire arménien Daschnaktzoutioun*[Report presented to the International Socialist Bureau by the Socialist and Revolutionary Party Dashnaktsutin] (Stuttgart, 1907).

27. Helpful sources on the demise of the Socialist-Revolutionary Party under the Soviet communist regime are L. Schapiro, *The Origin of the Communist Autocracy: Political Opposition in the Soviet State, First Phase, 1917–1922* (Cambridge, Mass., 1955); O. Radkey, *The Sickle Under the Hammer: The Russian Socialist Revolutionaries in the Early Months of Soviet Rule* (New York, 1963); and M. Jansen, "De ondergang van de Russische Socialisten-Revolutionairen" [The Fall of the Russian Socialist-Revolutionaries], *Het eerste jaarboek voor het democratisch socialisme* [First Yearbook of Democratic Socialism] (Amsterdam, 1979): 174–188.

9

United States Populism

Ferenc Szasz
University of New Mexico

Populism in the United States differed from such movements elsewhere, as was noted in the Introduction. It was the only genuinely rural movement which nonetheless met the other criteria used in this study, that is, multiclass, expansive, electoral, socially reformist, and led by charismatic figures. This chapter provides an overview of the "classic" populist movement of the 1880s and 1890s in the United States, and then it analyzes those characteristics which are most comparable with other studies in this volume. In particular, it examines the social bases of U.S. populism, its reaction to the urban East (a symbol for the metropolitan revolution), and its demand for greater state intervention in economic affairs. The chapter concludes with a look at the rich populist legacy in twentieth century U.S. politics.[1]

American populism emerged as a direct reaction to the adverse agricultural and social conditions of the South and West after the Civil War. The destruction of the southern economy and the end of slavery meant the demise of the plantation system. Soon, small independent farm units, almost all of which were raising cotton for market, dominated the landscape. Many of these were under twenty acres and run on a system whereby the landowner furnished land, seed, and perhaps some tools in exchange for a percentage of the crop. Since the South had little cash at hand, food and other needed supplies were advanced by local merchants. When the crop was sold, the farmer often divided his meager earnings between the landowner and the merchant. Then he signed on for another year of the same. By 1900, virtually the only success achieved by the farmers was the tripling of cotton production. Increased output had few benefits, however, because by 1890 cotton prices had fallen so low they allowed for no margin of profit.[2] They remained at that level for most of the 1890s.

West of the Mississippi River, the problems were different but the end result was the same. Here the story revolved around the familiar western theme of "boom and bust." Although it often is overlooked on maps, one of the cardinal facts of American geography is the 98th parallel, where the well-watered interior lowlands meet the semi-arid plains of the western Dakotas, Nebraska, Kansas, Texas, eastern Montana, Wyoming, Colorado, and New Mexico.[3] After the Civil War, the rainfall in this area seemed sufficient to support agriculture, and thousands of acres were opened to settlement. Although there were some experiments with communal or "bonanza" farms in the Red River Valley of the North and in parts of Texas, the dominant economic unit which prevailed in the area was the family farm.[4]

Externally, the family farm seemed little changed from antebellum times, but actually the farmers had shifted their orientation from family subsistence to the production of wheat and corn for market. In short, the American farmer had become a businessman; but he was only dimly aware of this change. As Theodore Saloutos has noted, few farmers kept any real business records, and managerial talent was most conspicuous by its absence. Men of real ability and capital went into other, more profitable fields.[5]

So long as farm prices remained high and rainfall in the plains abundant—as happened in the 1870s and early 1880s—settlement marched westward. Little towns boomed, railroads laid track far beyond stable agricultural zones, and thousands of farmers went deep into debt. The money to finance such activity came from readily available eastern loans.

The bitter winter of 1887–88 marked the end of the good years. Soon afterward prices plummeted and the boom towns went bust. Even nature failed to cooperate. Only once between 1886 and 1891 did the rainfall reach above normal; only twice from 1887 to 1897 did it reach the average of 21.83 inches established in the preceding years. In five of the dry years, the rainfall was so low it produced almost complete crop failure in the plains.[6]

Thousands of farmers abandoned their farms. In 1891 alone 18,000 Prairie Schooners crossed the Missouri River bridge at Omaha going east. Signs on their side told the story: "Going Back to the Wife's Family" or, "In God we Trusted, In Kansas We Busted." For those who stayed, cases of near starvation were recorded.[7]

By 1890, then, in both the South and the West a thoroughly disillusioned set of farmers had emerged. Isolated from the mainstream of society, they believed that, as a class, they had been "cheated" by unknown forces. The result was a mind-set ready to lash out against the existing order.[8] Thus was American populism born.

Anyone familiar with the conservative mood of the Republican and Democratic parties during this time can hardly help sympathizing with the farmers. Although the presidential elections were all bitterly contested and voter turnout high, the rival candidates seldom addressed themselves to economic issues. Instead, the parties refought the Civil War or conducted sham battles over Civil Service reform or the Tariff. None of the third parties of the period—Greenbackers, Prohibitionists, Socialist Labor Party, and so forth—made much headway either. The elections often revolved around real issues, but, as recent studies by Paul Kleppner and Richard Jensen have shown, they tended to be religious and cultural. Thus, they were less susceptible to immediate political solutions.[9] Such side-stepping may not have been entirely detrimental to the nation, for it did allow it to industrialize and absorb millions of immigrants without a revolution. But the story changed with the onset of the depression of the 1890s.

Most people associate the phrase "great depression" with the 1930s but many historians regard the economic slump of 1893–97—without the benefit of any New Deal relief measures—as even worse.[10] Two-and-a-half million men were out of work in the winter of 1893-94 and actual food riots broke out in Buffalo. Several urban mayors experimented with putting unemployed people to work planting vegetable gardens on vacant city lots. One expert estimated that over 50,000 able-bodied, out-of-work men were simply wandering aimlessly across the land.[11] In 1894 "General" Jacob Coxey led a march of some of these unemployed to Washington, D.C., which ended in fiasco when their leader was arrested for walking on the grass.[12] In 1893, historian J. Rogers

Hollingsworth noted, America was divided along economic lines more than at any other time in previous history.[13] The depression intensified and broadened the demands for social change. Because the agrarian movement was the dominant insurgent force of the time, it served as the channel for all these protests.

What did the populists propose? No single answer suffices: whether one places them in the liberal, radical, or conservative tradition often depends on which set of demands one looks at. When the agrarian revolt began—dominated in the early stages by the Southern Farmer's Alliance—it emphasized the establishment of farmer-run economic co-ops. "I hold," noted C.W. Macune, the architect of this position, "that co-operation, properly understood and properly applied, will place a limit to the encroachments of organized monopoly, and will be the means by which the mortgage-burdened farmers can assert their freedom from the tyranny of organized capital."[14] In *Democratic Promise: The Populist Movement in America* (1976), Lawrence C. Goodwyn argues that this initial cooperative program was a brilliant and radical proposal. Goodwyn maintains that such cooperation offered the last viable alternative before industrial capitalism assumed final control of the American economy.[15] Numerous cooperative ventures were put into effect, but most proved ephemeral. The farmers simply lacked the capital to make such ventures succeed. As the 1890s wore on, however, the idea of farmers' cooperatives began to take a back seat to other issues. The most prominent of these were: direct election of Senators; postal savings banks; governmental control of the railroads; federal supervision of corporations; the initiative and referendum; a graduated income tax; women's suffrage; prohibition; free and unlimited coinage of silver (more on this later). All of these proposals were designed to limit the power of the large corporations and restore the government to "the people."[16]

These issues broadened the range of reform considerably. Moreover, since the Populist party (formed 1891) provided the only real political alternative to the Republicans or Democrats, it soon attracted reformers of every stripe. In addition to agrarians, the famous 1896 Populist convention at St. Louis abounded with Single Taxers, Bellamyite Nationalists, Socialists, Prohibitionists, Greenbackers, and Suffragettes. Eugene V. Debs, later the perennial Socialist candidate, was much in the running for the 1896 Populist nomination. Historians have found that old Populists cast many of the early twentieth century socialist ballots.[17]

Since the agrarian vote alone was probably not enough to capture the White House, the Populists did their best to entice the nation's workers into their fold. Populist editorials constantly reminded their readers not to neglect the "toiling masses" of labor. Here, however, they were only partially successful. Although much of the Populist vote in the western mining states of Colorado and Montana relied on labor support, the party never appealed to workers in the East.[18] The votes garnered by James B. Weaver, Populist candidate in the 1892 presidential election, showed clearly that the party's main strength lay in rural areas. The urbanized states of New York, New Jersey, Pennsylvania, and Massachusetts, for example, gave Weaver less than 30,000 votes. In 1896, the same story was repeated, but by then Populism had become caught in the ground swell of "free silver."

Discussion of America's monetary policy goes far beyond the scope of this essay, but it is necessary to say a few words. By 1890, the farmers realized (correctly) that the low prices they received for their wheat, corn, and cotton were not caused solely by overproduction. They were directly related to the deflationary monetary policy followed by the government since the Civil War.

When Alexander Hamilton organized the American monetary system, Congress set the mint ratio at 15 to 1—that is, fifteen ounces of silver were worth one ounce of gold. In 1834 this was raised to 16 to 1, which tended to drive silver dollars out of circulation. In 1873, an act of Congress (the so-called Crime of 73) discontinued the silver dollar as a national monetary standard.[19] Yet few people anticipated any problems. Thanks to the heavy gold strikes in California and Australia—the richest since the Spanish exploitation of the New World in the sixteenth century—the gold supply seemed sufficient for the nation's monetary needs.

Soon afterward, however, increased silver imports from Mexico and important strikes in Montana, Colorado, and New Mexico increased the availability of silver. Numerous people began to advocate a return to bimetalism as the chief means of increasing the national money supply. These groups achieved two limited victories with the passage of the Bland-Allison Act of 1878 and the Sherman

Silver Purchase Act of 1890—both of which provided for limited purchasing and coinage of silver by the federal government. President Grover Cleveland, however, blamed these acts for the depression of the 90s and soon after taking office the second time urged repeal of the Sherman Act. In August of 1894 a group of Populists and Republicans met in Chicago to form the National Bimetalic League, which demanded the free (that is, unlimited) coinage of silver at the old ratio of 16 to 1. Thus, the two sides formed: "Gold bugs" versus "Silverites" (really "Bimetalites").

Historian Walter T. K. Nugent has argued that the money question eventually became a substitute for all the other questions of the period.[20] The gold standard stood for Newtonian, classical economics and the status quo; silver for inflation, "democracy," and change. Nugent likened the division between monometalists and bimetalists to a "theological dispute" in which meaningful arguments were, at best, very difficult.[21] "To the combatants of that era," noted Richard Hofstadter, "silver and gold were not merely precious metals but precious symbols, the very substance of creeds and faiths. . . ."[22]

The confrontation emerged in the presidential election of 1896 when Republican William McKinley clashed with Democrat and Populist William Jennings Bryan in the "Battle of the Standards." Thus all the complex issues of the period were subsumed under the cry of "gold" versus "silver."

As the other points of Populism faded, new leaders emerged. And here one must turn to the career of William Jennings Bryan. Because Bryan never officially joined the Populist party, some historians have claimed that he was not a "real" Populist.[23] Yet it is hard to find anyone else who was a better representative of the Populist cause. This was the man the Populists themselves chose as their standard bearer in 1896.[24]

Born in Illinois and educated as a lawyer, Bryan, like so many Populist leaders, was not strictly an agrarian. Yet he was from Nebraska, an agrarian state, and he voiced most of the positions they advocated. Moreover, Bryan possessed in abundance that element of leadership only hinted at by the other Populist figures. "Sockless" Jerry Simpson, William Peffer, Mary E. Lease, and Ignatius Donnelly, might be termed "colorful" or "eccentric"; William Jennings Bryan possessed real charisma.[25]

No political figure of the times could match Bryan's appeal. Three times he sought the Presidency—1896, 1900, and 1908—and three times he was defeated. Yet he kept his followers through each defeat. Without ever holding high office, he maintained his position as a major figure in political circles for almost thirty years. One loyal follower even had his tombstone engraved:

> Kind friends I've left behind
> Cast your vote for Jennings Bryan.

Much of Bryan's continued support came from his often-voiced trust in "the people" as the arbiter of all issues. As he put it when he addressed the 1920 Nebraska Constitutional Convention:

> There is no other source to be trusted. Not that the people will make no mistakes, but that the people have a right to make their own mistakes, and that a few people have no God-given right to make mistakes for the rest of the people.[26]

Never, throughout his long career, did Bryan abandon this concept. His magazine, *The Commoner* (begun 1901), was set up "to aid the common people in the protection of their rights, the advancement of their interests and the realization of their aspirations." Steadfastly he urged that all issues of government, morality, and justice be submitted to them for a final decision. The other side of this faith in people was Bryan's distrust of any minority who interfered with the people's desires. "A private monopoly," he wrote in 1896 "is indefensible and intolerable."[27] He held to this position until his death.

In addition to a raw egalitarianism—what is often meant now by the term "populism"—Bryan's message was always highly moral. His followers were largely Bible people, and Bryan used the language of Zion in all his speeches. Biblical metaphors abounded in everything he wrote or said. His most popular talks on the Chautauqua circuit were "The Value of an Ideal," "The Prince of Peace," and "The Price of a Soul." The oration which secured him the 1896 Democratic nomination spoke of a "crown of thorns" and a "cross of gold."[28] Such rhetorical flourishes kept him continually in the public eye.

In spite of his voter appeal, however, Bryan's selection as Populist standard-bearer in 1896 was largely an accident. It occurred because the Democrats held their national convention three weeks earlier than the Populists. When the Democrats met on July 11, 1896, Bryan was in his element. Thanks to some adroit political maneuvering, he secured not only the party's nomination but also a plank in the platform endorsing the 16 to 1 silver program. Thus, when the Populist convention met on July 25, their main issue had been stolen by the Democrats. After fierce discussion, they decided to back Bryan—in truth their only hope of success—but they selected their own vice-presidential candidate for good measure. Thus did the Populist Party merge with the Democrats, "that bourne," remarked Henry D. Lloyd, "from which no reform party returns. . . ."[29]

Bryan's dramatic appeal to the nation—he traveled perhaps 18,000 miles by train, speaking at every whistle-stop along the way—came to naught. He lost to McKinley by 600,000 votes. Like J. B. Weaver in 1892, Bryan could never get the necessary eastern urban support. In the traditionally Democratic urban centers, his plea for inflation fell on deaf ears. Thus did Populists go down to defeat. Although the party continued to run candidates until 1908, they were never a serious political threat.[30] Even worse, they seemed unnecessary. With a sudden upturn in farm prices after 1896, plus a new means of increasing the gold supply, the farmers returned *en masse* to the two major parties. Organized Populism had risen and fallen in fifteen years.

While they never attained the presidency, the Populists had considerable success on state and local levels. Following often heated contests, they sent numerous congressmen to Washington. They controlled the executive machinery of Kansas for four years (1893–95; 1897–99), and Populist-Democratic "fusionist" administrations governed the states of Washington, Montana, and Idaho from 1897–99. In Nebraska, they were in power from 1895–1901, and they were a force to be reckoned with in several other states.[31] In the South, Populist candidates often won their electoral contests at the ballot box but, because of Democratic vote-stealing and other fraudulent political maneuvers, were frequently cheated out of their victories. This was especially true in Alabama and Georgia.[32]

This Populist success at the polls was largely due to their appeal to "the people." Obviously no political group can represent all "the people," but the Populists claimed to speak for many who had been ignored by the traditional system. Agrarians and western laborers comprised two of these groups; women and blacks formed two others.

Women played a surprisingly large role in the agrarian uprising. Almost all of the group photographs in Goodwyn's *Democratic*

Promise show women standing prominently with the men. Robert McMath, Jr. has estimated that perhaps one-fourth of the Farmers' Alliance people were daughters and wives of the men who had joined the order.[33] Perhaps this was their way of escaping the isolation of the frontier. Mrs. Sarah E.V. Emery's *Seven Financial Conspiracies which have Enslaved the American People* (1888) was one of the most popular financial tracts of the time, and Mary E. Lease's *The Problem of Civilization Solved* (1895) found a wide readership.

The women performed many tasks. Widowed Mrs. Bettie Gay of Columbus, Texas, for example, managed her farm while she simultaneously spoke and wrote vigorously for women's suffrage, prohibition, and farmers' causes. Stump speaker Annie L. Diggs performed the same role in Kansas. In Montana in 1892, Ella Knowles—the "Portia of the People's Party"—ran for attorney general on the Populist ticket (even though she could not herself vote). Although she lost the election, she gathered considerable support, which was broadened when she subsequently married her incumbent opponent.[34] In New Mexico Territory, Anglo-American Populists were forced to deemphasize the women's issue so as not to offend their more traditional Spanish colleagues.[35]

The most vocal woman Populist of the era was Mary E. Lease, "The Kansas Pythoness." Gifted with good lungs and a clever way of phrasing, Lease spoke out on all the issues of the day. When reporters discovered that she provided good copy, they often devoted full columns to her speeches. Her most colorful phrase— still found in virtually every high school textbook—is her famous advice to farmers to raise "less corn and more hell." A dedicated radical, she ended her days in the Lower East Side of New York giving free legal advice to the poor.[36] Had women been able to vote on a national level, the outcome in 1896 might have been different.

The last group of "outsiders" picked up by the Populist crusade were the American blacks. Negro Alliance Movements sprang up along side their white counterparts from the very beginning, and they worked together in a limited fashion. At first these parallel black organizations aroused no more controversy than the Negro Masons or the African Methodist Episcopal Church. The black groups grew rapidly. Perhaps 75 percent of all Negroes were connected with agriculture, and they shared a sympathetic cause with the white agrarians.[37] Historian William H. Chafe has argued that blacks joined the Kansas populists primarily because they saw

Populism as favorable to their own immediate and distinct self-interest.[38] R.M. Humphrey, white organizer of the Colored Farmers Alliance, put it bluntly: "The colored people are part of the people and they must be recognized as such." Many Populist groups made token efforts along these lines. The Arkansas People's Party took an official stand on behalf of the "downtrodden, regardless of race."[39] The People's Party of Texas had two prominent blacks in leadership positions; and black orator John B. Rayner was one of Texas' main speakers in the important, ongoing lecture system. Others, more cynical, urged cooperation to keep the black vote from being used against them.

The most articulate Populist spokesman for racial cooperation was Georgia's Tom Watson, termed by C. Vann Woodward, his biographer, as: "perhaps the first native white Southern leader of importance to treat the Negro's aspirations with the seriousness that human strivings deserve."[40] Tom Watson phrased his biracial appeal in these words:

> Now the People's Party says to these two men [black and white], you are kept apart that you may be separately fleeced of your earnings. You are made to hate each other because upon that hatred is rested the keystone of the arch of financial despotism which enslaves you both. You are deceived and blinded that you may not see how this race antagonism perpetuates a monetary system which beggars both."[41]

The program of the Populists called for racial cooperation in a common venture against a common enemy. Numerous other party leaders echoed Watson's words.

How far these ideas of racial cooperation were carried out in actual practice has become a matter of dispute among historians. Using oral history techniques in Grimes County, East Texas, Lawrence C. Goodwyn has shown that the Populists did, indeed, develop a brief, workable alliance with the black community.[42] This ceased only when the Democrats resumed control. Sheldon Hackney has noted that the Populists provided effective legislative opposition to efforts to disenfranchise black voters.[43]

Yet other studies have argued that the white Populists showed the same racial attitudes as their opponents. The lack of any constructive legislation on racial matters from Populist-controlled state legislatures supports this view.[44] On the other hand, the

Populists did convince black and white farmers to sit down together to discuss their common economic grievances. This, in itself, was a real accomplishment.

After the Populists were defeated, any halting efforts toward racial cooperation collapsed. On this point historians do agree. Southern Populism was defeated by the Democratic Party, whose spokesmen convinced white voters that racial solidarity was more important than economic interests. When the Southern Farmer's Alliance merged into a third political party, especially one with biracial overtones, it became anathema to southern Democrats. "The South," grumbled black Populist lecturer John Rayner, "loves the Democratic Party more than it does God."[45]

Rayner did not exaggerate by much. When the southern Populists were defeated, racial relations everywhere took a turn for the worse. Black Populists were terrorized or driven out of areas where they had come close to holding power. By 1906 blacks had been systematically excluded by law from voting in Democratic primaries across the South. Tom Watson so soured on the issue of racial cooperation that he became a Negro-baiter and blamed the blacks for the failure of his political aspirations. As he said in 1910: "Consider the advantage of position that Bryan had over me. His field of work was the plastic, restless, and growing West: mine was the hide-bound, rock-ribbed Bourbon South. Besides, Bryan had *no everlasting and overshadowing Negro Question to hamper and handicap his progress:* I had."[46] Ironically, Populist appeals on behalf of black farmers probably left them in a worse plight than before.

The Populist revolt produced a significant, albeit small, body of literature. If one excludes editorials and money tracts such as those by William H. "Coin" Harvey and Mrs. Sarah E.V. Emery, three books dominate the list. Two of these spoke of despair and one of hope. The theme of despair can best be seen in Hamlin Garland's *Main-travelled Roads* (1891; second edition with six additional stories, 1893) and Ignatius Donnelly's *Caesar's Column* (1890). Garland was a son of the agricultural frontier of Wisconsin, Iowa, and South Dakota. Hence, his short stories captured the suffering of farm wives and the agony of the men who waited for rain that would not come. In the best-known tale of the collection, "Under the Lion's Paw," he delivered a short sermon on Henry George's ideas of the Single

Tax—a tax on unearned increment in land values. Garland's first and best work was a direct attact on easterners who praised the virtues of agrarian life.[47] Literary critic William Dean Howells saw the timeliness of the book. "If anyone is still at a loss to account for the uprising of the farmers in the West," Howells noted, "which is the translation of the Peasant's War into modern and republican terms, let him read *Main-travelled Roads* and he will begin to understand . . . ."[48]

Ignatius Donnelly's *Caesar's Column* was cut from a more militant piece of cloth. Published in 1890, just before Donnelly stepped onto the national stage with his ideas, this book spoke not just to agrarian discontent. It also dealt with the division of society into the haves and the have-nots. One of the numerous utopian novels published in the wake of Edward Bellamy's successful *Looking Backward* (1888), Donnelly's vision revealed a violence which the others ignored. Against the background of a hotel named "The Darwin," the "Brotherhood of Destruction" finds itself pitted in a death-struggle against "The Oligarchy." The book details the downfall of industrial civilization in the late nineteenth century because of class warfare. Only a saving remnant survives by fleeing to Africa, where it will begin the story of civilization once again.[49] One of Donnelly's biographers has suggested that the novel also contained some positive comments on American life, but this interpretation was not the most common reading given by the public.[50]

The Populist literary work that would have the most impact on American life was Lyman Frank Baum's *The Wonderful Wizard of Oz* (1900). Unbeknownst to contemporary critics, it would become a classic. Like Garland and Bellamy, Baum was also a son of the Midwest. When the farmers revolt began he was living in Aberdeen, South Dakota. By 1891 he had moved to Chicago, where he became a loyal supporter of William Jennings Bryan.

All of the characters of *The Wonderful Wizard of Oz* come directly from the Populist movement. Dorothy, of course, hails from Kansas, a land which was beautiful before the adversities of nature introduced drought. Her Aunt Em and Uncle Henry, who had once been cheerful, now no longer laughed. The Wicked Witch of the East (Industrialism) had enslaved the "little Munchkin People" (the workers) and forced them into a dehumanized factory existence. (The Tin Woodsman, remember, was searching for a heart.) Dorothy

(Miss Everyman) starts off down the Yellow Brick Road (gold standard) wearing her magic *silver* shoes on her way to visit the Land of Oz (Washington, D.C.). Her friend, the scarecrow, is really the American farmer (seemingly awkward but basically very shrewd) while the Cowardly Lion is none other than William Jennings Bryan himself. Their march toward the Emerald City echoed Coxey's March of 1894 but, unlike Coxey, they actually had an audience with the Wizard (Presidents McKinley, Cleveland, Harrison). Very quickly they discover that, not only is he a "humbug," he comes from nearby Omaha. "Why, that isn't very far from Kansas," says Dorothy. Finally, the Wicked Witch of the West is destroyed by water (proper rainfall, irrigation) and happiness is restored to the plains once again.[51]

Baum's delightful parable shows how deeply the socioeconomic conflicts of the 1890s were felt by the society at large. And every time Judy Garland appears as Dorothy in the popular 1939 movie version—as she does almost every Easter on television—the Populist crusade is re-enacted once again.

The Populist movement rose and fell in a fifteen year period. But it left a legacy that continues to the present day. Those who treat the Populists favorably praise the movement for initiating many of the reforms later enacted by the Progressives during 1901−14. Some even credit them with serving as the ancestors of Franklin Roosevelt's New Deal.[52] In the 1960s, they were viewed as a major source of the American radical tradition. Skeptics of this interpretation, however, see the Populists as conservative, or even reactionary. Thus, the Populist heritage has been ambiguous: it provided ammunition for both liberals and conservatives.

Although the Populist cause fell into disrepute after 1900, one of its enduring legacies was that of a distinctive campaign style. Any twentieth-century leader who rallied the "little people" against "the interests" was usually termed a "populist." During the 'teens and twenties such appeals were largely restricted to flamboyant southern politicians, such as Alabama's J. T. "Tom-Tom" Heflin, Mississippi's James K. Vardaman, and South Carolina's "Pitchfork" Ben Tillman. Using anti-Yankee, anti-Negro, and anti-Capitalist rhetoric, these men built a solid base of support among their poor white constituents. Except for the Radical Non-Partisan League of North Dakota, populism in the early twentieth century was largely a southern phenomenon.

The onset of the 1930s, however, refurbished populism on a national scale with the appearance of the three "Pied Pipers" of the Depression: Father Charles E. Coughlin, Dr. Francis Townsend, and Huey P. Long.[53] These three "neopopulist" figures soon became the most colorful critics of the decade.[54]

A canadian-born Roman Catholic priest of Irish extraction might, at first glance, seem an unlikely candidate for a "populist" spokesman. Yet in the 1930s, Father Charles E. Coughlin of the Shrine of the Little Flower in Royal Oak, Michigan, became the foremost advocate for one of their old ideas—the remonetizing of silver. To this program for inflation, Coughlin added strong statements on social justice as promulgated by Pope Leo XIII, "Rerum Novarum" (1891), and Pius XI, "Quadragesimo Anno" (1931). Through this unique combination, Coughlin interpreted the abuses of American capitalism for the ordinary people.[55]

A charismatic figure, Coughlin was one of the first reformers to realize the mass potential of radio. In fact, he began his career by delivering occasional Sunday night radio sermons over a local Detroit station. In these he denounced (among others) the Ku Klux Klan, prohibition, and the policies of Herbert Hoover. Then, on January 19, 1930, he broadcast a powerful anti-Communist sermon that brought in so many letters of support the national networks began to seek him out. Coughlin suddenly had a nationwide forum. Soon he began to blend the prestige of the Catholic Church's stand on social justice with his own pet schemes for ending the Depression. His ideas were often frustratingly vague, but they included revaluation of gold, creation of a central bank, a program to extend consumer credit, and the remonetization of silver.

Listening to tape recordings of his addresses maintained at the National Voice Library, one realizes that Coughlin possessed close to the perfect radio voice. His rich, booming brogue reached an estimated ten million listeners every week. Non-Catholics who had never met a priest in person tuned in faithfully to hear his views on world affairs, social justice, and how to end the Depression. One poll reported him as more popular than any other radio program, including Amos n' Andy, Fu Manchu, and Eddie Cantor.[56]

In the beginning, Father Coughlin supported Franklin Roosevelt's New Deal measures. But as Roosevelt gradually moved away from

204

inflationary policies to other relief programs, the priest began to turn against him. In 1934, Coughlin went on radio to announce the formation of this own organization—the National Union for Social Justice (NUSJ). Amidst much publicity, he also put forth his "sixteen principles" of social justice—his personal program to restore national prosperity. These "principles" included some important points: liberty of conscience, liberty of education, the right to organize, the right to a living wage, and so forth. They were far too vague to be of any practical use, yet the bishop of Detroit praised them as an attempt "to apply Christ's principles to every day problems."[57]

After 1935, when it was obvious that Roosevelt had no plans to adopt any major inflationary program regarding silver, Coughlin moved into outright opposition. Soon his attacks on Roosevelt knew no bounds. Mixed into these diatribes were anti-Semitic accusations, proinflationary statements, and vague claims for social justice. It was a curious mélange. In 1936 he swung the power of his NUSJ behind the radical Union Party candidate, William Lemke of North Dakota.

Both Rome and liberal American Catholics were embarrassed by Coughlin's activities, but it was not until 1942—under pressure from the federal government—that the Church finally silenced him. Father Coughlin complied with the order and promptly faded from public view. His passing also marked the last gasp of the old Populist idea of the "free and unlimited coinage of silver."

Dr. Francis E. Townsend seemed as unlikely a candidate for populist leadership as Father Coughlin. Born in a Illinois log cabin in 1867, Townsend received his M.D. degree in 1899 and practiced medicine for years in the Black Hills region of South Dakota. In 1919 he moved to southern California where, several years later, he lost his temporary job as assistant county health officer. Much distressed, in poor health, and with little money, in 1933 he wrote a series of eight letters to the editor of the *Long Beach Press Telegram*. The ideas expressed here soon became the basis for the most popular economic scheme of the entire decade: The Townsend National Recovery Plan.[58]

Drawing from personal experience, Townsend pointed out how modern urban and industrial life had undermined the worth and wealth of older people. Few state or corporate pension systems then existed, and when older people lost their savings, they had nowhere to turn. California, with a large body of recent immigrants and heavy concentration of people over sixty, proved a fertile ground for the sowing of such ideas.[59]

Like the earlier Populist leaders, Townsend spoke out for a minority—this time the aged—who had long been ignored by the two major political parties. Moreover, the inflationary scheme he proposed also echoed Bryan's plan of Free Silver. Through numerous speeches, a newsletter, and the organization of Townsend Clubs—over 2,000 by the spring of 1936—the doctor focused the nation's attention on the problems of the elderly.[60]

Strictly speaking, however, Townsend's plan was not just to benefit older citizens. Reform of the entire economy was his ultimate goal. Accordingly, the plan argued the following: through a 2 percent tax on all business transactions, the nation could accumulate a substantial fund. This would be distributed in the form of $200 a month to everyone over sixty, on the condition that it be spent within thirty days. This "rapid and continuous and compulsory circulation of existing money," Townsend felt, would restore economic prosperity. Several politicians became interested. One of them, California Representative John S. McGroarty, twice introduced the Townsend Plan on the floor of Congress. As a result, Roosevelt's administration was put on the defensive. It had to justify its own proposed Social Security plan—which had a much lower monthly stipend—and fend off the aggressive proponents of Townsend's ideas.[61]

Neither Townsend nor his followers were economists, of course. Their scheme was sold to the public on moral as much as economic grounds. Townsend, a tall, ascetic-looking man, frequently referred to scripture when he spoke of "justice" and the "American way." One of his supporters, Chicago politician "Big Bill" Thompson, described the doctor's ideas as "the most Christ-like plan that has been conceived since the crucifixion."[62]

Economists, however, were harder to convince. Administration officials argued that $200 a month was too much to give to the least economically productive segment of society. In 1936 the University of Chicago held a Round Table discussion on the economic merits of the plan. The economists assembled concluded that it simply could not work. The proposed pension was too high to be met by any ordinary means of taxation; the "transaction tax" was far too complicated to be implemented; its most probable result would be to slow down the economy. "To propose such an ill-advised scheme," they concluded, "can do nothing but distract attention from more reasonable pension plans."[63]

By 1935 Townsend's failure to capture Roosevelt's ear pushed him into permanent opposition. The next year he cooperated with Father Coughlin and other "hate-Rooseveleters" in lending support for William Lemke and the Union Party. Thoroughly unhappy with the passage of the federal Social Security measures, Townsend continued to advocate his ideas through his autobiography *New Horizons* (1943) and occasional speeches until his death in 1960.

The flamboyant "Kingfish" of Louisiana, Huey P. Long, fits more neatly into the traditional Populist mold. Born in 1893 in northern Winnfield, Louisiana, Long rose from modest circumstances to become governor in 1928 and senator two years later. Only an assassin's bullet in 1935 kept him from seeking the presidency.

For historians, placing Huey Long in political perspective has proven a difficult task. His numerous opponents called him a "demagogue," a "fascist" and an "American Dictator."[64] Historian T. Harry Williams, however, feels that these labels are far too facile to fix this brilliant, enigmatic man. Williams argues that Huey Long can best be understood as a traditional American boss, nurtured on Populist and Socialist ideals, who had to enact his program against the very real confines of southern politics.[65] But Huey Long differed from the traditional southern politician, such as Vardaman, Tillman, and Heflin, in three important respects. First, unlike the others, he avoided "Negro baiting," which pitted the poor whites against the poor blacks. Instead, Long tried to speak for the poor of both races. Second, he avoided calling up the ghosts of the Confederacy to damn the amorphous "Yankee" and all things Northern. Finally, while his southern counterparts all remained local figures, Huey Long created a reform program with truly national dimensions.

In 1928, when Long was elected governor of Louisiana, it ranked as one of the most backward states of the Union. Ordinary people had almost no spokesmen for their interests, and the state's political and economic power was concentrated in the corporate and commercial hands of New Orleans. Long's reform program of more equitable taxation—a clear attack on the large corporations—free school textbooks, better hospitals, improved roads, and so forth, brought the state along with rapid strides.

State measures occupied all his time until 1934, when he finally assumed the senate seat to which the voters had elected him two years earlier. Thus, Long did not emerge on the national scene until the effects of the Depression had been felt for almost five years. Then, drawing from the populist background of his northern Louisiana parish, plus enormous reading on his own, Long devised his own scheme to end the Depression. He would redistribute America's wealth.[66]

By selected reading of certain portions of Nehemiah, Leviticus, and James, Huey Long argued that scripture demanded a release of all debts every seven years and a redistribution of wealth every fifty years.[67] Drawing about him the mantle of Andrew Jackson, Abraham Lincoln, and William Jennings Bryan, he advocated the following: a "homestead" allowance of $6,000 for every family; a guaranteed annual income of $2-3,000; "adequate" old age pensions; free college education for youth; and government control of the labor market. To fund such a scheme, Long recommended 100 percent tax on all annual incomes over one million a year and 100 percent tax on all inheritances over five million.[68]

Like Father Coughlin, Huey Long had great personal magnetism, and he, too, realized the power of radio. In February 1934, he went on a nationwide hook-up to announce the formal organization of the "Share Our Wealth" Society (SOW), with the motto of: "Every man a king." Soon SOW clubs began forming across the nation, and by the end of 1935 the Society claimed groups in every state over 4.5 million members. A private Democratic poll concluded that Long might well take away 4 million votes if he ran for president in 1936.

Long's assassination in the Louisiana State Capitol of Baton Rouge in September of 1935 ended all his ambitions. But many of his followers—the most prominent being his lieutenant Gerald L. K. Smith—ended up supporting Lemke's Union Party in 1936.

The net effect of these Depression "neopopulist" critiques of American life was to drive the Democratic administration into more extensive reform measures, including passage of such legislation as: the Works Progress Administration (WPA); the National Youth Administration (NYA); the National Labor Relations Act (which set up the National Labor Relations Board); the Social Security Act; the Rural Electrification Authority (REA); increased appropriations for the Civilian Conservation Corps (CCC); and stiffer regulation of business—all of which helped deflate the populists' proposals. Although Roosevelt himself could hardly be called a "populist," the reform measures of his administration eventually absorbed most of the following of his more radical critics. It was ironic that the ultimate effect of the "neopopulism" of the 1930s was to produce a generation of very loyal Democrats.

The next wave of interest in Populism came in the late 1940s and 1950s. Wisconsin Senator Joseph R. McCarthy utilized the cold war tensions of these years to call on "ordinary" Americans to root out "traitors" in high governmental circles—chiefly the State Department. McCarthy was not exactly a "populist," but the atmosphere his accusations created so influenced Richard Hofstadter that he formulated in his brilliant *Age of Reform* (1955) a view of the original Populist movement that dominated a generation of scholarship. Populism, according to his interpretation, was basically a retrograde movement. It fostered isolationism, demagoguery, anti-Catholicism, anti-Semitism, and a general anti-intellectualism. Its legacy could be seen in McCarthyism. Some of Hofstadter's followers, less careful of the facts than he, even branded the Populists as American fascists. This view of the "seamy" side of the Populist movement held sway for much of the 1950s.[69]

In the 1960s, a new group of historians challenged these views. The scholarly revival of populism—the stress now lay on its "radicalism"—probably facilitated the reemergence of populist candidates for national office.[70] The elections of 1972 and 1976 abounded with people who claimed to be "populists." That this new populism was often espoused by people who would surely have voted for McKinley in 1896 didn't seem to matter. Overnight, populism had become "respectable."

Populism of the 1960s had both conservative and liberal wings, but a sense of frustration provided the connecting link. The foremost theoretician of 60s' conservative populism was Robert W. Whitaker, who was listed as Director of the Populist Forum and who termed himself "a practicing populist."[71] In *A Plague on Both Your Houses* (1976) Whitaker read liberals out of the populist camp to praise his hero of the moment, Alabama Governor George Wallace.[72] Both Republicans and Democrats, he said, were equally part of the Establishment. As such, they were unresponsive to the needs of ordinary citizens. Their only reaction to social problems was to throw vast sums of money after them and search for an "expert" to run things. "America is so big," he complained, "that we can only reach each other through institutions." Yet none of these institutions was responsive to ordinary citizens.[73] Only George Wallace, "the populist of our day," could lead what he termed the fight against the Interests on behalf of the People.

Kevin Phillips in *The Emerging Republican Majority* (1969) argued along similar, albeit more balanced lines. Phillips claimed that President Nixon was in position to reshape American politics by forging a Republican majority based on these groups: the Sun Belt, Wallace Democrats, working-class Catholics, the heartland, and ordinary suburbanites. The black vote could be left to the Democrats without fear.[74] Phillips' account created quite a stir when it was first published, but Watergate and the Democratic victory of 1976 have undermined his credence as a prophet. Still, he was one of the first to point to the rise of the so-called "ethnic" issue, which was picked up by numerous other writers. Probably the most important of these was Michael Novak, whose *The Rise of the Unmeltable Ethnics* (1970) will surely rank as one of the most important books of the decade.

Novak argued that white ethnic Americans—Poles, Italians, Hungarians, Greeks, Slavs, and so forth, so long ignored or ridiculed by liberals and by the Power Elite—would be the political force of the future. The seventies, he predicted, would be "the decade of the ethnics." Talk of ethnic power automatically assumes a populist stance, because by definition no ethnic group has ever been large enough to gain power on its own. The frustrations of these "little people" sometimes bore a resemblance to the frustrations of the small farmers some eighty years earlier.[75]

Awareness of this frustration was not lost on the liberals. "The nicest thing anyone can say about a Democratic presidential candidate this year," *Time* magazine remarked in 1972, "is to call him a populist."[76] Even the suave mayor of New York City, John Lindsay, wrapped himself in the populist blanket; but no one expressed this sentiment better than Oklahoma Senator Fred Harris. In *Now is the Time: A New Populist Call to Action* (1971) and more fully in *The New Populism* (1973) this son of a sharecropper set forth his attacks on bigness and impersonality: "The new populism," he said, "—and it doesn't matter what you call it—means that most Americans are commonly exploited, but that, if we get ourselves together, we are a popular majority and can take back our government,"[77]

In *A Populist Manifesto: The Making of a New Majority* (1972), Jack Newfield and Jeff Greenfield outlined another plan of action.

There are "people, classes, and institutions that today possess an illegitimate amount of wealth and power," they noted; "they use that power for their own benefit and for the common loss. This power, which is at root economic, corrupts the political process and insulates itself from effective challenge." [78] Reformer Ralph Nader predicted a coming together of those whom he termed the "victimized"—family farmers, small businessmen, consumers, blacks, Chicanos, some segments of labor, and young people against "the common victimizer." Just who this "victimizer" was depended largely on the observer. Nader saw it as corporate interests; others blamed big government; still others saw international conspiracies. But the thrust of this "new populism" was clear; it was the politics of the small, poor, and out-of-power against the large, wealthy, and Established.

The Presidential election of 1972 seems to have marked the high point of this rhetoric, but one could still hear echoes of it four years later. Lillian Carter's father had worked with Tom Watson in some of his campaigns, and family stories must have somehow rubbed off on her son. When asked by a reporter if he considered himself a populist, Jimmy Carter replied, "I think so."[79] Much of his successful campaign was based on promises to restore government to the hands of "the people."

By 1980, then, American populism had fragmented considerably. It could mean the revolt of poor farmers, angry ethnics, inner city blacks, suburban housewives, or soured liberals, such as Ralph Nader and Bess Myerson (whom Simon Lazarus has termed *The Genteel Populists*). But behind everything, it spoke for the politics of frustration against the bigness and impersonality of an Established System. As political observer Harry Boyte noted in 1976, "Only the active informed strength of a mobilized people can prevail against the weight of corporate empire." To this William Jennings Bryan, Mary Ellen Lease, Huey Long, and the farmers of the 1890s would have said, "Amen."[80]

Notes

1. The author would like to thank Margaret Connell Szasz for valued assistance in the preparation of this article.

2. Herbert J. Doherty, Jr., "Voices of Protest from the New South, 1875–1910," *Mississippi Valley Historical Review* 42 (1955):46. Melvin J. White, "Populism in Louisiana During the Nineties," *Mississippi Valley Historical Review* 5 (1918):5–7. William Warren Rogers, *The One-Gallused Rebellion: Agrarianism in Alabama, 1865–1896* (Baton Rouge, 1970)

has a good account of these conditions. C. Vann Woodward, *Origins of the New South* (Baton Rouge, 1951) is the standard work.

3. Louis Bernard Schmidt, "The Agricultural Revolution in the Prairies and the Great Plains of the United States," *Agricultural History* 58 (1934):171.

4. The communal bonanza farms were often seen as "un-American." Cf. LaWanda F. Cox, "The American Agricultural Wage Earner, 1865-1900," *Agricultural History* 22 (1948):106-7.

5. Theodore Saloutos, "The Agricultural Problem and Nineteenth Century Industrialism," *Agricultural History* 22 (1948): 164.

6. Hallie Farmer, "The Economic Background of Frontier Populism," *Mississippi Valley Historical Review* 10 (1924):416. Raymond Curtis Miller, "The Background of Populism in Kansas," *The Mississippi Valley Historical Review* 11 (1925):467-89; Gilbert C. Fite, "Daydreams and Nightmares: The Late Nineteenth-Century Agricultural Frontiers," *Agricultural History* 40 (1966):285-93.

7. Miller "The Background of Populism in Kansas," 477; Fite, "Daydreams and Nightmares," 292-93; Farmer, "The Economic Background of Populism," 420-23.

8. Fred A. Shannon, *The Farmer's Last Frontier: Agriculture, 1860-1897,* 2d ed. (New York, 1968), pp. 291-328. James Turner, "Understanding the Populists," *Journal of American History* 67 (September, 1980): 354-73.

9. Paul Kleppner, *The Cross of Culture: A Social Analysis of Midwestern Politics, 1851-1900* (New York, 1970), and Richard Jensen, *The Winning of the Midwest: Social and Political Conflict, 1885-1896* (Chicago, 1971), argue that the real issues were cultural and religious, not political and economic. Thus the high turnout of voters.

10. Samuel Rezneck, "Unemployment, Unrest, and Relief in the United States During the Depression of 1893-97," *Journal of Political Economy* 61 (1953):423-25.

11. J.T. McCook, "The Tramp Problem," *Lend A Hand* 15 (1895):167.

12. Donald L. McMurry, *Coxey's Army: A Study of the Industrial Army Movement of 1894* (Seattle, 1968; originally published in 1929), is the best study of Coxey.

13. J. Rogers Hollingsworth, *The Whirligig of Politics: The Democracy of Cleveland and Bryan* (Chicago, 1963), p. 106.

14. Macune, quoted in Robert C. McMath, Jr., *Populist Vanguard: A History of the Southern Farmers' Alliance* (Chapel Hill, 1975), p. 106.

15. Goodwyn, *Democratic Promise, passim.* In 1978, the Southern Historical Association reserved one entire session of their annual meeting for a discussion of the book. The consensus was that it is the best volume on Populism now available.

16. As the *New York Times* remarked on Mary Lease's passing, all her causes (except free silver) were eventually enacted. *Times,* 30 October 1933.

17. Henry D. Lloyd, "The Populists at St. Louis," *Review of Reviews* 14 (1896):298-303. Samuel Walker, "George Howard Gibson, Christian Socialist Among the Populists," *Nebraska History* 55 (1974):553-72. For discussion of the more radical elements in Populism see: J. Martin Klotsche, "The 'United Front' Populists," *Wisconsin Magazine of History* 20 (1937):275-389; David A. Shannon, "The Socialist Party Before the First World War: An Analysis," *Mississippi Valley Historical Review* 38 (1951):283; Grady McWhiney, "Louisiana Socialists in the Early Twentieth Century: A Study of Rustic Radicalism," *Journal of Southern History* 20 (1954):317-18; Leon W. Fuller, "Colorado's Revolt Against Capitalism," *Mississippi Valley Historical Review* 21 (1934):343-60.

18. Richard Hofstadter, "Introduction," to *Coin's Financial School* (Cambridge, 1963), pp. 17-18; Thomas A. Clinch, *Urban Populism & Free Silver in Montana: A Narrative of Ideology in Political Action* (Helena, 1970), p.49.

19. On the "Crime of 73" see Allen Weinstein, *Prelude to Populism: Origins of the Silver Issue, 1867-1878* (New Haven, 1970), ch. 1.

20. Walter T.K. Nugent, *The Money Question During Reconstruction* (New York, 1967), p. 22.

21. *Ibid.*, pp. 57-58.

22. Hofstadter, "Introduction," p. 1.

23. Goodwyn feels that Bryan, as a latecomer to the Populist cause, properly belongs to what he terms the "shadow movement" of the agrarian crusade.

24. Robert F. Durden, *The Climax of Populism: The Election of 1896* (Lexington, 1956), and Stanley L. Jones, *The Presidential Election of 1896* (Madison, 1964), are the best studies of this election. See also the account by Paolo E. Coletta in *William Jennings Bryan: Political Evangelist, 1860–1908)* (Lincoln, 1964).

25. Roger G. Kennedy, "Ignatius Donnelly and the Politics of Discontent," *American West* 6 (1969):10–14; Karel Denis Bicha, "Jerry Simpson: Populist Without Principle," *Journal of American History* 54 (1967):291–306; the best biography of Bryan is Paolo E. Coletta's three volume *William Jennings Bryan.* Louis W. Koenig treats his political career in *Bryan* (New York, 1971); Paul W. Glad's *The Trumpet Soundeth: William Jennings Bryan and his Democracy, 1846-1912* (Lincoln, 1960) is also comprehensive.

26. Pamphlet, William Jennings Bryan Manuscripts, Library of Congress, Washington D.C.

27. *The Commoner* 1 (1901); W. J. Bryan, *Heart to Heart Appeals* (New York, 1917), pp.25–51.

28. Bryan, "Why I Lecture," *The Commoner* 15 (1915).

29. Henry D. Lloyd, "The Populists at St. Louis," 298.

30. Robert F. Durden, "The 'Cowbird' Grounded: The Populist Nomination of Bryan and Tom Watson in 1896," *Mississippi Valley Historical Review* 50 (1963):397–423; William Diamond, "Urban and Rural Voting in 1896," *American Historical Review* 46 (1941):281–305; James A. Barnes, "Myths of the Bryan Campaign," *Mississippi Valley Historical Review* 34 (1947):367–404; Paul W. Glad, *McKinley, Bryan and the People* (Philadelphia and New York, 1964); George F. Whicher has edited a collection of documents in *William Jennings Bryan and the Campaign of 1896* (Boston, 1953); C. Vann Woodward has a good account of Populism's latter days in *Tom Watson: Agrarian Rebel* (New York, 1938).

31. K. D. Bicha, "The Conservative Populists: A Hypothesis," *Agricultural History* 47 (1973):17.

32. Rogers, *The One-Gallused Rebellion*, William Ivy Hair, *Bourbonism and Agrarian Protest: Louisiana Politics, 1877-1900* (Baton Rouge, 1969), and Woodward, *Tom Watson,* detail these frauds.

33. McMath, *Populist Vanguard,* p. 67.

34. Thomas A. Clinch, *Urban Populism and Free Silver in Montana: A Narrative of Ideology in Political Action,* pp. 55–65; 84.

35. Robert W. Larson, *New Mexico Populism* (Boulder, 1974), offers the best account of Populism in a territory.

36. *New York Times,* 30 October 1933; Richard Stiller, *Queen of the Populists: The Story of Mary Elizabeth Lease* (New York, 1970).

37. Gerald H. Gaither, *Blacks and the Populist Revolt: Ballots and Bigotry in the "New South",* pp. 2-3; Goodwyn, *Democratic Promise,* p. 277; Robert C. Hart, *Redeemers, Bourbons, and Populists: Tennessee, 1870-1896* (Baton Rouge, 1975), p. 123.

38. William H. Chafe, "The Negro and Populism: A Kansas Case Study," *The Journal of Southern History* 34 (1965):404.

39. Goodwyn, *Democratic Promise,* quoted pp. 290,298; Goodwyn's account, pp. 296–306, and Gerald H. Gaither, *Blacks and the Populist Revolt: Ballots and Bigotry in the "New South"* offer the best treatment of this issue.

40. C. Vann Woodward, *Tom Watson: Agrarian Rebel,* p. 221.

41. Quoted *Ibid.*, p. 220.

42. Lawrence C. Goodwyn, "Populist Dreams and Negro Rights: East Texas as a case Study," *American Historical Review* 76 (1971):1135–71.

43. Hackney, "Introduction," to Gaither, *Blacks and the Populist Revolt,* p. 14.

44. Hart, *Redeemers, Bourbons, and Populists,* p. 125.

45. Goodwyn, *Democratic Promise,* p. 304.

46. Woodward, *Tom Watson: Agrarian Rebel,* quoted, p. 220.

47. Lazer Ziff, *The American 1890s: Life and Times of a Lost Generation* (New York, 1966), pp. 93–108.

48. George Arms, et al., eds., *William Dean Howell's Prefaces to Contemporaries 1882–1920* (Gainesville, 1957), p. 38.

49. Ignatius Donnelly, *Caesar's Column: A Story of the Twentieth Century* (Chicago, 1890; reissued 1960).

50. Martin Ridge, *Ignatius Donnelly: The Portrait of a Politician* (Chicago, 1962), pp. 248, 265; Cf. John Patterson, "From Yeoman to Beast: Images of Blackness in Ceasar's Column," *American Studies* 12 (1971):21–31; Allyn B. Forbes, "The Literary Quest for Utopia, 1880–1900," *Social Forces* 6 (1927): 184–85.

51. Henry M. Littlefield, "The Wizard of Oz: Parable on Populism," *American Quarterly* 16 (1964): 47–58.

52. John Hicks, *The Populist Revolt* (Minneapolis, 1931), is the traditional account of this liberal interpretation of populism.

53. Francis Brown, "Three 'Pied Pipers' of the Depression," *New York Times Magazine,* 17 March 1935, in Carl N. Degler, ed., *The New Deal* (Chicago, 1970). Gerald D. Nash, *Organizing America, 1933–1945* (New York, 1979), pp. 37–46.

54. Arthur M. Schlesinger, *The Politics of Upheaval* (New York, 1960), especially chapter 1.

55. Cf. Wallace Stegner, "The Radio Priest and his flock," in Isabel Leighton, ed., *The Aspirin Age, 1919–1941* (New York, 1949), pp. 232–57.

56. Sheldon Marcus, *Father Coughlin: The Tumultuous Life of the Priest of The Little Flower* (New York, 1973): pp. 66–67. Louis B. Ward, *Father Charles E. Coughlin: An Authorized Biography* (Detroit, 1933), pp. 78 ff. Richard D. Lunt, "Agitators: Long, Townsend and Coughlin versus the New Deal—1932 through 1936" (unpublished Masters Thesis, University of New Mexico, 1959), pp. 12, 87–89.

57. Marcus, *Father Coughlin,* quoted p. 73.

58. These eight letters have been reprinted, with an introduction by J. D. Gaydowski, in *The Southern California Quarterly* 52 (1970): 365–82.

59. Abraham Holtzman, *The Townsend Movement: A Political Study* (New York, 1963), pp. 23–24.

60. Lunt, "Agitators," pp. 65–71.

61. Frances Perkins, *The Roosevelt I Know* (New York, 1936), p. 294.

62. Holtzman, *The Townsend Movement,* quoted, p. 28.

63. Harry D. Gideonese, ed., *The Economic Meaning of the Townsend Plan* (Chicago, 1936), p. 24.

64. Hodding Carter, "Huey Long: American Dictator," in Isabel Leighton, ed., *The Aspirin Age, 1919–1941* (New York, 1949), pp. 339–63. Hugh Davis Graham, ed., *Huey Long* (Englewood Cliffs, New Jersey, 1970), offers a good collection of such statements.

65. T. Harry Williams, "The Politics of the Longs," in *Romance and Realism in Southern Politics* (Athens, Ga., 1961), pp. 65–84. Williams, *Huey Long* (New York, 1969).

66. T. Harry Williams, *Huey Long,* pp. 44–45.

67. Huey P. Long, *Every Man a King* (New Orleans, 1933; reissued Chicago, 1964).

68. Williams, *Huey Long,* pp. 726–28.

69. Richard Hofstader, *The Age of Reform* (New York, 1955). Victor Ferkiss, "Populist Influences on American Fascism," *Western Political Quarterly* 10 (1957): 350–73; Oscar Handlin, "American Views of Jews at the Opening of the Twentieth Century," *Publications of the American Jewish Historical Society* 40 (1951): 323–44.

70. Christopher Lasch, "Populism, Socialism, and McGovernism," in *The World of Nations* (New York, 1973), pp. 162–63. The Populists were rehabilitated by numerous authors,

including O. Gene Clanton, *Kansas Populism: Ideas and Men* (Lawrence, 1969); Norman Pollack, *The Populist Response to Industrial America: Midwestern Populist Thought* (Cambridge, 1962); Walter Nugent, *The Tolerant Populists* (Chicago, 1963); Theodore Saloutos, "The Professors and the Populists," *Agricultural History* 40 (1966): 235–54.

71. Robert W. Whitaker, "Populist Views on Opposing Carter," *National Review* 28 (1976): 1182.

72. Robert W. Whitaker, *A Plague on Both Your Houses* (Washington-New York, 1976).

73. Whitaker, *A Plague on Both Your Houses,* pp. 11, 13, 40; the quotation is from p. 7.

74. Kevin Phillips, *The Emerging Republican Majority* (New York, 1969).

75. Michael Novak, *The Rise of the Unmeltable Ethnics* (New York, 1970). Cf. Richard Krickus, *Pursuing the American Dream: White Ethnics and the New Populism* (New York, 1976).

76. Edwin Warner, "The New Populism: Radicalizing the Middle," *Time,* 17 April 1972, p. 27. Peter Barnes, "Populist Rumblings," *New Republic* 166 (1972): 19.

77. Fred Harris, *The New Populism* (Berkeley, 1976), p. 13.

78. Jack Newfield and Jeff Greenfield, *A Populist Manifesto: The Making of a New Majority* (New York, 1972), p. 17.

79. "How Populist is Carter?" *Time,* 2 August 1976, pp. 13–15.

80. Harry Boyte, "Building A New Democracy," *The Progressive* 40 (1976): 16. Simon Lazarus, *The Genteel Populists* (New York, 1974).

10

Conclusion:
Requiem for Populism?

Paul W. Drake
University of Illinois

Perhaps a wave of studies of populism is upon us because historians like to analyze things that are dead. Although a funeral oration for populism may be premature, such movements clearly faded in the 1970s. After electrifying Latin American politics from the 1920s into the 1960s, populists found themselves frustrated, scorned, banned, exiled, and even buried. In 1974 Juan Perón expired after unsuccessfully trying to reunite contradictory social and ideological interests that were no longer so reconcilable as in the Argentina of the 1940s. Luis Echeverría failed in his efforts to revive the Mexican multiclass reform coalition of the 1930s. Fred Harris, Jimmy Carter, and other reformers in the United States evoked feeble responses with their flirtations with the populist spirit of bygone years. In 1979 Víctor Raúl Haya de la Torre finally passed from the scene after half a century as Peru's and Latin America's most enduring populist leader. For the first time in decades, Ecuador held an election in which José María Velasco Ibarra ("Give me a balcony and I will be president") was not a leading candidate. An attempted return to office by Víctor Paz Estenssoro of Bolivian revolutionary fame fell short. Therefore it seems time to perform at least a checkup if not an autopsy on populism.

A diagnosis of the health of Latin America populism partly depends on how the patient is defined. If it is viewed as primarily an outcropping of a persistent Ibero-American patrimonial political culture laced with Weberian strains of charisma and legitimation, then populism may well flourish again throughout the hemisphere. Once the current corps of military dictatorships exhaust their technocratic solutions and repressive arsenals, personalistic leaders may sprout once more to rally the masses behind nationalistic state intervention to reform society and the economy. Conversely, if populism is seen as basically an offspring of unstable economic conditions and class alignments evolving during changing crises of so-called modernization, then its recurrence may be less likely. Classic populism may have run its course in more urbanized, industrialized, politicized countries like Argentina and Chile. By the same logic, it could still be viable in "less-developed" neighbors like Ecuador. However, since scholars remain unsure about the definition, causes, and consequences of populism, it is still problematic whether this volume is dealing with a revival or a relic.

Like *dependency,* the concept of *populism* has been most skillfully elaborated by Latin Americans themselves. The term has principally been used in Latin America, with ample latitude, to refer to three interrelated political patterns. First, *populismo* has been applied to a recognizable style of political mobilization employing recurrent rhetoric and symbols designed to inspire "the people" against their oppressors. This approach relies on a magnetic, paternalistic leader who emphasizes dramatic, emotional appeals. While waving nationalistic banners, he promises immediate psychic and material gratification of the needs of society's underdogs. Second, populism has described a heterogeneous social coalition aimed primarily at the working classes but including and led by significant sectors from the middle or upper strata. The proportional mix of social elements varies from movement to movement, but all tend to be "mass" rather than narrowly "class" constructs. Third, populism has connoted a reformist set of policies tailored to promote development without explosive class conflict. Eschewing unbridled capitalism or socialism, these programs seek national integration. They normally respond to the problems of underdevelopment by expanding state activism to incorporate the workers in a process of accelerated industrialization through ameliorative redistributive measures.[1]

The above three characteristics of Latin American populism are obviously interconnected. Ideally, a charismatic *jefe máximo* generates the cohesive force to weld together a polyclass coalition that compromises on eclectic policies to spread the costs and benefits of development. Presumably, a movement strongly exhibiting all three traits mentioned above would fit within a reasonably acceptable descriptive definition of populism. Such classification is a question of degrees. Other movements might have so-called populistic mobilization, social, or policy proclivities woven in with contradictory tendencies.

Although a definition of populism might be stretched from Argentina through Nebraska to Russia, this essay will focus on Latin American examples while merely noting comparable variations elsewhere. Further case studies such as those in this collection may soon spawn more sophisticated, rigorous, and transferrable conceptualization. Meanwhile, even the rudimentary notion of populism offered here may illuminate some corners of an untidy and murky historical record.

To isolate the species to be examined, certain political animals should be excluded from the populist camp. Varieties of nonpopulist parties would theoretically include those overwhelmingly appealing to one social class, for example the Communists, who focus on the proletariat. By the same token, technocratic or aristocratic parties such as nineteenth-century conservatives and liberals, who do not champion the masses or redistribution from the wealthy to the wretched, would fall outside the populist category. In addition, mainly middle-to-upper-class reform parties, such as the Chilean Radicals, their Argentine namesakes after Hipólito Yrigoyen, the Venezuelan COPEI, and the Colombian Liberals, with little reliance on charismatic leaders, public paternalism, manual laborers, or crusades for nationalistic redemption of the downtrodden, would normally lack the mystique, zest, and scope of populists in and of themselves. Equally unlikely candidates would be primarily pragmatic, clientelistic, aggregative machine parties with tepid mobilization practices and weak social or ideological orientations, such as the Mexican revolutionary party from 1940 to 1970 or the U.S. Democrats and Republicans most of the time. Moderate Argentine or European Socialists would also seldom be branded as populists. Finally, fervently ideological movements, such as Nazis or, again, Communists, would usually be set aside. Since such typologies are anything but airtight, however, all the movements eliminated above could conceivably display some "populistic" symptoms, for example occasional cults of personality. Cutoff points create thorny problems. How personalistic, polyclass, and integratively reformist does a movement have to be to qualify as populist?

Obviously, the three central features of populism proposed here contain serious ambiguities and contradictions. The patrimonial style of campaigning and recruitment conflicts with mass desires for more direct participation. It also clashes with the need to institutionalize the movement within an ongoing party or, more importantly, within the government to deliver on reform promises. The multiclass makeup of the movement builds in friction among disparate groups. Such discord becomes especially likely between the middle and working classes, particularly once the movement takes office and has to allocate rewards among its constituents. Finally, the programmatic commitment to simultaneous industrialism and welfarism leads to difficult tradeoffs and dilemmas. Dependent economies plagued by inflation possess scarce surplus for assuaging competing demands. For these reasons, most populist movements proved more effective out of government than in it.

These three aspects of populism will now be examined, with reference to the chapters in this collection as well as other examples, particularly from Chile. Thereafter the causes and consequences of populism will be probed, with an eye to its historical metamorphoses under changing conditions. In closing, some suggestions for further research will be sketched out.

POPULIST MOBILIZATIONS

A cultural approach to Latin American populism would emphasize the paternalistic bond between the leader and the masses. According to many analysts, this reciprocal but hierarchical relationship grows out of a rural, seignorial, Roman Catholic, Ibero-American heritage of ingrained inequality with at least 500-year-old roots. Theoretically, it can be traced back to the deference paid the crown, viceroys, the church, nobility, and *caciques* in the colonial period. It can be witnessed in mass submission to landowners and *caudillos* in the nineteenth century. From this perspective, there are significant carryovers in political styles from garish nineteenth-century bosses like Juan Manuel de Rosas to flamboyant twentieth-century politicians like Juan Domingo Perón. Although dealing with different political environments, tools, issues, and constituencies, both Argentines capitalized on their personal authority over the poor to claim the presidency from the rich.

After World War I, populist leaders promoted mass mobilization in countries with a largely nonparticipant political culture. Many studies have concluded that workers pouring into the cities could not immediately shed a legacy of enforced social and political subordination to landlords, clergy, generals, and the fortunate few. New urban groups brought habits of coping with authority in from the countryside. Although not passive, many workers often tried to handle their new environment in traditional ways. For example, they attached themselves to protective labor leaders, factory managers, or municipal politicians. This apparent propensity for deferential reliance on patron-client linkages, while hardly unique to Latin America, cropped up in urban as well as rural areas and even in seemingly participatory movements against the status quo.

Although difficult to measure, these cultural-behavorial continuities from the colonial, rural, peasant past to the urban present have been widely noted by students of Latin America. They were allegedly associated with the desire for a charitable state to replicate the authoritarian, condescending relations historically prevailing between the upper and lower social orders. Very little is known about the extent of such attitudes and actions among illiterate (or at least unpublished) rural and urban workers in the opening decades of the twentieth century. Their preference for paternalistic guidance might be assumed from their widespread but seldom articulated support for such leaders. It would be difficult to prove, however, that mass subservience to personalistic authorities sprang mainly from a psycho-cultural impulse to latch on to a generous *patrón* or from an inbred conservative timidity. Rather, such followership might be better explained by quite objective and lucid calculations on the part of deprived social groups. The workers probably realized the odds against more autonomous or radical alternatives and in favor of garnering at least marginal benefits through adherence to bosses. The motives of followers and leaders may have been significantly different. There seems little doubt, however, that most populist politicians believed that the masses desired such a patronizing figure and accordingly offered the workers a fatherly, domineering approach.

Most studies of Latin American populism have found that such an updated *caudillo* was more essential to a movement's dynamism than were class solidarity, ideological purity, or intricate programmatic provisions. These leaders reached down to the masses often because they were alienated from their own higher social sectors. Examples would include the displaced northern elites of Peru forging APRA or unsatisfied professionals, intellectuals, and students founding Democratic Action in Venezuela or socialist movements in Chile. Blakely also shows the Russian masses receiving paternalistic leadership from disgruntled urban intellectuals. The Latin Americans developed a characteristic style of an exalted leader far above the mass level but speaking for the underprivileged. A case in point was Getúlio Vargas casting his image as the "father of the poor." Another rather typical example would be the following quote from a 1941 Socialist Party pamphlet exhorting Chilean rural laborers to worship its populist paladin, Marmaduke Grove:

> . . . this soldier . . .who has not felt a muscle in his face tremble before death . . . who listens to threats of shooting with a smile on his lips, this man . . . made of steel . . . often has the tenderness of a child, when listening to a worker describe his poverty. More than once Grove has dried a tear from his eyes, taking upon his shoulders the misfortune of the humble . . . one ought to read his biography to gather its lessons. . . . . We can see him in this instant, with . . . his clear eyes, hard in order to whip the enemies of proletarian demands and affectionate when shaking the weathered hand of a son of the common people.[2]

In the 1930s the Socialists touted Grove as the savior of the disadvantaged, claiming that his "voice has a humble intonation, a familiar vibration, that evokes in us the voice of the father."[3] A Socialist senator later observed about his party's early years, "If well it is true that the Socialist Party . . . counted upon intellectual values of the highest order, nonetheless its growth was due in the first place to Grove, to that emotional attraction he exercised over the people. . . ."[4] Thus even the Chilean Socialist Party, which evolved over the decades into one of the hemisphere's more radical ideological movements, began life in the 1930s with pronounced populist inclinations.

One danger in emphazing the charismatic quality of populist leadership is that it may explain everything and thus nothing. Bundling together figures such as Bryan, Hitler, Churchill, Perón, and Castro could obscure the profound dissimilarities in the movements they commanded. Although the charismatic ingredient was crucial, it must be understood within the context of the stressful socioeconomic conditions that set the stage for a such a leader, the symbols which allowed him to galvanize available forces, the social groups attracted to his call, the programs supported, and the reactions of his opponents.[5] Rather than merely explaining their populist leaders as charismatic, Navarro and Stein seriously plumb the meaning of that concept. They explore its definition, apply it systematically to the language and symbols used, examine the sources and character of the responses elicited, and probe the political culture and social structure which surrounded that phenomenon. Interestingly, the political rhetoric and rituals of both Eva Perón and Haya de la Torre as well as William Jennings Bryan carried religious overtones. A broader, comparative, in depth analysis of populist oratory and propaganda in Latin America might yield very suggestive findings, especially in the imagery of *el pueblo, el líder,* and their enemies.

Different populists aroused mass followings through divergent means. Some like Perón and Haya were stirring leaders. Others like Vargas and Grove were not. More modern means of communication enhanced populist possibilities. Conniff shows Pedro Ernesto's magnetism based on radio speeches and his image as a *médico bondoso*. Szasz portrays U.S. populists in the 1930s also wooing listeners over the airwaves. Many Latin Americans established their reputation and mystical authority through daring deeds, such as Grove's lightning formation of a twelve day Socialist Republic in 1932, Vargas' seizure of power in 1930, and Perón's resurrection on October 17, 1945. Exile and suffering enhanced Haya's charisma. A few, like Echeverría, were scarcely charismatic at all, though he profited from the institutional aura of his regal office. Symbolic gestures also counted heavily. The story is told in Chile of Arturo Alessandri, the Lion of Tarapacá, mesmerizing and dialoguing with a vast audience of workers during the winter of his 1920 presidential campaign. He lambasted the "oligarchy" as "gilded scoundrels" and praised the masses as "my beloved rabble." When one of the workers hollered that he was cold, Alessandri magnanimously hurled an overcoat from the podium into the crowd. That the mob tore the garment to shreds may say something about the value of populist payoffs. That the coat belonged to someone on the speaker's stand other than Alessandri may say something about the idealism of populists.

Populist leaders used multiple means to build their movements and to reach and hold power. They emphasized elections. This was partly because of democratic convictions. More importantly, winning ballots was one power and means of legitimation that populists wielded more effectively than did the established elites, who relied more on economic and military resources. Populists also resorted to authoritarian means, especially within their own parties or when in office. They were devoted to expanding popular participation but not necessarily through formal, Western democratic mechanisms. Perón, Vargas, Haya, and other populists repeatedly exhibited dictatorial propensities toward their followers and opponents. They apparently favored controlled, paternalistic mobilization of the masses more than uninhibited, pluralistic democratic competition. More important than the political instruments employed was the question of what social groups were included and served by different authoritarian or democratic techniques.

The selection of tactics by populists probably depended less on their philosophical and cultural inclinations than on the realistic options within the political systems they confronted. When hostile ruling classes and their military allies denied full democratic rights to populists, they became more likely to engage in undemocratic behavior themselves. As Blakely says, "Given the autocratic nature of tsarist Russia, populism there was necessarily revolutionary." Although many Latin American populists displayed authoritarian strains, their devotion to electoral contests was striking, especially when adverse armed forces in Peru, Ecuador, Argentina, and other countries refused time and again to let them take or keep offices won through the ballot box. Stymied populists probably did not turn to insurrectionary methods more often because that would have triggered even harsher resistance. As Ellner notes in Venezuela, Brazil, Argentina, and elsewhere, populist reliance on generally moderate means also suggests that their commitment to social reform was overshadowed by their desire to be accepted into the regular rules of the political game. Even within the electoral arena, they rarely demanded extension of the franchise to illiterates, which would have enormously expanded the electorate, especially among peasants. Yet cautious and peaceful means often proved disappointing ways to pursue social change in conservative countries with imbedded elites adamantly opposed to pluralism, equality, or displacement.

Given these constraints, both mobilization and institutionalization constituted double-edged swords for populists. Mobilization raised demands, followers, and claims to a share in political power. It provided legitimacy and a social base for carrying through programs once in office. It also, however, threatened to outrun populists' capacity for control and ability to deliver on promises. As Basurto shows, even populist mobilization launched from the presidential palace rather than from the street corners may spill over the boundaries intended by the leadership. As mass mobilization gains momentum, it can destabilize or capsize populist governments. Elevating worker expectations may overload systems with limited resources so long as populists remain reluctant to attack the privileges of established elites. In most cases, political instability or breakdown resulted not because mass demands were so excessive but rather because elite willingness to grant concessions was so slender. Consequently mobilization, especially at a swift pace, often ignited repression from the upper class, the armed forces, or the insecure middle classes, who came to fear that alignment with the workers was jeopardizing their own well-being. Therefore populists encountered grave difficulties in converting their ability to lift mass expectations and organizations into institutional strength and programmatic achievements through disciplined parties with ongoing access to national decision-making.

Institutionalization also presented opportunities and hazards. Consolidation of a populist movement in a party and, more importantly, into the government offered continuity, sinecures, and spoils. It furnished administrative avenues to recruit and serve more supporters as well as involvement in the drafting and implementation of reform programs. Immersion in standard party structures, coalitions, practices, and government, however, also dissuaded populists from disruptive social activism. Institutionalization could cost the movement its protest credentials, its dynamism, and its followers. Success opened the door to compromise and possible cooptation. As a result, populists frequently behaved more temperately in the corridors of power than on the hustings. They often shifted to the right, as domestic and foreign elites brought pressures to bear. Examples would include the Chilean Popular Front during 1939−41, Democratic Action in Venezuela during 1945−48, and the Peronist government of 1946−55. To reach office from World War I on, it became increasingly necessary to appeal to the workers. But to function effectively and survive once in office, it remained necessary to pacify the controllers of the major means of production, distribution, communication, and coercion. Populist mixtures of social classes and program planks allowed politicians great latitude in switching from leftist campaign rhetoric to conservative administrative behavior. It required impressive political agility to win fervent support from the masses as well as grudging acceptance from the elites. How to enflame enough enthusiasm to propel themselves to power and then govern within tolerated limits once there remained a delicate dilemma. Not only accommodation with elites but also entanglement with the bureaucracy blunted populist reforms. Their skimpy accomplishments in office, however, do not gainsay their enormous contribution to the early political mobilization and education of the masses. After all, it was mainly populists who enshrined issues of foreign domination, oligarchic exploitation, economic underdevelopment, social injustice, and cultural nationalism as the common currency of Latin American politics.

If the paternalistic dynamic between leaders and followers is the key to Latin American populism, then it remains unclear why such movements blossomed after World War I and decayed by the 1970s. Perhaps the current hiatus is mainly explained by a cycle of conservative repression. Maybe the generation of populists who emerged in the interwar years have simply spent their energies. Another explanation might be that the political culture and consciousness of many Latin Americans has changed from the twenties to the seventies, leaving the masses less susceptible to the charms of populists. Or it could be that charismatic mobilization was never really the crux of the matter, especially by itself. An alternative hypothesis would be that the essense of populism was its adaptation to certain socioeconomic imperatives widespread during the first half of the twentieth century but no longer prevailing in the major countries. If so, greater attention must be paid to the social content and ramifications of populism.

POPULIST COALITIONS

That Latin American populism was multiclass does not mean it was classless. It had some class content in that certain groups were emphasized (for example, urban labor) while others tended to be excluded (the traditional oligarchy), as groups if not as individuals. Populists denounced the old upper class and imperialists as negative references for the masses. In many ways, this approach to recruitment and coalitions resembled the Popular Front formula of the Comintern in the 1930s, which recommended broad reform alliances among peasants, workers, the middle class, and progressive elements of the national bourgeoisie.

In countries lacking prior middle-class revolutions or massive urban concentrations of industrial workers, reform movements had to reach beyond a narrow middle-class or proletarian base. The vast majority of the population still dwelled in the countryside, but mobilization there encountered less organization and literacy among the workers and more resistance among the landed elites. Arising mainly in the mushrooming cities, populists tried to unite defectors from the upper class and professional ranks with "manual and intellectual workers." They concentrated on fusing blue-collar *obreros* with white-collar *empleados,* known jointly as *trabajadores.*

As Conniff has ably argued, it was mainly this urban orientation that distinguished Latin American from U.S. or, to a lesser extent, Russian populism. Szasz shows that U.S. populism also emphasized charismatic leaders, multiclass coalitions, and state interventionist economic programs, albeit not for import-substituting industrialization; rural mobilization proved far more effective among the family farmers of the U.S. than amidst the latifundia and minifundia of Latin America. In Brazil, Chile, and their neighbors, it required a certain threshold of economic growth, urbanization, labor specialization, education, and social articulation for populism to emerge. As "the metropolitan revolution" accelerated in the twentieth century, so grew the pool of mobilizable groups amenable to populist appeals. Therefore Latin American populists supported induced industrialization not only as an economic policy attractive to their consituents but also as a means of expanding their constituency. However, the swelling size and demands of urban labor made the accommodation of diverse class interests increasingly difficult. As Basurto demonstrates, it became an extremely delicate balancing act to sustain polyclass movements in dependent economies with sparse resources. Although populism often surfaced during economic crises, it needed a period of relative growth to satisfy its components without extracting unacceptable sacrifices from encrusted elites.

Almost as important to determining the trajectory of a populist movement as the support of the middle and lower classes was the response of the upper strata to these new political contenders. Traditional landowners, industrialists, and financiers might try to accommodate or squash such a mass movement. It might be argued that populism ultimately served the interests of established domestic and foreign elites by deflecting class antagonisms into social coalitions behind mild incremental reforms. This suggests that upper-class flexibility and cooptation preserved more of their privileges than overt intransigence might have. Few ruling groups, however, perceived populism as a harmless nostrum or safety valve during its heyday. If most populists were manipulating the masses on behalf of the bourgeoisie, most members of that dominant class failed to appreciate it. Although some Latin American elites were sophisticated enough to try to cooperate with and channel populist movements, most fought tenaciously against them. The Peruvian military's decades of resistance to *Aprismo,* the Argentine aristocracy's hatred for *Peronismo,* and the Brazilian rightists' crusade against the political descendants of Vargas show privileged groups reacting to populism as a threat. Populists sought to be cut into the system by wringing concessions from the upper class rather than overthrowing it. Nevertheless, most elites balked at that challenge. Even more conciliatory members of the upper class proved far more willing to cede political offices to populist leaders of the masses than to surrender economic or social benefits to their followers.

For example in Chile, upper-class leaders during the first two decades of the twentieth century responded to middle and lower-class ferment in the cities and mines with outrage and troops. They fought desperately against the election of liberal populist Alessandri in 1920. The more far-sighted rightist leaders, however, came to realize that his ascension to the presidency might mollify the workers symbolically without producing drastic substantive reforms. By the 1930s, those elites supported their old nemesis Alessandri as president in preference to more reformist options, which had arisen to the left of him. Those new political forces formed the Popular Front, which again aroused passionate resistance from traditional elites. After the Front took office in 1938, however, some conservative groups learned to live with it and toned down its reformist content. More adept rightists saw the virtue of incorporating the most articulate urban groups into a subordinate role in the political system to avert open conflict. Many showed similar flexibility toward the Christian Democrats in the 1960s. The growing radicalism of the left, which issued in the Popular Unity government and unprecedented mass mobilization of the 1970s, however, convinced besieged elites that confrontation was preferable to conciliation. As a result, they opted for the destruction and prohibition of mass politics, whether of a socialist or populist variety.

In economies heavily reliant on foreign trade and capital, populists also clashed with or succumbed to external interests, particularly from the U.S. For example, the U.S. government evinced hostility toward the nationalism of the *Apristas* in the 1930s, the Peronists in the 1940s, and Echeverría in the 1970s. Over time, however, U.S. officials apparently came to evaluate most populists as preferable to more radical alternatives. They also managed to win over some leaders like Haya and Betancourt, partly through antifascism during World War II and anticommunism during the Cold War.

The Latin American middle classes provided leaders and followers for populist movements. Doctors, dentists, lawyers, engineers, architects, and teachers staffed the upper ranks. Intellectuals in Russia as well as Latin America blended diverse ideologies to concoct populist platforms. Idealistic university students helped knit together middle-lower-class coalitions by supporting trade unions, establishing "Popular Universities" for worker education and politicization, and mounting demonstrations against conservative governments. Bureaucrats provided backing and implementation for populist programs. Particularly in countries with scant industrial opportunities and numerous economic command posts monopolized by foreigners, the middle classes sought mobility and security through political employment and an expanding state. Although often serving as a bulwark against change, the military also generated populist precursors and leaders, such as the *tenentes* in Brazil, Grove and Carlos Ibáñez in Chile, Luis Sánchez Cerro and

Juan Velasco Alvarado in Peru, military "socialists" in Bolivia, and Perón in Argentina.

Reflecting their ambiguous and precarious station in society, the "middle sectors" played contradictory but crucial roles in the emergence and later submergence of populism. Professionals and white-collar employees were more likely to back such movements in the early years as battering rams to open up the upper-class system to their participation. After the interwar years, the middle strata, especially the upper-middle-class professionals, became increasingly concerned with defending hard-won gains. Many became more worried about encroachments from below than about denials from above. That the middle class later resisted mounting working-class demands, however, should not obscure their contributions to populism.

The primary target of populist movements was wage laborers (Vargas' *trabalhadores,* Perón's *descamisados*), especially in the mines and cities. Because of legal and social restrictions on their political capabilities, workers naturally turned to leaders from the higher social spheres. By the turn of the century, the presence, organization, and protests of the urban working groups in politics opened new possibilities. Strikes and demonstrations by laborers preceded populist movements, but workers seldom became the originators or directors of such parties. Labor's increasing visibility as a political issue (the so-called social question) and availability as a political resource presented both threats and opportunities to the upper and middle classes.

Populists transmitted benefits to workers and, in turn, thrived on their support. They usually outbid more radical alternatives through their personalism, ability to attract multiclass allies for the labor movement, and concrete, clientelistic rewards for the faithful. Appeals to the practical benefits of patron-client linkages with parties and governments, to deferential loyalty, to liberalism, to nationalism, to socialism, and to class conflict and ideological radicalism all evoked favorable responses among varying segments of the working class. To the extent that populist labor movements depended on the idealism or opportunism of leaders from above worker ranks, it indicated the frailty of the handicapped and mistreated lower classes as political actors, a situation obviously not unique to Latin America. If nothing else, populists at least eased the chronic repression of workers and allowed them greater freedom to organize and press grievances. Moreover, populism was not merely paternalistic or manipulative. Its vigor also demonstrated the determination of workers to express dissatisfactions with and through the prevailing political system. As organizers and voters, laborers rewarded those who empathized with their problems and tried to better their lot. Both followers and leaders used each other to their own, and sometimes mutual, advantage.

Most Latin American populist movements neglected rural laborers both electorally and materially, notwithstanding rhetorical dedication to the tillers of the soil. Indeed, populists usually promoted industrialization and welfare reforms for the urban middle and working classes at the expense of the rural poor. They often won upper-class acquiescence for urban modernization by not disturbing elite sanctuaries in the countryside. Some populists, like Rómulo Betancourt in Venezuela and Jorge Gaitán in Colombia, did not ignore rural labor. However, populists found most farmers and peasants still tightly controlled by traditional landowners, hard to organize, and typically rather localized in their outlook and conservative in their political consciousness. As Blakely points out in Russia, "From all indications, the peasant remained essentially a monarchist, not a republican; he just wanted a good tsar in place of the one reigning." Nevertheless, the need to expand the base of populism over time, especially in the face of competitive reform movements, increasingly added a rural focus to political mobilization. By the 1960s, heightened attention to rallying the work force in the countryside strained the crowded and brittle political systems of Latin America to the breaking point, as seen in Chile and Brazil. Basurto also shows in Mexico that rural and urban groups and issues remained very difficult to reconcile.

Particularly by the end of World War II, women also became a distinctive and significant component of populist movements, notably in Argentina, Chile, and Colombia. Dynamic leaders like the wife of Perón and the daughter of Gustavo Rojas Pinilla erupted on the national scene, as they had earlier in the U.S. Although these female leaders called into question the paternalistic essence of populism, they failed to establish lasting movements independent from their male originators. Navarro argues the "Evita cannot be studied isolated from Perón because her leadership originated in him and it was explicitly exercised as a complement of his." Moreover, many women, particularly those from the middle and upper classes, remained highly mobilizable around traditional issues against populism, as seen in their support for reactionary military takeovers in Brazil and Chile.

Although new social groups and concerns became the lifeblood of populism, those movements also arose through appeals to more venerable conflicts in Latin American politics, particularly regionalism. APRA took wing not only in the name of the oppressed masses but also as a defender of northern Peru against the Lima aristocracy. Reformers in Chile spoke not only for white-collar employees and blue-collar workers but also for the far northern and southern provinces against the oligarchy in and around Santiago. Ecuadorean populism became entangled with the historic cleavage between Quito and Guayaquil. Conniff uncovers populism arising in a Rio de Janeiro resentful of declining national influence. U.S. populism also sprang from regionalist roots. Outlying zones, like the lower classes, felt exploited by the central elites, especially as capitalist modernization further concentrated wealth and power in the historic nucleus of the country. From Alessandri to Echeverría, a constantly repeated and virtually never fulfilled populist promise was "decentralization." This was contradictory because populist expansion of industry and the state helped assure growing dominance by the national core.

Most scholars have interpreted populists as creating and managing such diffuse coalitions mainly in order to further social control and integration rather than conflict. Both Stein and Navarro depict leaders clearly manipulating followers in part to shore up the essense of the social hierarchy. However, as Navarro indicates with labor initiatives under Perón, Ellner with wildcat strikes under Betancourt, and Basurto with rural land seizures under Echeverría, populists also sometimes saw their followers outdistance them in both tactics and demands.

POPULIST PROGRAMS

Given their multiclass composition, populist movements have naturally been ideologically eclectic. To provide a broad umbrella for diverse social sectors, they have stressed nationalism. Populists extolled the virtures of the common people as the essence of national identity while denouncing "antinational" cultural and economic elites as well as foreign imperialists. They espoused nationalism in countries still in search of nationhood. Seeking to close the gap between the rich and the poor internationally and domestically at the same time, Latin American *populistas* had both a nationalist and a class orientation. At the same time, populism borrowed foreign elements, such as campaign techniques from European fascists like Benito Mussolini and program planks from European ideologists like British and French socialists.

Their ideological elasticity represented adjustments to Latin American political-cultural traditions, social structure, and economic underdevelopment. Populists sought a path in between capitalism and communism—a "Third Way"—to national development. In that middle ground, leaders like Haya, Grove, and Betancourt mainly adapted socialist ideas and slogans to countries they believed lacked sufficient elaboration of industry and the proletariat to embrace fullblown socialism. For most, this diluted Marxism promised to preempt more militant socialism; for a few, it offered a preliminary step toward more combative socialist efforts. Not only in Latin America but also in the U.S. and especially Russia, populism had socialist overtones and could provide the seedbed for later socialist movements.

Populists' programs, like their social coalitions, resembled the premises of the Popular Front, especially in the 1930s in Chile, Mexico, and Venezuela. In this view, Latin America needed a national, reformist, industrial surge forward, even with controlled participation by foreign capital, before any leap toward socialism was conceivable. Indeed, many populists hoped that state capitalism with the central government encouraging private enterprise in the development of a mixed economy and welfare society would preclude rather than lead to state socialism.

Along with socialism, populists also wove in strands from anarchism, liberalism, and even corporatism. Depending on the historical period, populism and corporatism could be compatible or in conflict. From the 1930s to the 1950s, many corporatist-functionalist proposals punctuated the programs of Lázaro Cárdenas, Haya, Perón, and other populists. They referred to the need to build a new state structure composed of functional groups more than autonomous and competive individuals, classes, and parties. By incorporating the masses and elites into national governing processes through officially sanctioned interest group organizations, such inclusionary corporatism could provide social representation and control during industrialization, or so its advocates claimed. In between liberalism and socialism, such absorptive state corporatism promised "controlled mobilization" of awakening working-class groups before they became more powerful independent forces. Both corporatism and populism purported to be integrative and multiclass. Both offered paternalistic approaches to encapsulating the workers into a program of planned modernization. Both sought adjustments in the traditional order rather than its destruction. In contrast to corporatism, populism was more effective in the opposition than in the government. Populism was also more suited to arousing than institutionalizing lower-class activism, more of an offensive strategy for the middle and working classes than a defensive strategy for the ruling elites, aimed more at the unorganized masses than at occupational interest groups, and more concerned with social welfare and redistribution than simply technocratic economic growth. In the interwar years, populism was seen as an instigator of disorder, corporatism as an instrument of order. Nevertheless, once in office, populist leaders sometimes adopted corporatist mechanisms to institutionalize their followers in functional and sectoral groups linked to the state. By the same token, cooptive corporatists sometimes used populist appeals to enroll workers in government-certified interest organizations. This interplay offered one way of solving the tension between mobilization and institutionalization.

As Conniff has pointed out, both redistributive, democratic, populist and technocratic, authoritarian, corporatist currents could be found coursing through the same movement. As urbanization and industrialization progressed from the 1920s into the 1960s, these two political tendencies increasingly came into conflict. As the stakes rose, populism came to be seen more and more as a harbinger of inflation and anarchy rather than an integrative means of social control. Corporatism came to be seen as an exclusionary alternative for controlled demobilization rather than mobilization. Corporatism evolved into a model for neocapitalist growth for endangered elites by suppressing already assertive rather than just newly emergent lower-class competitors. No longer viewed as a conservative means for orderly inclusion of new elements, corporatism became a rationale for dictators to clamp down on mass participation and demands.[6]

Whatever their ideological inspiration, populist programs tended toward national integration. Conceptually, their approach differed from conservative strategies, which explicitly favored the capitalist elites' accumulation at the expense of the working classes. It also departed from revolutionary strategies that attempted to replace the bourgeoisie with the workers and peasants. Instead, populists tried to subsidize both property-owners and laborers, especially in the cities. They sought to conciliate the elites while gradually incorporating the urban masses into participation and benefits. They attempted to share the costs of development, with a rising proportion to be paid by wealthier natives and foreigners. Social welfare became almost as high a priority as material growth, both under state auspices.

Import-substituting industrialization served as a mild form of economic nationalism and as a response to spiralling urbanization. It did not live up to populist expectations for creating greatly improved national independence, employment, and abundance. Nevertheless, it did temporarily reconcile the interests of urban elites, middle classes, and workers without threatening the structure of power and privilege in the countryside or the external sector. Only in times of relative prosperity, however, did it prove possible to synchronize simultaneous industrialism and welfarism. Populists found it necessary to make tradeoffs, usually in favor of growth over redistribution. Economies heavily dependent on foreign trade and capital inhibited populist policies. Protected industrialization repeatedly led to balance of payments disequilibria, which required stabilization measures inimical to expansive, redistributive domestic programs. Populism sired inflation, whether in the 1940s in Chile or the 1970s in Mexico. The incumbent international economic constraints then forced the sacrifice of worker welfare. [7]

Populist social reforms—higher wages, stronger unions, better housing, improved health, social security, education, and so forth—broke important new ground even though they fell far short of campaign promises. While shying away from necessary structural changes, populists captivated the masses not only with dashing slogans and psychic payoffs but also with concrete benefits well in excess of those delivered by most other political options. For example, Conniff describes Pedro Ernesto in Rio using the wherewithal made available by recovery from the depression to hand over significant material rewards to his followers; this helped make him and the government effective substitutes for past urban charity dispensers to the poor. Such substantive achievements, however fleeting, often established a positive historical memory, which froze mass loyalty to populist leaders for many years therefter, as seen in Brazil and Argentina. The accomplishments as well as the charisma of populists often shone brighter in contrast with the reactionary regimes that frequently succeeded them.

POPULIST CAUSES, TIMING, AND CONSEQUENCES

The following hypotheses about the structural determinants of Latin American populism are based largely on the Chilean and Argentine cases. It appears that the failures and dislocations of tardy and dependent capitalist development, rather than its absence, tended to produce populism. Stimulated by the growth of the export economy in the latter decades of the nineteenth century, urban modernization began generating the necessary mobilizable mass and socioeconomic issues for populism to take hold in the opening decades of the twentieth century. Urbanization outstripped industrialization. Fluctuations in the international economy caused disruptions in local production and state finances which helped spawn populist movements. When raw material-producing economies were jolted by market forces beyond local control, openings appeared for mass mobilization against traditional upper-class, laissez-faire policies. Populism burst forth earlier in the more modernized U.S. when the 1890s depression sparked protests in regions slighted by industrialization; those dissenters felt exploited by a new breed of monopoly capitalists and their institutions, as Szasz explains. Similar disturbances in the increasingly pervasive world economy occurred with World War I and Alessandri in Chile, the 1930s depression and Haya in Peru and Vargas in Brazil, and World War II and Perón in Argentina. In this sense, populism constituted a reaction against expanding and unstable capitalism. It was perhaps analogous to peasant revolts in many parts of the world against the destruction of local modes of production, labor practices, and folkways by the onslaught of capitalist appropriation, concentration, and routinization. Those sectors of Latin American society first and most affected by intensifying capitalist changes were usually in the cities. They were most attracted to populist movements, which promised to revitalize indigenous cultural values and control over the economy and society. Groups disadvantaged and alienated by modern urban, oligopolistic capitalism and foreign penetration looked to the state to restore the protection and cohesion of older communities. Because these movements arose out of reactions against capitalist dislocations and abuses, however, does not mean that they were coherently anticapitalist. Whether for elites seeking a new social base for their shaken authority or for workers demanding a stake in the system, populism only promised modifications to cushion the shocks of capitalist growth.

Latin American populism usually emerged earliest in those countries most advanced in export growth, urbanization, literacy, and light industrialization—notably Argentina and Chile. It became both a reaction against the industrial systems of the developed West and a drive for industrialization at home. It aimed to improve production by the nation as well as consumption by the middle and working classes. Populism constituted a protest by countries on the periphery of the global economy and by marginal groups within those countries. The irony of populism was that the very processes of partial urbanization and industrialization to which that political phenomenon initially responded and then helped promote later inhibited its continuation.

Taking a cue from Conniff and Basurto, it might be worthwhile to consider notions of "early," "classic," and "late" populism. Without being mechanistic, it can be argued that the timing of appropriate conditions for these types of populism varied from country to country. In the opening decades of the twentieth century, Latin America remained an overwhelmingly agrarian area. Highly aristocratic, narrow political systems still dominated. Many in the lower and middle classes were politically ignored or repressed at relatively low cost to government authority. Most societies lacked strong interest group organizations, solid unions, or mass parties. As the strains of contemporary capitalist and urban growth began eroding traditional upper-class hegemony, populist precursors emerged in the larger cities and more prosperous countries. These might be called the early or liberal populists. Although attracting some labor backing, they relied on disaffected elites and the emergent middle classes. They generally limited their reform promises to legalistic democratization for the literate few. Admittedly an important first step, such juridical changes made little impact on the economy or society. In retrospect, probably the major contribution of the early populists, like Yrigoyen in Argentina and Alessandri in Chile, was to pioneer a personalistic style of campaigning invoking mass support at the national level, thus opening political possibilities for the next generation.

During the 1930s and 1940s, the classic populists appeared. The most outstanding figures include Haya, Grove, Cárdenas, Betancourt, Gaitán, and Perón. Far more than the early populists, these leaders mobilized broad segments of the urban masses behind programs enlivened by selected socialist ideas and slogans. The early radicalism of some members of the APRA in Peru, the Cárdenas movement in Mexico, the AD in Venezuela, and the Popular Front in Chile should not be lost in the haze of hindsight. Moreover, these movements saw themselves as bound together in favor of social reform for workers, electoral democracy, and continental ("Indo-American") nationalism against imperialism and fascism. These sentiments were expressed during the First Latin American Congress of Leftist Parties hosted in Santiago in 1940 by the Chilean Socialists; major participants included APRA, AD, and the official Revolutionary Party of Mexico.[8]

Populism took hold in several countries as a coherent response to the acceleration of industrialization, social differentiation, and urbanization. Populists reflected and fueled those pressures by promising tandem welfare measures and protected industrial growth. Although divided, most leaders of the upper classes would still doubtless have preferred to preserve the orderly arrangements of the past without the intrusion of these mass movements. To many reform leaders and even some established elites, however, continued exclusion of the urban middle and working classes soon appeared more costly than gradual incorporation. Strikes, protests, and espousal of radical ideologies by some laborers made populism look preferable to numerous politicians. Into the 1950s in many countries, this accommodationist, integrationist strategy was tenable. It did not require frontal assaults on domestic capitalists, latifundia, or the vital foreign sector. For a time, populist policies often satisfied, in varying degrees, manufacturers with tariffs and credit; agriculturalists with expanding urban markets and continued control over the rural workforce; the middle class with nationalistic state growth, employment, and social security; and the more skilled urban workers with consumer, welfare, and union benefits superior to those accorded other lower-class groups. These compromises postponed showdowns over scarce resources so long as the relatively easy stage of replacing consumer goods from abroad lasted and so long as political institutionalization kept pace with mobilization. At the same time, structural barriers to autonomous development and social equality remained intact.

By the 1950s and 1960s, the prospects for multiclass populism dimmed. Significant populists continued to stride forth, including Paz Estenssoro in Bolivia; Vargas, Quadros, Brizola, and Goulart in Brazil; Ibáñez and some Christian Democrats in Chile; and Velasco Ibarra in Ecuador. Even such prominent leaders, however, encountered mounting difficulties sustaining their political momentum, holding their coalitions together, and putting through programs. Import-substituting industrialization began running into bottlenecks in many countries. Relative industrial stagnation and acute inflation set in amidst continued perplexing reliance on volatile international commodity and credit markets. The proliferation of urban dwellers and politically relevant actors, which had given birth to populism, continued and strained the fragile economy's capacity for absorption. Added to the demands raised earlier by labor and reformers were expectations from peasants, rural-urban migrants, and women. Mobilization began outpacing institutionalization. In response to changing conditions, some populists, like Haya and Betancourt, shifted to the right and therby became more acceptable to native and foreign elites. Others, notably in Peru and Venezuela, moved leftward from the mother party and even formed guerrilla spinoffs. In most of the hemisphere, populists were outflanked. Both rightists and leftists began denouncing each other as excessive burdens on an allegedly cramped and overextended state and economy. While the lower classes became less satisfied with minor concessions, the upper and middle classes became less tolerant of social reform.

Late populists in the 1970s included Echeverría and Perón. They found it extremely difficult to revitalize the populist alliances and programs of earlier days. Such an approach proved ever more inadequate to contend with the social pluralism and conflicts that years of modernization and populist policies had nurtured. As what Basurto labels "the network of entrenched interests" multiplied and solidified, the space for maneuvering in the political arena shrank. The cruel arithmetic of a zero-sum game seemed to be squeezing the possibilities of consensus or compromise. Despite cultural continuities, paternalism proved less satisfying to growing numbers of workers. To many in the Latin American upper and middle classes, it appeared that reformers were moving leftward, allowing radicals to get out of hand, and losing control over the masses. To these elites, the perceived price of including the masses—rising wages, inflation, property transfers, and even social displacement (the spectre of Cuba and Chile)—now appeared greater than the risks of enforced exclusion. Consequently, under severe economic and social pressures, the armed forces outlawed populism in most of Latin America by the mid-1970s. Whether these recent efforts at authoritarian, corporatist exclusion of the workers will be more successful than past attempts at democratic, populist inclusion remains very doubtful.

Whatever the future holds, both the right and the left have condemned populism in Latin America. Indeed, their complaints against populists have changed little in fifty years. From the 1920s to the 1970s, conservatives have repeatedly lashed populists as demagogic agitators who spur excessive mass expectations, fuel inflation, frighten domestic and foreign capital, and engender political instability. Meanwhile, leftists have excoriated populists as charlatans who dupe the masses into supporting palliative reforms that subtly preserve the existing hierarchy of power and privilege. As early as 1920 the Worker's Socialist Party of Chile warned that Alessandri's election signified "the ascension to power of a new oligarchy deceiving the working masses with false promises of a false evolutionism that tries to obtain the support of the working classes in order to become their masters tomorrow."[9] One cause of rightist and leftist discontent has been that populists have drawn support from both extremes to themselves. Social scientists have echoed these criticisms of populism, pointing out that the main failure has been not solving the structural problems of underdevelopment.

All the critics are correct that populism has failed. It did not even deliver on its own moderate promises of integrated economic and social modernization through relatively democratic means. It is unclear, however, what have been and are the preferable and viable alternatives. There is no convincing case that rightwing, coercive, technocratic, military or civilian regimes have been more efficient in providing political development, economic growth, or social justice. Neither is there much persuasive evidence that, in the absence of populism, socialist governments with coherent and realizable programs for development would have leapt to power.

Populism, like muddling through, is at least a relatively humane answer to the question of what to do until the unlikely social revolution comes along. Perhaps Latin Americanists have imposed excessive standards of dedicated leadership, mass participation, class coherence, ideological consistency, and programmatic deliverance on reform movements in the hemisphere. Glancing at Europe or the United States would hardly convince a neutral observer that personalistic politicians, contradictory class alliances, patchwork ideologies, and programmatic shortcomings are unique to Latin America. Although appearing in distinctive forms in particular national settings, populism is scarcely a disease and by no means confined to Latin America. Critics have been so harsh partly because populists have promised so much in an area where the needs of the majority are so severe and the likelihood of remedies so limited by domestic and international constraints.

While populists have contributed little to the needed structural transformation of Latin America, it would be ahistorical to deny the advances they have fostered. They furthered political participation, democratic rights, unionization, industrialization, and welfare reforms for the urban workers and especially middle classes. Even when they failed to reach power, their proposals were often enacted by other administrations. As Basurto indicated, because reforms such as those by Cárdenas paved the way to continued domination by domestic and foreign capitalists does not mean the reforms themselves were necessarily reactionary or intended at the time to lead to the conservative outcomes they did. The interesting historical questions are what were the motivations of the populists and the reactions of their opponents in the era, how were their movements transformed by countervailing interests, and how might the results have been different?

Even granted that Latin American populism has not aspired to revolutionary changes, why has it failed on its own terms? Populist parties often lacked the intellectual rigor and institutional durability to bring their movements to fruition. With their patron-client connections, personalism, and heterogeneity, they proved particularly prone to vitiating compromises, cooptation, opportunism, factionalism, and fragmentation. Witness the frustration of APRA, the meteoric but ephemeral careers of Gaitán and Quadros, the easy dismantling of Brazilian parties in the 1960s, or even the weak party organizations created by U.S. and Russian populists. Not only the structural contexts but also the internal structures of populist movements merit further investigation.

RESEARCH NEEDS

Now populism is under attack not only as a political phenomenon but also as a social science concept. It has fallen into disrepute as a movement because of its past failures and its current repression. It has been called into question as a construct because it seems too fuzzy and too culturally and nationally bound to serve comparative studies. It seems likely to survive as an analytical category with greater vitality the more it can address socioeconomic or structural features and variables that will give it cross-national relevance. Therefore students of populism should probably concentrate on the societal conditions that gave rise to and set limits on various varieties of populism. They should examine intensively the social composition, program, and consequences of these movements. Inserting political history more deeply into social and economic history offers the best hope of building a foundation for improved conceptualization and comparisons.

As the tentativeness and oversimplifications of this essay reveal, more in depth case studies are needed before further attempts are made at generalizations. Following the thrust of the chapters in this collection, perhaps the concept of populism should be refined first by focusing on the most universally accepted major examples to establish a baseline. Probably the Argentine, Brazilian, Bolivian, Peruvian, and Venezuelan cases are the richest.

The next candidates for special scrutiny might be precursors and neglected movements. Looking back into the first two decades of the twentieth century at early labor organizations and activities, rural and urban *caciquismo,* and the underrated influence of anarchism-anarchosyndicalism might yield valuable insights. One object for dissection could be the Democrat Party of Chile, a nineteenth-century clientelistic amalgam of middle sectors, artisans, and workers that incubated most later reform movements in that country. Conniff's treatment of urban mayors in Brazil could be applied elsewhere, for example to Buenos Aires and Guayaquil. In all cases, can the rise and fall of populism somehow be correlated with shifting international economic forces and their impact on the domestic political economy?

Looking at the three central features of Latin American populism, the mobilization style might be better understood through crafting serious biographies of the leaders, both collectively and individually. Their associations, thinking, rhetoric, and actions should be placed in the context of their upbringing and social affiliations. Haya, Cárdenas, Perón, Velasco Ibarra, Betancourt, and others cry for sophisticated treatment. Those still alive deserve in depth interviewing. More importantly, their tactics and behavior might be better explained through more penetrating analysis of the formal and informal political systems and "rules of the game" within which they operated.

In terms of social composition, the field needs critical and quantitative breakdowns of the followers, adversaries, and beneficiaries of populist movements. Beyond the leadership's claims to represent "the people," which people were in fact involved and why? The more specific and measured class analysis becomes, the more difficult it will be to sustain, for example in determining which precise social groups were best served by a particular movement's composition or program. Research from the bottom up might be especially fruitful, surveying popular culture as Stein does and anchoring it with oral history. Did the masses really prefer paternalistic appeals and moderate reformist programs? If so, which groups within the lower classes and why? More research is particularly desirable on instances when Latin American workers took matters in their own hands. Under what conditions and from what occupational sectors did leaders from the working class turn out to be more militant than those from farther up the social pyramid? What circumstances caused populism to deter more combative labor politics or to breed greater worker radicalism over time? Reform movements did not simply flow from the top down, and the dynamic interaction between followers and leaders deserves more attention. Further investigations could also be conducted into the political roles of women and of different occupational groups within the middle strata. Since populism in the long run often served the interest of the dominant class, why did so many elites battle against it for so many years? Were there significant variations in upper-class responses, perhaps depending on their production sectors, historical experiences, or ideological formations? The reactions of foreign powers to populist movements also warrant additional study.

243

Finally, more microscopic examination of the origins and impacts of populist programs under varying economic circumstances would be welcome. When are growth and redistribution compatible? How are decisions made about tradeoffs among policy preferences and competing segments of a populist coalition? Do different proportions of class mixtures among leaders as well as followers tend to produce different agendas and results? To what extent are the developmental strategies, social makeup, and leadership character of populist movements inextricably linked and immutable?

Can populism be readapted to fit the changing conditions of the 1980s and beyond? Although it seems unlikely, perhaps slight modifications in the social-political orientation of leaders, followers, and programs might produce a resurgence, especially if improving economic conditions cleared more space for experimentation. One facet of populism which might reappear would be the charismatic or patrimonial leadership style, which could serve multiple purposes and movements. As democracy returns to Latin America in myriad forms, any populist reincarnation seems destined to have different meanings, for different groups, with different reverberations and consequences, under different conditions than in previous decades. The ingenuity of Latin American politicians in devising temporary solutions to the crises of underdevelopment and in breathing new life into ostensibly moribund institutions and approaches should never be underestimated. At the same time, many Latin Americans are groping for new political models or combinations, with populism apparently bankrupt, bureaucratic authoritarianism repugnant to the vast majority, and socialism still blocked by awesome vested interests. To speculate further about the dubious future of populism, however, requires a more thorough comprehension of its past.

Notes

1. To avoid repetition, let it merely be noted that this conclusion is founded on the basic literature on populism cited in the notes and bibliography for Conniff's introduction, especially DiTella, Weffort, Germani, Ianni, Véliz, Cardoso and Faletto, Ionescu and Gellner, Newton, Pike and Stritch, and Malloy. It also owes a heavy debt to Charles W. Anderson, *Politics and Economic Change in Latin America* (Princeton, 1967); Guillermo A. O'Donnell, *Modernization and Bureaucratic-Authoritarianism* (Berkeley, 1973); Howard J. Wiarda, *Politics and Social Change in Latin America: The Distinct Tradition* (Amherst, 1974); and Barrington Moore Jr., *Social Origins of Dictatorship and Democracy* (Boston, 1966). It is further informed by the chapters in this collection and the fundamental secondary literature footnoted for each. Finally and above all, this conclusion draws

extensively on my own book *Socialism and Populism in Chile* and the bibliography referred to therein.

2. Partido Socialista, *Cartilla sindical campesina* (Santiago, 1941), pp. 5—7.

3. *Acción,* No. 1 (Santiago, October, 1933), p. 1.

4. Alejandro Chelén Rojas, *Trayectoria del socialismo* (Buenos Aires, 1967), p. 85.

5. Rafael Quintero, "Preliminares de una critica sobre el llamado 'velasquismo'," Quito, 1979.

6. Philippe C. Schmitter, "Still the Century of Corporatism?" in Pike and Stritch, pp. 85–131. Also see my "Corporatism and Functionalism in Modern Chilean Politics," *Journal of Latin American Studies* (May 1978), pp. 83–116 and the further literature cited there.

7. Thomas E. Skidmore, "A Case Study in Comparative Public Policy: The Economic Dimensions of Populism in Argentina and Brazil," *The New Scholar*, No. 7 (1979), pp. 129–66.

8. Partido Socialista, *Primer congreso de los partidos democráticos de latino-américa* (Santiago, 1940).

9. Luis Vitale, *Historia del movimiento obrero* (Santiago, 1962), pp. 12–19, 40–64.

Contributors

JOHN D. WORTH (Ph.D. Stanford University) is professor of history at Stanford and the author of several books on Brazil, including *Minas Gerais in the Brazilian Federation, 1889–1937* (1977).

DAVID TAMARIN (Ph.D. University of Washington) is visiting assistant professor of history at the University of Oregon.

MARYSA NAVARRO (Ph.D. Columbia University) is professor of history at Dartmouth College. Her most recent publication is a biography of Evita Perón.

MICHAEL L. CONNIFF (Ph.D. Stanford University) is associate professor of history at the University of New Mexico and author of *Urban Politics in Brazil: The Rise of Populism, 1925–1945* (1981).

JORGE BASURTO (Doctorate, University of Paris and Autonomous National University of Mexico-UNAM) is professor of political and social sciences at the UNAM and he has been a coordinator of the Center for Historical Studies of the Mexican Labor Movement. He is author of *El proletariado industrial en México* (1975) and *El conflicto internacional en torno al petroleo de México* (1977).

STEVE STEIN (Ph.D. Stanford University) is associate professor of history at SUNY-Stony Brook and author of *Populism in Peru* (1980).

STEVEN ELLNER (Ph.D. University of New Mexico) is assistant professor at the Universidad del Oriente, Barcelona, Venezuela, and author of *Los partidos políticos en el movimiento sindical en Venezuela, 1936-1948* (1981).

ALLISON BLAKELY (Ph.D. University of California, Berkeley) is associate professor of history at Howard University.

FERENC SZASZ (Ph.D. University of Rochester) is associate professor of history at the University of New Mexico and author of *The Divided Mind of Protestant America, 1880–1930* (forthcoming).

PAUL W. DRAKE (Ph.D. Stanford University) is associate professor of history and director of the Center for Latin American and Caribbean Studies at the University of Illinois. He is author of *Socialism and Populism in Chile* (1978).

248

Index